Studies in Medieval Literature

The Phillips Studio, Philadelphia

Albert Croll Baugh

Studies in Medieval Literature

In Honor of
PROFESSOR ALBERT CROLL BAUGH

Edited by

MacEdward Leach

Editorial Committee

Frederick L. Jones
William H. Marshall
Harold S. Stine
MacEdward Leach, Chairman

Philadelphia
University of Pennsylvania Press

Printed in the United States of America

Foreword

The most difficult problem faced by the Editorial Committee charged with the task of preparing a festschrift in honor of Professor Albert C. Baugh was one of selection of papers. Professor Baugh's influence and associations, extending so far beyond the University through his activity in such organizations as the Modern Language Association of America, the Medieval Academy, and the Modern Humanities Research Association, made it desirable to plan this volume on as wide a base as possible. Then, too, many medieval scholars and others, indebted to Professor Baugh directly or indirectly, wished to show their appreciation by participation in this tribute. Unfortunately the number of pages at our disposal was limited. We have had, consequently, to restrict the book to those papers that represent Professor Baugh's special interests. This meant that we could not include papers from colleagues and students in other fields though we realize that many of these scholars owe much to Professor Baugh and wish to pay tribute to him. This is especially true of those at Pennsylvania who were taught the materials and methods of scholarship in Professor Baugh's famous course in methodology.

These seventeen papers have been selected to represent Professor Baugh's major interests in the medieval field: five are concerned with Chaucer, eight with general medieval literature, two with linguistics; two reflect his interest in editing medieval texts.

The Committee wishes to thank all who helped to make this book a possibility. Mr. Thomas Yoseloff of the University Press, the Press Committee of the University of Pennsylvania, Professor Matthias Shaaber, Chairman of the Department of English, have been very helpful with counsel and advice. The Committee wishes to acknowledge with many thanks the unfailing help of Mr. Bernhard Kendler in getting this difficult manuscript into print. To Dr. Nita Baugh, wife of Professor Baugh, we owe special thanks for constant help and advice. To all who participated through their contributions we owe deepest thanks.

We present this volume, then, to Professor Albert C. Baugh as an expression of the admiration and affection of all of us who have been associated with him through the years at Pennsylvania, of his students who have gone out in the world, and of his colleagues in medieval studies here and abroad.

MacEdward Leach

Albert Croll Baugh

Albert Croll Baugh was born on February 26, 1891, the son of Horace L. Baugh and Margaret (Croll) Baugh. His ancestors were largely Pennsylvania Dutch; for 250 years the family has lived along the Schuylkill. Albert Baugh attended the Philadelphia public schools, graduating from Northeast High in 1908. From Northeast he received a City Scholarship to the University of Pennsylvania, where he matriculated in the same year. He took his A.B. degree in 1912, his A.M. in 1914, and his Ph.D. in 1915. His dissertation, written under the direction of Professor Felix E. Schelling, was *William Haughton's Englishmen for My Money, or A Woman Will Have Her Will: Edited with Introduction and Notes* (Philadelphia, 1917).

Professor Baugh's teaching career began in 1912, when he was appointed Assistant Instructor at the University of Pennsylvania. After serving as Instructor and Assistant Professor he received his professorship in 1928. In 1946 he was appointed to the Felix E. Schelling Memorial Professorship in English, a position which he still holds. He served as Chairman of the Department of English at Pennsylvania from 1944 to 1957. Professor Baugh has held many visiting professorships: at Stanford University in 1928; at Duke in 1935, 1937, 1939, and 1941; at Northwestern in 1940; and at the University of Southern California in 1949.

Notable among the courses in English Literature and Language which he has given from year to year are his course Materials and Methods of Research, his very popular and very rewarding course in Chaucer, and his deeply scholarly History of Middle English Literature. The fruits of his teaching and his scholarship may be seen in the many young scholars he has stimulated, as well as in the large list of his scholarly publications.

Professor Baugh has been very active in a number of learned societies. During his whole academic life he has worked in the Modern Language Association. He was a member of the Editorial Board from 1930 to 1941 and from 1946 to 1951, a member of the Executive Committee from 1943 to 1946, Second Vice-President in 1950, and President in 1952. He is a long-time member and Fellow of the Medieval Academy; he served as a member of its Advisory Board from 1939 to 1941 and as Clerk in 1949-50. He has long been active in the American Dialect Society and in the Linguistic Society and has held important offices in both. He is Associate Editor of the *Philological Quarterly* and of *Word*. In 1960 Professor Baugh was elected President for three years of the Fédération Internationale des Langues et Littératures Modernes. He is the first American to hold this important office.

Professor Baugh has likewise been very active in the American Philosophical Society. He is a member of its Committee on Publications, 1948——; of its Committee on Research, 1953——; of its Committee on Jayne Lectures, 1959——; and of its Council 1959——. Professor Baugh is a member of Phi Beta Kappa, having been elected in his junior year at Pennsylvania. He was awarded an Honorary LL.D. degree by Ursinus College in 1939, a L.H.D. by Franklin and Marshall in 1956, and a Litt.D. by the University of Pennsylvania in 1961.

Great fame has come to Albert Baugh in America and abroad through his numerous scholarly publications—books, articles, reviews. A listing of the most important of these follows on pages 11-17. Two deserve special mention. *A History of the English Language,* first published in 1935 and revised in 1957, has from its initial publication been regarded both here and in England as the very best book on its subject. It is widely used as a reference book and as a basic text. *The Middle English Period, 1100-1500,* in *A Literary History of England* is unquestionably the best short history of Middle English literature. Its style is clear and graceful; its scholarship is deep, and its information is abundant.

Professor Baugh married Nita Emeline Scudder on June 20, 1925. Mrs. Baugh, herself a medieval scholar, has been actively interested in her husband's work. They have two children, William Scudder and Daniel Albert, and two grandchildren. The Baughs have always lived near the University, where their home has been a rendezvous for medieval scholars from home and abroad. Here, housed in a beautiful study, designed and built by Professor Baugh himself, is probably the finest medieval library in the country. It is rich not only in the vast number of rare works dealing with the Middle Ages but also in its complete runs of all important scholarly periodicals, English and foreign.

Albert Baugh has carried on and enriched the great tradition of distinguished scholarship and inspiring teaching established over the years at Pennsylvania and exemplified by his own great teachers, such as Felix E. Schelling, Edward P. Cheney, and Arthur H. Quinn.

MacEdward Leach

A Partial List of the Publications of Albert Croll Baugh

1917. *William Haughton's* Englishmen for My Money, *or* A Woman Will Have Her Will. *Edited with Introduction and Notes.* Philadelphia (University of Pennsylvania Ph.D. dissertation).

1917-38. "English Language and Literature." *American Year Book.*

1918. "A Seventeenth Century Play-List." *Modern Language Review,* XIII: 401-11.

"The Mak Story." *Modern Philology,* XV: 169-74.

"A Note on the Shakespeare First Folio." *MLN,* XXXIII: 505.

"The English of Oral English." *Univ. of Pennsylvania Schoolmen's Week Proc., 1918,* pp. 277-83.

1922. "Some New Facts about Shirley." *Modern Language Review,* XVII: 228-35.

1922-51. "American Bibliography: English." *Publications of the Modern Language Association,* XXXVII-LXVI.

1923. *Schelling Anniversary Papers by His Former Students* [edited by A. C. Baugh]. New York: The Century Co.

"The Chester Plays and French Influence." *Schelling Anniversary Papers,* pp. 35-63.

1924. *Writing by Types: A Manual of Composition for College Students.* New York: The Century Co. With Paul C. Kitchen and Matthew W. Black.

1925. *Century Types of English Literature, Chronologically Arranged.* Edited by George Wm. McClelland and Albert C. Baugh. New York: The Century Co.

"Beowulf" [Translated into modern English prose]. In *Century Types of English Literature,* pp. 4-43.

1927. "Synonyms, Antonyms, and Discriminations." *The New Century Dictionary of the English Language.* 3 vols. New York: The Century Co. Vol. III, pp. 2251-2405. With Paul C. Kitchen.

1928. Introduction to *The Return of the Native,* by Thomas Hardy, pp. ix-xxii.

1929. *The Literature of America: An Anthology of Prose and Verse.* Edited by Arthur Hobson Quinn, Albert Croll Baugh, and Will David Howe. 2 vols. New York: Charles Scribner's Sons. Volume I: *From the Beginning to the Civil War.* Volume II: *From the Civil War to the Present.* (Second edition, revised, 1938.)

Essays Toward Living: A Book for College Students. [Edited] by Albert C. Baugh and Norman E. McClure. New York: Ronald Press (Modern America Series of English Texts).

"Graduate Work in English." *English Journal* (College ed.), XVIII: 135-46.

"A Source for the Middle English Romance, *Athelstan.*" *Publications of the Modern Language Association,* XLIV: 377-82.

Review: *The Middle English Stanzaic Versions of the Life of St. Anne,* edited by R. E. Parker (Early English Text Society, Original Series, No. 174), London, 1928. *Philological Quarterly,* VIII: 414-16.

1930. Review: Edward Hicks, *Sir Thomas Malory, His Turbulent Career: A Biography,* Cambridge, Mass., 1928. *Journal of English and Germanic Philology,* XXIX: 452-57.

1931. "Further Facts about James Shirley." *Review of English Studies,* VII: 1-5.

1932. "Kirk's Life Records of Thomas Chaucer." *Publications of the Modern Language Association,* XLVII: 461-515.

"Osbert of Clare, the Sarum Breviary and the Middle English *Saint Anne* in Rime-Royal." *Speculum,* VII: 106-13.

Review: Edmond Faral, *La Légende arthurienne— études et documents,* Première Partie: *Les plus anciens textes;* 3 vols., Paris, 1929. *Modern Philology,* XXIX: 357-65.

1933. "Documenting Sir Thomas Malory." *Speculum,* VIII: 3-29.

"A Recent Theory of the *Ludus Coventriae*." *Philological Quarterly,* XII: 403-06.

"Thomas Chaucer, One Man or Two?" *Publications of the Modern Language Association,* XLVIII: 328-39.

"Robert Shelton Mackenzie (1809-1881)." *Dict. of Amer. Biography,* XII: 96-97.

"Morton McMichael (1807-1879)." *Ibid.,* XII: 142-3.

"Peter Markoe (c. 1752-92)." *Ibid.,* XII: 287-8.

Review: *When Rome Is Removed to England.* Eine Politische Propheziehung des 14. Jahrhunderts, edited by Reinhard Haferkorn, Leipzig, 1932. *Modern Language Notes,* XLVIII: 128-29.

1935. *A History of the English Language.* New York: Appleton–Century Co. (Second edition, revised, 1957.)

"The Chronology of French Loan-Words in English." *Modern Language Notes,* L: 90-93.

1937. "The Original Teller of the Merchant's Tale." *Modern Philology,* XXXV: 15-26.

Review: Heinrich C. Mathes, *Die Einheitlichkeit des Ormulum,* Heidelberg, 1933. *Journal of English and Germanic Philology.* XXXVI: 263-68.

1939. "Biblia cum glossis (1481)." *University of Pennsylvania Library Chronicle,* VII: 28-33.

"Bigger or Better." [University of Pennsylvania] *General Magazine and Historical Chronicle,* XLI: 422-33 (Founders' Day address, Ursinus College).

Review: Sister Imogene Baker, *The King's Household in the Arthurian Court from Geoffrey of Monmouth to Malory,* Washington, D. C., 1937. *Modern Language Notes,* LIV: 145-46.

1940. "The End–Product of Research." *Modern Language Journal,* XXIV: 268-78.

"Richard Sellyng." *Essays and Studies in Honor of Carleton Brown,* New York, pp. 167-81.

"Thomas Jefferson, Linguistic Liberal." *Studies for William A. Read,* pp. 88-108. University, Louisiana: Louisiana State University Press.

"What Can Scholarship Do for the College Teacher?" *College English,* I: 389-196.

Review: E. E. Wardale, *An Introduction to Middle English,* London, 1937. *Englische Studien,* LXXIV: 91-94.

1941. Review: R. M. Wilson, *Early Middle English Literature,* London [1939]. *Modern Language Notes,* LVI: 218-21.

1947. Review: E. K. Chambers, *English Literature at the Close of the Middle Ages,* Oxford, 1945. *Journal of English and Germanic Philology,* XLVI: 304-07.

1948. *A Literary History of England.* Edited by Albert C. Baugh. New York & London: Appleton–Century–Crofts. (*The Old English Period, to 1100,* by Kemp Malone. *The Middle English Period, 1100-1500,* by Albert C. Baugh. *The Renaissance, 1500-1660,* by Tucker Brooke. *The Restoration and Eighteenth Century, 1660-1789,* by George Sherburn. *The Nineteenth*

Century and After, 1789-1939, by Samuel C. Chew. (Also published in four volumes.)
The Middle English Period (1100-1500). Book I, Part ii of *A Literary History of England*, pp. 109-312.
Appleton–Century Handbooks of Literature. Albert C. Baugh, General Editor. 1948 *et seq*. Five volumes published to date.

1949. "A Fraternity of Drinkers." *Philologica: The Malone Anniversary Studies*, pp. 200-207. Baltimore: The Johns Hopkins Press.

Review: Roger S. Loomis and Rudolph Willard, *Medieval English Verse and Prose in Modernized Versions*, New York, 1948. *Speculum*, XXIV: 128-31.

1950. "The Authorship of the Middle English Romances." *Annual Bulletin of the Modern Humanities Research Association*, No. 22, pp. 13-28 (M.H.R.A. Presidential Address).

1951. "Fifty Years of Chaucer Scholarship." *Speculum*, XXVI: 659-72.

1953. "Justification by Works." *Publications of the Modern Language Association*, LXVIII: 3-17 (Presidential Address, Modern Language Association).

"Literature in College." [University of Pennsylvania] *General Magazine and Historical Chronicle*, LV: 107-13.

1954. *English Literature: A Period Anthology*. Edited by Albert C. Baugh and George Wm. McClelland. New York: Appleton–Century–Crofts (a revision and expansion of *Century Types*, 1925).

1955. "Chaucer." *Encyclopedia Americana*, VI: 361-5.

Review: J. A. Sheard, *The Words We Use*, New York, 1954. *Language*, XXXI: 309-11.

1956. *The English Text of the* Ancrene Riwle. *Edited from*

British Museum MS. Royal 8C.1. London: Early English Text Society (No. 232).

1957. Review: Hardin Craig, *English Religious Drama of the Middle Ages,* Oxford, 1955. *MLN,* LXXII: 207-10.

1959. "The Date of Walter of Bibbesworth's *Traité." Festschrift für Walther Fischer,* pp. 21-33. Heidelberg.

"Improvisation in the Middle English Romance." *Proceedings of the American Philosophical Society,* CIII: 418-54.

"A Medieval Survival in Elizabethan Punctuation." *Studies in the English Renaissance Drama: In Memory of Karl Julius Holzknecht,* pp. 1-15. New York: New York University Press.

1960. "Chaucer and the Panthère d'Amours." *Britannica Festschrift für Hermann M. Flasdieck,* pp. 51-60. Heidelberg.

Review: *The French Text of the Ancrene Riwle,* ed. W. H. Trethewey (EETS, No. 240). *Speculum,* XXXV: 156-8.

Review: C. E. Wright, *English Vernacular Hands from the Twelfth to the Fifteenth Centuries,* Oxford, 1960. *Journal of English and Germanic Philology,* LIX: 722-4.

1961. "Chaucer's *Troilus,* iv. 1585: A Biblical Allusion?" *Modern Language Notes,* LXXVI: 1-4.

Contents

18 Contents

Studies in Medieval Literature

Was Chaucer a Free Thinker? [1]

Many critics have refused to accept Geoffrey Chaucer as a thinker at all. Matthew Arnold denied him the quality of high seriousness. Many readers, I feel sure, even though they admit that Chaucer had ideas about such topics as true gentility and Christian piety, take him as a representative of the Middle Ages, of the Age of Faith, and assume that he never came up against the problems which have haunted the eighteenth century, the so-called age of reason, and the nineteenth century, the age of science, and our own age, in which it seems possible that mankind together with its problems may cease to exist. For such readers, Chaucer speaks only through the Prioress and the Second Nun, as an unquestioning devotee of the Trinity and the Blessed Virgin. They fail to take into account, or dismiss as rhetorical flourishes, the heterodox ideas which he sometimes expressed.

When I say that Chaucer *expressed* these heterodox opinions, I do not mean that he actually held them as firm convictions; I do not mean that they formed articles in his creed. What I do mean to say is that these skeptical ideas crop up again and again in his poems when there was no particular occasion for them and when there was nothing in his sources to suggest them. What I do mean is that certain basic doubts, which went beyond Wyclif's questioning of the authority of the papacy and denunciation of the mendicant orders—doubts of God's justice and wisdom in dealing with mankind, doubts as to the freedom of the will, doubts as to immortality of the soul—were sufficiently familiar to Chaucer as to obtrude themselves into the *Troilus*, the Knight's Tale, the *Legend of Good Women*, the Franklin's Tale, and even so pious a legend

21

as the Man of Law's Tale of Custance. It is noteworthy that
these questionings crop up in writings of the period when
Chaucer was making his translation of Boethius, in which
these very problems were raised.

Of course, there is plenty of evidence that the poet was
no confirmed skeptic but a devout and orthodox Christian.
The *ABC* may be discounted as evidence of Chaucer's personal devotion to the Virgin, since it is essentially a translation from Deguileville and was, according to Speght, made at
the request of Blanche the Duchess for her private use. The
pious tales related by the two nuns may also be discounted
as required by the profession of the narrators. But no such
objection can be raised against the epilogue to *Troilus*, against
the *Balade of Good Counsel*, or against the *Retractions*. Even
the portrait of the Parson, though it displays from a Catholic
point of view a heretical taint, from the Protestant point of
view is orthodoxy itself.[2]

In the *Retractions*, though the poet frankly confesses to
inditing worldly vanities, tales that "sounen unto sin," and
many a lecherous lay, he apparently feels himself innocent
of any provocation to skepticism. If more proof were needed,
there are the references to Chaucer by such impeccably
orthodox writers as Hoccleve and Lydgate, who probably
would have heard if their master had been *at any period*
notorious as an agnostic. I am quite ready, therefore, to agree
with those who maintain that Chaucer was, in spite of a
temporary sympathy with the heresiarch Wyclif and in spite
of temporary lapses into ribaldry, a professing Christian and,
in certain moods at least, a devout one.

I have used two expressions which show perhaps how I
would reconcile my belief in Chaucer's religious orthodoxy
with my belief in the skeptical tendency of certain passages
in his writings: those expressions are "at any period," and

"in certain moods." For it is characteristic of most human beings to change with the passing of time and to respond to
different moods. Professor George Stewart in a penetrating
essay on "The Moral Chaucer," in the *University of California Publications in English*, remarked thirty-two years
ago:[3] "Even the simplest of us play in our lives, often in the
same day, many and sometimes incongruous parts: a keen-
eyed friend may see in *us*

> Buffoon and poet, lover and sensualist,
> A deal of Ariel, just a streak of Puck,
> Much Antony, of Hamlet most of all,
> And something of the shorter Catechist.

So with Chaucer—a little of the Miller, more of the Squire,
a bit of the Wife, a touch of the Manciple, something (not
very much I feel) of that strange elvish creature with down-
cast eyes, most of all probably of the Clerk, and finally no
inconsiderable portion of the Parson." To Professor Stewart's
analysis of the many-sided Chaucer I would add that there
was in him something of the rationalist, something of the
skeptic. Can we not all agree that the greatness of Chaucer,
as of Shakespeare, lies in his universality, his ability to enter
sympathetically into the thoughts and feelings of the most
diverse characters? Can we not agree that a poet who expressed with such poignancy and naturalness the contrary
views on marriage of the Wife of Bath and of the Clerk of
Oxenford was able to feel and to express very diverse attitudes toward the ultimate problems of man's destiny? Permit
me to quote a passage from an essay on Bernard Shaw written
by one of the best of American critics, Edmund Wilson. Wilson wrote:[4]

One of the prime errors of recent radical criticism has been the
assumption that great novels and plays must necessarily be written

by people who have everything clear in their minds. People who have everything clear in their minds, who are not capable of identifying themselves imaginatively with, who do not actually embody in themselves, contrary emotions and points of view, do not write novels and plays at all—do not at any rate write good ones. And—given genius—the more violent the contraries, the greater the works of art.

If Edmund Wilson was right in enunciating this by no means novel idea, and if it applies to Shakespeare, it surely applies to the author of the *Canterbury Tales* and *Troilus*. If it applies to the creator of Hamlet and Falstaff, it applies to the begetter of Troilus the romanticist and of Pandarus the ironist, to the begetter of the Parson, who caught his words out of the Gospel, and also of the Doctor, whose study was but little on the Bible. So, granting that Chaucer regarded himself and was regarded by others as essentially a conformist to the religion of his day, let me ask you to consider a number of passages which show a questioning spirit.

But before reviewing these passages, may I remind you that this also was in conformity with the spirit of his day. It was a period of doubt and challenge. Kittredge in his excellent book, *Chaucer and His Poetry*, declared:[5]

We hear . . . that our times are blessed with a critical or questioning spirit, whereas our medieval ancestors believed what they were told, with blind faith. This, however, is at best a very crude antithesis, and it has no merit whatsoever when applied to Chaucer's lifetime. Then, if ever, the spirit of radicalism was abroad in the land. To describe as an era of dumb submissiveness the age of Wyclif, and John Huss, and the Great Schism, of the Jacquerie in France and Tyler and Ball in England, is to read both literature and history with one's eyes shut.

Anyone who surveys the literature of the fourteenth century for evidence of this questioning spirit will quickly discover that it not only challenged, as the Protestants did later, the validity of excommunication, the spiritual value of pilgrimages, the miracle of transubstantiation, and the authority of the Pope, but also went far beyond, to question the justice of God, the freedom of the will, the doctrine of the fall of man and his redemption, and the immortality of the soul.

One of the most representative and popular homiletic works of the later Middle Ages was the *Gesta Romanorum,* written probably in England about 1330. It contains two exempla, or parables, particularly designed to answer doubts as to the justice of the divine dispensation. One is the famous, perhaps notorious, parable of the Angel and the Hermit.[6] A hermit, who lived in a remote cave, one day saw a shepherd tending his flocks. The shepherd fell asleep and a sheep was stolen, whereupon his master had him put to death. Appalled at this injustice, the hermit cried out: "O Lord, see how this man placed blame on an innocent person and killed him. Why do you permit such things to happen? I will go out into the world and live as other men do." Leaving his cave, the hermit set out into the world. An angel appeared to him in human form and became his travelling companion. In the course of the next few days the angel killed the child of a knight who had given them shelter, stole a gold cup from a burgess who had entertained them, threw into a river a pilgrim, and presented the stolen cup to a man who had refused them the shelter of his home. Thus the hermit was even more deeply convinced that injustice prevailed in the world. But the angel revealed his celestial mission, explained the divine plan to prevent sin and reform character by means of his acts, and concluded saying: "Know that nothing on earth is done without reason." The second exemplum tells how a knight accused an innocent servant of theft, cut off his foot, and left him to die.[7] A hermit went to the servant's aid and was moved by his story to reproach God for permitting such wrongs to exist. Once more an angel was sent to justify the Deity. "All His ways are truth and His judgments equity. Do not say: Why did He make me and then let me fall?"

The presence of these two exempla in a manual for preachers is evidence that the problem of the theodicy was one with which preachers of the fourteenth century found it necessary to deal. Among their parishioners doubtless there were those who asked, "Why did God make me and then let me fall?"

In Chaucer's own time the monk and chronicler Thomas of Walsingham wrote that the Londoners were of nearly all peoples the most arrogant, and had no faith in God.[8] Walsingham also referred to the lords who believed that there was no God, no sacrament of the altar, no resurrection after death, but that as an animal dies, so also ends man. Chaucer's friend Gower in the *Mirour de l'Homme* confirms this accusation as regards the merchant class.[9] "One of them," he writes, "said to me the other day that he who can have the sweetness of this life and rejects it, would in his opinion act like a fool, for after this life no one knows the truth, whither to go or by what way." Langland asserts that men of high degree were accustomed to mock at the most sacred doctrines.[10] "I have heard high men, eating at table, talk as if they were clerics, of Christ and his power. They found fault with the Father who formed us all. . . . Why would our Savior allow such a serpent into His garden of bliss, who beguiled first the woman and the man after, and through whose wily words they went to hell, and all their seed for their sin suffered the same death? Why should we who now live rot and be rent for the sins of Adam? Reason would never have it." Here in Christian England of Chaucer's day men were anticipating the charge which Fitzgerald made in the nineteenth century in his *Rubaiyat:*

> O Thou, who didst with pitfall and with gin
> Beset the road I was to wander in,
> Thou wilt not with predestined evil round
> Enmesh and then impute the fall to Sin.

Again Langland speaks of the blasphemous talk of the rich.[11] "Now it is the mode at meat when minstrels are silent for laymen to dispute about holy lore with the learned, and talk of the Trinity, how two slew the third. . . . Thus they drivel on the dais to explain the Deity, and gnaw God with the gorge when their guts are full." It will be remembered that Dante assigned a whole circle in hell to the Epicureans, "those who with the body make the spirit die." And among those who denied the after-life were Farinata degli Uberti, Cavalcante Cavalcanti, Cardinal Ubaldini, and the Emperor Frederick II. Dante speaks of more than a thousand of these unbelievers, and his commentator Benvenuto da Imola remarks that it would take too long to enumerate the eminent men of the Epicurean sect.[12] "Ah, how many heretics there are who hypocritically pretend to be Catholics for fear of punishment or infamy!" It would seem that these men, and other skeptics, such as those mentioned by Langland and Gower, conformed outwardly to all the teachings of the Church, heard mass, went to confession, took the sacraments, and except for the Emperor Frederick were not excommunicated. But among their intimates they made no secret of their sadduceeism.

It is to be noted that Dante classed even the Cardinal Ubaldini among the Epicureans, and Ubaldini seems not to have been unique among the clergy in his materialistic philosophy. Froissart, the chronicler, was in orders and became

a canon of Chimay. For eight years he moved in the same
court circles as Chaucer. When he returned to England in
1395, he made inquiries of a certain squire as to how Richard
II's campaign against the Irish had gone. The squire explained that four Irish kings had submitted to the King of
England "by the grace of God." Froissart, churchman though
he was, could hardly believe that this was sufficient cause,
and, as he tells us himself, he remarked: "La grâce de Dieu est
moult bonne, qui la puet avoir, et puet grandement valloir,
mais on voit petit de seigneurs terriens présentement aug-
menter leurs seigneuries, se ce n'est par puissance." [13] Here is a
sentiment exactly analogous to the cynical dictum often,
though mistakenly, attributed to Napoleon, that God is always on the side of the big battalions. Froissart was essentially
a worldling, and his worldliness extended itself beyond a fond-
ness for the fleshpots and for the pageantry of life to something very close to a materialistic interpretation of history.

It may perhaps be thought that I have overdrawn the picture. Of course, I have said nothing about the millions who
never wrestled with doubt, and the other millions who after
wrestling with doubt came for one reason or another to the
conclusion that the clergy were wiser than they. And when it
comes to estimating the exact proportion of believers, secret
doubters, and downright skeptics, it would be impossible
even for a contemporary, even for Chaucer himself, to make
more than a rough guess. All that one can say is that there
was a considerable minority who though conforming to the
demands of the Church sufficiently to escape excommunication and burning, actually were agnostics, Sadducees, or even
atheists. Some of the more powerful and wealthy even in-
dulged in open mockery at the most sacred doctrines. It is
necessary to remember the existence of these scoffers when

the Middle Ages are pictured as an Age of Faith, exempt from any taint of materialism, fatalism, or rationalism.

Now Chaucer lived in the same world with Thomas of Walsingham, Gower, Langland, and Froissart, and he, if anyone, knew what was going on in the minds of his contemporaries, not to mention the ideas they discussed openly. It is well to remember that though he was a bookworm and though much of his poetry consists of translation and quotation, he was also very much a man of affairs. John Livingston Lowes, one of the greatest interpreters of the poet, declared in an article over fifty years ago that [14] "Sources other than the books Chaucer read—sources that lie in his intercourse with men and in his reaction upon the interests, the happenings, the familiar matter of his day—entered likewise into 'that large compasse' of his, and must be taken into account in estimating his work."

Now, given Chaucer's contact with men and women who were covertly or openly skeptical of the most sacred dogmas of Christianity, it would be strange if he did not in some measure feel the impact of their skepticism. His was a mind which combined a strong element of docility and imitativeness with an equally strong element of originality and inventiveness. His was a spirit given to inquiry and exploration. And when he was presented with some of the perennial questions which men have asked about the universe and man's place in it, about undeserved suffering and the immortality of the soul, about fate and free will, he more than most men was likely to examine with tolerance and understanding the various answers. The poet who could so sympathetically present the erotic feminism of the Wife of Bath and portray so admiringly the Wyclifite Parson, was not one who saw life entirely from a conventional angle. So it is only natural that in reading Chaucer we should find him repeatedly expressing in his own person or through the mouths of his characters certain heterodox opinions. Let me repeat that I do not believe that he was an agnostic, a materialist, a rebel by conviction, but simply that such speculations were familiar to him, that they were much on his mind, and that they crop up in his work with significant frequency even when nothing in his sources called for them.

Thus Chaucer seems to have passed through a period of disillusionment and dark musings, a period when the sense of assurance and hope was weakened by doubts. Between 1379 and 1385 he was probably writing the *House of Fame,* which, with all its fun, manifests a completely ironic, disillusioned view of the inequities of fame and reputation; the Knight's Tale, with Palamon's violent outburst against the inequities of man's lot and Arcite's despairing "What is this world? What asketh men to have? Now with his love, now in the colde grave, alone withouten any companye." Certainly in this period he wrote the *tragedye* of Troilus, told of his "double sorwe," and concluded with this comment:

> Swych fyn hath al his grete worthynesse,
> Swich fyn hath his estat real above,
> Swich fyn his lust, swich fyn hath his noblesse.

And it was in this period that Chaucer took the time to translate into English the *De Consolatione Philosophiae* of Boethius, which offered a reasoned antidote to all these doctrines of doubt and despair.

Let me quote again from Professor Stewart's article on "The Moral Chaucer." [15] "Like Hardy's *Dynasts,* although not quite so schematically, the *Troilus* attempts to probe the motivation of human existence, and again like the *Dynasts* its conclusion is strikingly black." Stewart goes on to make the following personal comment: "The Knight's Tale, the Boethius, and *Troilus and Criseyde*, make me believe that in this middle period Chaucer became greatly interested in the deeper problems of life, to which he was able to see no solution except through religion." Indeed the *Troilus* may be regarded as an exemplum as much as the story in the *Gesta Romanorum* of the Angel and the Hermit—an exemplum in which the fickleness of Fortune, the undeserved torment of a noble soul, are in the end reconciled with a belief in Him who died upon a cross our souls to redeem, and who will betray the trust of no man, I dare say, who will lay his heart wholly on Him.

But Chaucer reaches this solution not by logic but by faith. He puts into the mouth of Troilus the long discussion of fate and foreknowledge, taken over from Boethius, but he does not add the defense of human freedom which Boethius supplied. He allows Troilus to stop with a fatalistic conclusion.[16] Now it is highly significant that Chaucer's principal source, Boccaccio's *Filostrato*, has not the barest suggestion of this debate on God's foreknowledge and man's free will. It is Geoffrey Chaucer who has introduced it, rather inappropriately, since it is odd to find the Trojan prince an adept in metaphysics and pondering this complex problem with all the subtlety of those great clerics "who have their tops full high and smoothly shorn." There can be no doubt that it is the poet's own interest in the problem which has foisted it, somewhat artificially, upon the Trojan prince as a soliloquy.

Much the same problem is introduced by Chaucer into the Knight's Tale, this time, I believe, much more naturally. Again there was little to correspond in the Italian source, the pseudo-classical epic, Boccaccio's *Teseida*. In fact, the Knight's Tale reveals a preoccupation with the idea of destinal forces moulding men's lives. The planets Mars, Venus, Diana, and Saturn

exercise their conflicting influences and determine the out-
come of the lovers' rivalry. The notion of chance and its
ironies is a sort of *leitmotif*. The Theban queen who greets
Theseus on his return to Athens addresses him as "Lord, to
whom Fortune hath given victory," and ascribes her wretched-
ness to Fortune and her false wheel. Arcite ascribes his imprisonment to Fortune or to some disposition of the stars.
"So stood the heaven when that we were born." Palamon likewise refers to his destiny shaped by the eternal word. Arcite
indulges in a longish soliloquy on the ironies of life. There is
mention of Fortune's dice and Fortune's mutability. Straight
from Boethius comes a passage on man's ignorance of where
his true happiness lies. We are like a drunk man who knows
he has a house, but does not know the way thither. Later in
the poem Chaucer repeats from Boccaccio the comment on
the role of chance: "Sometyme it shal fallen on a day that
falleth not eft within a thousand yeer."

The chief expression, however, of protest against the divine
order is put into the mouth of imprisoned Palamon. Shut off
from his Emelye, he inveighs against the gods.

> "O crueel goddes that governe
> This world with byndyng of youre word eterne,
> And writen in the table of atthamaunt
> Your parlement and youre eterne graunt,
> What is mankinde more unto you holde
> Than is the sheep that rouketh in the folde?
> For slayn is man right as another beest,
> And dwelleth eek in prisoun and arreest,
> And hath siknesse and greet adversitee
> And ofte times gilteless, pardee.
> What governance is in this prescience
> That giltelees tormenteth innocence?
> And yet encresseth this al my penaunce

That man is bounden to his observaunce,
For Goddes sake, to letten of his wille,
Ther as a beest may al his lust fulfille.
And whan a beest is deed he hath no peyne;
But man after his deeth moot wepe and pleyne,
Though in this world he have care and wo.
Withouten doute it may stonden so.
The answere of this lete I to dyvynys,
But wel I wot that in this world greet pyne ys."

Palamon's protest begins with paraphrasing a metrical pass-age in Boethius, but the words are more audacious, the passion more violent. And Chaucer added the complaint that man-kind is bound by God's law to curb his desires, whereas noth-ing hinders an animal from indulging its appetites. Man alone is doomed to suffer after death, but when a beast is dead, he has no pain. Is there in English literature, except in James Thomson's *City of Dreadful Night*, a stronger appeal against "the governaunce which gilteless tormenteth innocence"?

And it is to be remarked that this charge of Palamon's against the cruel gods receives no direct refutation such as Boethius attempted. Later the old Egeus, who knew this world's transmutation, gives the cold comfort that the world is but a thoroughfare full of woe, and death is the end of every worldly sore. Theseus himself, after a discourse on the inevitability of change and death, declares:

"Then is it wisdom, as it thinketh me,
To maken vertu of necessitee,
And take it weel that we may not eschue. . . .
And whoso gruccheth ought, he dooth folye,
And rebel is to him that al may gye."

This is, of course, no real answer to Palamon's complaint. In fact, there is, according to the Knight's Tale, no rational

justification of the universe. It is folly to rebel. Submit to
what cannot be helped. That is the moral. I think we may
safely conclude that the poet had found no satisfactory
rational answer to the problem; otherwise he would have
given it to us. His failure to answer is practically a confession
of agnosticism—at least of incompetence so far as this particular difficulty is concerned.

Two generations ago, in 1892, Professor Lounsbury of
Yale University published his erudite *Studies in Chaucer,*
in which he adduced another passage in the Knight's Tale
which seemed to strengthen the case for Chaucer's agnosticism.[17] He quoted the lines about the fate of Arcite's soul
after death.

> His spirit chaunged hous and wente ther,
> As I cam never, I can not tellen wher.
> Therefore I stinte, I nam no divinistre.
> Of soules finde I noght in this registre,
> Ne me ne list thilke opinions to telle
> Of hem, though that they writen wher they dwelle.

Lounsbury commented: "Can modern agnosticism point to a
denial more emphatic . . . of the belief that there exists for
us any assurance of the life that is lived beyond the grave?"
Lounsbury had a point; the lines are capable of such a construction; but they are also open to another interpretation
which relieves them of any unorthodox tendency. One of the
issues on which there was debate among the orthodox was
the fate of the righteous heathen—men who never had heard
of the Christian's God or of His plan of salvation, who by no
possibility could have received God's grace through baptism
and the sacraments.[18] Dante, you will remember, brought up
the problem in the *Paradiso*.[19] "A man is born upon the bank
of Indus, and there is none to tell of Christ, nor none to read,

nor none to write; and all his volitions and his deeds are good
so far as human reason seeth, sinless in life or in discourse.
He dieth unbaptized and without faith; where is that justice
which condemneth him? Where is his fault in that he not
believes?" [20] In England and in Chaucer's own day the question of the salvation of righteous heathen was argued pro and
con. The problem weighed heavily on the mind of Langland.[21]
The author of the Middle English *Saint Erkenwald* makes it
possible through a miracle for a pagan judge of King Belinus's
time to escape from limbo and join the celestial cenacle.[22]
Dame Juliana of Norwich, on the one hand, accepts as an
article of faith the damnation of those who die out of the
faith of Holy Church, that is, the heathen;[23] but on the other
hand approaches the doctrine of universal salvation.[24] "In
mankind that shall be saved is comprehended all; that is to
say, all that is made and the Maker of all; for in man is God,
and God is in all." It seems pretty clear that Chaucer preferred not to impale himself on the horns of that dilemma. In
confessing his ignorance as to the house where Arcite's spirit
dwelt, Chaucer was merely refusing to commit himself as to
the fate of so noble a pagan as Arcite. That is all that we can
infer from the passage.

Not long after the completion of the *Troilus,* Chaucer began
the *Legend of Good Women,* and it opens with some lines
which show that the question of the after-life was still much
on his mind. The passage is written in imitation of Froissart's
agnostic lines about the Fountain of Youth. Froissart wrote:[25]
"I have heard talk of the Fountain of Youth and of invisible
stones. But these are impossibilities, for never, by the faith
I owe to Saint Marcelli, have I seen anyone who has said:
'I have actually been there.'" Now Chaucer deliberately
rejected the Fountain of Youth as a place about which there
was no valid testimony and substituted heaven and hell. "A

thousand times have I heard men tell that there is joy in heaven and pain in hell, and I accord well that it is so. Nevertheless I wot well also that there is no one dwelling in this country who has ever been in heaven or hell or who knows of it in any other way but as he hath heard said or found it written. For by experience no man may prove it." After making the point that the existence of heaven and hell has never been verified by anyone living in England in his day, Chaucer goes on to assure us that this is no reason for disbelieving. "But God forbid that one should believe only what one sees with the eye. One should not consider everything a lie unless he has seen or done it himself. Then may we give full credence to books through which old things are kept in mind, and to the doctrine of wise men of old. . . . Well ought we then to honour and believe these books, when we have no other proof." Chaucer when he revised the Prologue of the *Legend of Good Women* some nine years later retained these lines intact. Obviously they do not mean that the poet rejected the belief in heaven and hell, as Lounsbury maintained; in fact, they state emphatically that we ought to accept many things of which we have no ocular demonstration. Nevertheless, they furnish another instance in which Chaucer departed from his source in order to bring up and to state clearly a case for unbelief. Even though he rejects it, he had at least entertained it, and if we may take the witness of his contemporaries, Gower and Thomas of Walsingham, there were men in business and among the aristocracy who were known to deny the immortality of the soul. It was a live issue, not a dead one.

If we hark back to the problem of God's tolerance of evil and unmerited suffering, it is noteworthy that it crops up again and again as a *leitmotif* in several other poems where the source had no corresponding note. Even in that most pious legend of Custance, the Man of Law's Tale, the ten⋅⋅ ⋅cy of which is to counsel patience under misfortune, to see a beneficent Providence operating through calamity and wrong, and to bring about a happy ending, this cry is heard, though uttered in all meekness. The Constable, having received the Uriah letter about the innocent Custance, exclaims:

> "O mighty God, if that it be thy wille,
> Sith thou art rightful juge, how may it be
> That thou wolt suffren innocents to spille,
> And wikked folk regne in prosperitee?"

Custance herself, about to be set adrift on the sea, though welcoming God's dispensation, cannot resist turning to the babe in her arms, and asking "O litel child, allas! What is thy gilt, That never wroghtest synne as yet pardee?" The opening lines of "Filomena" in the *Legend of Good Women* raise the question why the Creator created so black-hearted a villain as Tereus. "Thou giver of the forms, who hast wrought this fair world and borne it in thy thought eternally before thou didst begin thy work, . . . why dost thou suffer Tereus to be born, who is so false in love and so forsworn, that when folk name his name he corrupteth all, from this earth to the first heaven!" Here Chaucer in his own person expresses the same bewilderment that Dame Juliana of Norwich, his contemporary, felt and recorded:[26] "I wondered why, by the great foreseeing wisdom of God, the beginning of sin was not letted, for then, methought, all should have been well."

Dorigen in the Franklin's Tale finds unaccountable the existence of the black rocks off the Breton coast, rocks which serve only to destroy God's own creatures.

> "Eterne God, that thurgh they purveiaunce
> Ledest the world by certein governaunce,
> In ydel, as men seyn, ye no thing make.

> But, Lord, thise grisly feendly rokkes blake,
> That semen rather a foul confusioun
> Of werk than any fair creacioun
> Of swich a parfit wys God and a stable,
> Why han ye wroght this werk unresonable? . . .
> See ye nat, Lord, how mankynde it destroyeth?
> An hundred thousand bodyes of mankynde
> Gan rokkes slayn, al be they nat in mynde,
> Which mankynde is so fair part of thy werk
> That thou it madest lyk to thyn owene merk. . . .
> I wot wel clerkes wol seyn as hem leste,
> By argumentz, that al is for the beste,
> Though I ne kan the causes nat yknowe.
> But thilke God that made the wynd to blowe
> As kepe my lord! this my conclusioun.
> To clerkes lete I al disputisoun."

Here once more is poignantly expressed the agonized perplexity of a soul faced with the problem of reconciling the benevolence and wisdom of the Creator with the hostility and confusion of the world He created.

It is possible to argue that these complaints, addressed to the Deity and questioning His ordinances, which we find in the tales of Custance, and Filomena, and Dorigen, were mere literary commonplaces, samples of the rhetorical question and the apostrophe. It is also possible to argue that in two out of the three cases the sentiments are not those of Chaucer himself but those of his characters; and he canont fairly be held responsible for every emotional outburst to which they give vent.

But neither of these arguments seems to stand up against the force of certain facts. One of these protests, in the "Filomena," is that of Chaucer speaking in his own person. Moreover, in no case is the protest to be found in the source whence Chaucer derived the narrative setting. This is also true of the passage on heaven and hell which opens the *Legend of Good Women*, and of Palamon's passionate protest to the cruel gods in the Knight's Tale, and of Troilus's dissection of the problem of free will versus foreknowledge. According to the testimony of Chaucer's contemporaries, these were live issues. Least of all can the notion that these passages are hackneyed commonplaces or mere "colours of rethorike" stand up against the fact that Chaucer went to the trouble of making a careful translation of Boethius's work, which raised precisely these problems and offered ingenious and plausible solutions. In the face of these facts I see no other conclusion possible than that in his later thirties the poet went through a period of *Sturm und Drang* and was almost obsessed with these disturbing theological and metaphysical issues. Though he pretended to no special competence as a philosopher and more than once transferred to the "grete clerkes" the task of solving the riddles, he could not dismiss them from his mind. He may be placed, then, in the line of those men of letters who have taken seriously the problems of undeserved suffering and of evil in our world, a line which includes the author of the Book of Job, Plato, Boethius, Voltaire in *Zadig* and *Candide*, Matthew Arnold in *Mycerinus*, Fitzgerald in the *Rubaiyat*, and Thomas Hardy in *Tess of the D'Urbervilles* and *The Dynasts*. Some of these authors, needless to say, answered the problem with mockery or a sad irony. They found no reasonable creed which would justify the ways of God to man, and declared the heavens empty.

But Chaucer came to no such conclusion. Though he may *in a sense* be considered an agnostic since he repeatedly leaves the doubt he has raised without any answer, and repeatedly disclaims his ability to find an answer in logic, he seems to have found, like multitudes of others, an answer in faith. I believe that he was essentially a modest man, ready to kiss the steps where he saw pass Virgil, Ovid, Homer, Lucan, and Stace; ready also to put his trust in the "olde bookes," particularly Boethius's golden book. And for the benefit of his compatriots he rendered it into English, for here if anywhere there was a reasoned theodicy, a Christian apologetic (at least it was accepted as such) to counter the infidelity of his day, an apologetic which could be read by the layman—though, strange to say, the style must have discouraged most laymen from reading it.

But what is remarkable and highly significant is the fact that though Chaucer chose the way of faith and supported it with his translation of the *Consolation of Philosophy,* he does not, so far as I can remember, attack those who were lost in perplexity or who were vocal in their complaints against an omnipotent Deity. Indeed his doubters and complainants— Palamon, Troilus, Dorigen—are sympathetic, noble figures. They come in for no such castigation, in spite of their wild and whirling words, as do the hypocrites, not even for such gentle ridicule as the Prioress. Why such tolerance for persons who dared to question the decrees of Heaven and the teachings of the Church? The only explanation I can offer is that Chaucer himself had felt too keenly the force of their questionings and complaints, and though he could not go along with them and in fact opposed them, he could not blame them very much for following their reason to its logical conclusion. After all, unless the authority of reason is to be rejected, they could not honestly do otherwise.

It is pertinent to note that four of Chaucer's literary contemporaries, all four of English birth, displayed a similar tolerance, even a sympathy, for those who did not hold the Christian faith. Three of the four were unquestionably devout believers. The author of *Piers Plowman* was much exercised over the problem of whether Saracens, that is the heathen, could be saved, and in four passages he asserts the possibility of their salvation. At the end of the A text Scripture declares: "It is our belief that an unchristian, because of his just belief may have heritage in heaven, as truly as a high Christian." In the B text, Passus XI, Trajan, the Roman Emperor noted for his justice, interrupts the argument to cite his own case to prove that without singing of masses he could be saved. The poet continued: "Thus loyal love and living in justice pulled out of torment a pagan of Rome." Later in the twelfth Passus the case of Trajan is cited, and the principle is laid down that for him who lives as his religion teaches, and believes there is no better, a just God would never permit but that such a true man were approved. And finally, in Passus XV of the B text, in accordance with the same principle, Langland declared: "So may Saracens be saved and Scribes and Jews." The author of that contemporary masterpiece *Saint Erkenwald*, as I have already remarked, tells a story much like that of Trajan and of how a heathen judge of Belinus's time had executed justice with such flawless impartiality that not only was his corpse preserved uncorrupted for centuries in the tomb, but also his spirit was released from purgatory and joined the cenacle above because of a single tear shed by the Saxon saint.

The author of Mandeville's *Travels,* who now, thanks to Professor Josephine Bennett,[27] may be regarded as an Englishman, wrote of the Brahmins of India.[28] "Albeit that these folk have not the articles of our faith as we have, nevertheless, for their natural good faith and their good intent, I trow fully that God accepts their service, right as he did of Job, who was a paynim, and held him for his true servant. And therefore, albeit there be many diverse religions in the world, yet I trow that God loveth always them that love him meekly in truth. . . . No man should have in despite none earthly man for their diverse religions, for we know not whom God loveth, nor whom God hateth." As I have already noted, the devout visionary Dame Julian of Norwich wrote in her *Revelations of Divine Love:*[29] "In mankind that shall be saved is comprehended all; that is to say, all that is made and the Maker of all; for in man is God, and God is in all."

To such a doctrine of universal salvation Chaucer never approaches. But I think it is safe to say that, though he was not in our modern sense a free thinker, an agnostic, he displays in his poetry a broad tolerance and even a sympathy with honest doubt. He might have been willing to accept Tennyson's dictum:

> There lives more faith in honest doubt,
> Believe me, than in half the creeds.

ROGER SHERMAN LOOMIS,
Columbia University

Notes

[1] In 1950 Miss Mary Edith Thomas published a doctoral dissertation under the title *Medieval Skepticism and Chaucer* (William–Frederick Press, 391 East 149th St., New York). It was met with skepticism by several reviewers. Since it was prepared chiefly under my direction, I consider myself responsible for the material and the conclusions; and I am by no means ready to concede that the testimony of Dante, Benvenuto da Imola, the author of *Piers Plowman*, John Gower and many others, cited by Miss Thomas, is negligible or mendacious, as her critics imply. Accordingly, with acknowledgments to Miss Thomas, I propose to present the case briefly again, since I regard it as essential to the estimate of the poet as a serious thinker.

[2] R. S. Loomis, "Was Chaucer a Laodicean?", *Essays and Studies in Honor of Carleton Brown* (New York, 1940), pp. 141-46. Reprinted in *Chaucer Criticism*, ed. Richard J. Schoeck and Jerome Taylor (Notre Dame, 1960), pp. 302-4.

[3] P. 109.

[4] *The Triple Thinkers* (New York, 1948), p. 180.

[5] G. L. Kittredge, *Chaucer and His Poetry* (Cambridge, Mass., 1915), pp. 7 ff.

[6] *Gesta Romanorum*, ed. H. Oesterley (Berlin, 1872), pp. 397 ff.

[7] *Ibid.*, pp. 478 ff.

[8] Thomas Walsingham, *Historia Anglicana*, ed. T. H. Riley (Rolls Series, London, 1863-64), II:208.

[9] Gower, *Complete Works*, ed. G. C. Macaulay (Oxford, 1899-1902), I:287.

[10] *Piers Plowman*, B text, X:101-3, 105-12.

[11] *Ibid.*, C text, XII:35-7, 40 ff.

[12] *Comentum super Dantis Aldigherij Comoediam*, ed. J. P. Lacaita (Florence, 1887), I:357.

[13] *Oeuvres de Froissart*, ed. Kervyn de Lettenhove; *Chroniques*, XV (Brussels, 1871):179.

[14] *MP*, III (1905): 45 ff.

[15] *University of California Publications in English*, I (1929), p. 000.

[16] In *Speculum*, VI (1931):234, Prof. Howard Patch writes: "In the famous soliloquy of Troilus in Book IV, the hero gives, it is true, considerable expression to what, for the sake of argument, we may call determinism—although I think he is rather complaining against predestination and trying to exonerate himself without impiety. In any case, there is no reason to suppose that this monologue is spoken for other than dramatic effect."

[17] T. R. Lounsbury, *Studies in Chaucer* (New York, 1892), II:514 ff.

[18] R. W. Chambers, "Long Will, Dante, and the Righteous Heathen," *Essays and Studies by Members of the English Association*, IX (Oxford, 1924):50-69.

[19] *Paradiso*, Canto XIX.

[20] *The Divine Comedy*, Carlyle–Wicksteed translation, Modern Library (New York, 1932).

[21] Chambers, *loc. cit.*, p. 54.

[22] *Saint Erkenwald*, ed. H. L. Savage (New Haven, 1926).

[23] Juliana of Norwich, *Revelations of Divine Love*, ed. Roger Hudleston (London, 1927), p. 57.

[24] *Ibid.*, p. 17

[25] *Oeuvres*, ed. A. Scheler (Brussels, 1870-72), II:24.

[26] Juliana of Norwich, *op. cit.*, p. 48.

[27] Josephine W. Bennett, *Rediscovery of Sir John Mandeville* (New York, 1954), pp. 176-80.

[28] *Ibid.*, p. 73.

[29] See note 24.

The Development of the Wife of Bath

Although the Wife of Bath is generally interpreted from a static point of view which allows critics to see her just as she was left by Chaucer at the time of his death in 1400, a fuller understanding of her portrait may be revealed by an evolutionary point of view. In the course of years the poet's conception of her changed and developed; the complexity and appeal of her personality are no accident; for, when all the evidence is in, she appears to have interested Chaucer more, to have stimulated his imagination and creative power more fully and over a longer period, than any other of his characters.

The personality of the Wife of Bath is one of contradictions and paradox. She is old in years (beyond forty) but young in spirit. She speaks vividly of woe in marriage, but is eager to welcome a sixth husband as soon as possible. She declares that she can well understand that gentle text, "God bad us for to wexe and multiplye";[1] but like her barnyard rival and fellow devotee of Venus, daun Chauntecleer of the Nuns' Priest's Tale, she performs "the actes of mariage" all for love and nothing for reward—or, as Chaucer says of Chauntecleer, "Moore for delit than world to multiplye." Alice of Bath was born under the domination of Venus, but also under Mars. Venus gave Alice "lust" and "likerousnesse," but Mars gave her "sturdy hardynesse." She is "al Venerien In feelynge," but her "herte is Marcien." Again, as Professor Curry says, "she is . . . so coarse and shameless in her disclosures of the marital relations with five husbands, and yet so imaginative and delicate in her story-telling, that one is fascinated against his will. . . ."[2] She can tell of love and marriage from her own bitter, and sweet, experience; she distrusts clerks;

nevertheless in support of her views she is ready and able to cite and quote innumerable authorities—biblical, classical, and medieval. Jankyn, the "joly clerk" of Oxford, she classifies among her bad husbands; yet she declares that after their climactic brawl, both he and she were ever kind and true to each other. Thus contradiction is piled on contradiction, paradox on paradox. Such clashing inconsistencies help make the Wife human and add an extra dimension of reality to Chaucer's portrait of her.

Contributing to the vitality and complexity of the Wife is the intellectual background against which Chaucer portrayed her—the antimatrimonial and antifeminist tradition that flourished in his time." This tradition took the form chiefly of rather abstract, static materials: aphorism, anecdote, allegory, monitory advice to men, and vicious satire and invective against women. Chaucer uses the traditional material in a number of ways." Alice embodies in herself many of the qualities, characteristics, and habitual actions ascribed to womankind by the antifeminists; on occasion she sets forth the antimatrimonial doctrines and then argumentatively refutes them; again, she accuses various men of being antifeminists themselves; or she combats men who accuse her of possessing the traditional qualities of wicked wives. As Chaucer gradually assimilated and reworked the riches of his antimatrimonial inheritance, combining with them such other resources as astrological learning, folk materials, and his direct knowledge of contemporary English life, he developed the Wife over a period of years, and through a number of distinct stages, with increasing depth, reality, and significance.

The first section of this analysis of the development of the Wife of Bath is based on three related assumptions concerning Chaucer's early arrangement of tales and links: that the Man of Law originally told the story of *Melibee;* that his

Epilogue originally introduced the Wife of Bath; and that she originally told the tale of adultery now assigned to the Shipman. According to these assumptions, it was the Wife who originally protested against the possibility of having the Parson (whom the Host suspects of Lollardry) preach to the pilgrims, and hence offered her own services as storyteller (II 1178-90):[3]

> "Nay, by my fader soule, that schal he nat!"
> Seyde the Wyf of Bathe; "he schal nat preche;
> He schal no gospel glosen here ne teche.
> We leven alle in the grete God," quod she;
> "He wolde sowen som difficulte,
> Or springen cokkel in our clene corn.
> And therfore, Hoost, I warne thee biforn,
> My joly body schal a tale telle,
> And I schal clynken you so mery a belle,
> That I schal waken al this compaignie.
> But it schal not ben of philosophie,
> Ne phislyas, ne termes queinte of lawe.
> Ther is but litel Latyn in my mawe!"

Clearly the Wife has been bored nearly to sleep by the preaching, the philosophy, the physicians, the law terms, and the Latin in the tale just finished (the *Melibee*), and fears not heresy but more preaching. She is a proponent not of religious orthodoxy but of merry tales. The story first assigned to her is a Boccaccian fabliau of the Lover's Gift Regained, concerning the encounter of a merchant's wife and a monk, who borrows money from the merchant and then pays it to the wife, who spends it on new clothes. The narrator fulfills her promise: it is a merry tale; and the merchant's wife must have been a woman right after the Wife of Bath's own heart: for at the end of the story, the wife owes her husband money and promises to pay him her debt with her "joly body." Thus the early Wife of Bath was presented as a woman who thought of her body as "joly," and who liked a merry tale of adultery.

We learn more about her as she introduces the heroine of her tale (VII 3-19):

> A wyf he hadde of excellent beautee;
> And compaignable and revelous was she,
> Which is a thyng that causeth more dispence
> Than worth is al the chiere and reverence
> That men hem doon at festes and at daunces.
> Swiche salutaciouns and contenaunces
> Passen as dooth a shadwe upon the wal;
> But wo is hym that payen moot for al!
> The sely housbonde, algate he moot paye,
> He moot us clothe, and he moot us arraye,
> Al for his owene worshipe richely,
> In which array we daunce jolily.
> And if that he noght may, par aventure,
> Or ellis list no swich dispence endure,
> But thynketh it is wasted and ylost,
> Thanne moot another payen for oure cost,
> Or lene us gold, and that is perilous.

In these prefatory remarks, the Wife of Bath presents her conception of a typical wife (and husband?) and also tends to identify herself with that wife: a woman who is companionable and "revelous," who enjoys feasts, dances, and rich, fancy clothing, and who is eager to have and to spend money. Later in the story the heroine tells the monk that she is grieved by her husband's niggardliness, and says (VII 173-81):

> "And wel ye woot that wommen naturelly
> Desiren thynges sixe as wel as I:
> They wolde that hir housbondes sholde be
> Hardy, and wise, and riche, and therto free,

And buxom unto his wyf, and fressh abedde.
But by that ilke Lord that for us bledde,
For his honour, myself for to arraye,
A Sonday next I moste nedes paye
An hundred frankes, or ellis I am lorn."

Thus the Wife of Bath sets herself up as an authority on women, husbands, and love, and indicates her appreciation of elegant clothing.

Certain lines describing the Wife of Bath in the General Prologue of the *Canterbury Tales,* fit the woman mirrored by this tale: those which tell of her gay clothing; of her fair, bold, red face; of her large hips; of her laughter and joking; and of her knowledge of the "olde daunce" of the art of love. The prologue to the tale, the tale itself, and these portions of the General Prologue, however, offer no hint of old age; of a man-hungry widow; of a wife-wielded whip of tribulation and woe; or of many marriages—much less a defense of them. Only one danger appears to threaten the husband: that another will take his place if he is not generous with his love and gold; the spirit is all gaiety and joyous pleasure. In short, this early Wife of Bath really has little or nothing to do with antimatrimonialism or antifeminism. Further, the Wife as first conceived by Chaucer in this early simple portrait, does what we should naturally expect the average pilgrim to do: simply tells a conventional tale more or less suited to her personality and to her position in life: the autobiographical and doctrinal passages appear later.

If such was the early Wife of Bath, the next question is just how Chaucer proceeded to enlarge and develop her portrait. There are various possibilities, each involving the three main segments of the Wife of Bath's Prologue. This Prologue contains, first, the Wife's defense of many marriages, and of marriage itself as contrasted to virginity; then (after the Pardoner's interruption), her account of the tribulation she inflicted on her first three husbands, all "goode . . . , and riche, and olde," but completely undifferentiated from each other; and finally, the interrelated accounts of her adventures with her fourth and fifth husbands, the two quite distinct "badde" ones.

After carefully examining the Prologue, R. F. Jones pointed out that the first section, the Wife's "defense of the sensual pleasures of marriage," forms a "unified and well developed" conception, "distinctly different" from the remainder of the Prologue in tone, purpose, and source. I believe that the same distinction should be made concerning each of the other two sections; so I make use of and elaborate on Jones's conclusions. The first section, the Wife's defense of marriage and lust, is "combative and argumentative"; the second section, on her browbeating her first three husbands ("goode men, and riche, and olde") is "expository and descriptive";[4] the third section, on her adventures with the fourth and fifth (young and "badde") is narrative and dramatic.[5] The first section makes marriage seem attractive—except to the *eunuchus ex nativitate* who is on the pilgrimage, the Pardoner; the second section makes marriage seem unattractive—at least to men; the third shows (Alice hopes) how marital submission by the husband is rewarded by eternal kindness. The first is based on St. Jerome's *Epistola adversus Iovinianum;* the second, on Eustache Deschamps and on Theophrastus; the third on excerpts from St. Jerome, on Walter Map's *Epistola Valerii ad Rufinum,* and on Valerius Maximus, whom Chaucer presumably took to be the same author.

At first glance it may look as if Jerome's *Epistola* were a common source for all three sections. However, soon after Map's letter began to circulate, it attracted to itself, in many manuscripts, other Latin pieces in the antimatrimonial tradition, in particular the *Liber Aureolus Theophrasti de Nuptiis* as an independent item, separated from its position as chapter 47 in Book I of Jerome. Further, along with Valerius and Theophrastus there appears in several manuscripts a collection of antifeminist excerpts also from Jerome. That Chaucer was acquainted with such a manuscript compilation is suggested both by his description of the contents of the "book of wikked wyves" (669-81) belonging to Alice's fifth husband (its first three items were "Valerie and Theofraste . . . and . . . Seint Jerome . . . agayn Jovinian"), and also by his use of just such a collection as basic source material for the Wife's description of her first three husbands and her story of the fifth. Thus, whereas the first section of the Wife's Prologue is based on St. Jerome's *Epistola*, the sections on the five husbands are based not on this opus but on the initial pieces of Jankyn's "book of wikked wyves." Further, in the second section of the Prologue (the three old husbands) Chaucer used one part of Jankyn's "book" (the "Theofraste") while for the third section (fourth and fifth husbands) he used different parts (the "Valerie" and the "Seint Jerome").

Three different pieces of evidence suggest that the narrative of the five husbands was written before the "sermon." First, the Wife's many marriages and her lustfulness are the *raison d'être* for her "sermon," the purpose of which is to justify her conduct and beliefs.

Second, the "sermon" does not fit well between the Epilogue of the Man of Law's Tale and the tale of the Lover's Gift Regained, whereas the Wife's account of her browbeating her old husbands fits nicely in this position. The "sermon" cannot logically follow the Epilogue of the Man of Law's Tale; although the first six lines of the Wife's Prologue follow well enough after this Epilogue, the "sermon" as a whole does not: it is not "a tale" (II 1185), but involves learning (1168), preaching of a sort (1179), glossing, and teaching (1180), and skirts far too close to "philosophie" (1188) and even Latin (1190). In fact the "sermon" sounds as if the subject of marriage were already under discussion and may indicate Chaucer's achievement of the brilliant shift of the Wife of Bath's Prologue to a position following the Nuns' Priest's Tale. Nor does the "sermon" lead logically to the tale of the Lover's Gift Regained, with which it has little or nothing in common; nor can it lead to the fairy tale of the loathly hag directly, but only (as it eventually does) through the intervening account of the five husbands. Although the "sermon" does not fit between the Epilogue of the Man of Law's Tale and the tale of the Lover's Gift Regained, on the other hand, Alice's account of her browbeating her old husbands fits each juncture of this position. It follows neatly after the Man of Law's Tale of *Melibee*, where touches of antifeminism are matched by touches of feminism, all supported by authorities. It follows neatly after the Epilogue of the Man of Law's Tale, for it is narrative rather than argumentative and so can be called "a tale" (as it is called by Alice on several occasions); it is the antithesis of all Alice says she is avoiding and fits her promise that

> My joly body schal a tale telle,
> And I schal clynken you so mery a belle,
> That I schal waken al this compaignie.

These lines lead easily and naturally to the antimatrimonial, antifeminist materials adapted from Theophrastus and Eustache Deschamps. Further, the account of the old husbands leads nicely to the tale of the Lover's Gift Regained; in fact, of all the sections of the Wife of Bath's Prologue, this is the closest in details to the original Wife's tale, each picturing the husband as rich and hoarding, but ineffectual, and the wife as eager for money, involved in clothing, dances, and deceit, and proud of her *bele chose*

Third, the echoing of lines 1-6 by the Wife's rejoinder to the Pardoner is most easily explained through the assumption that "sermon," interruption, and rejoinder, were written together and inserted between lines 1-6 and the account of Alice's browbeating her old husbands. These opening lines of the Wife's Prologue are actually an introduction not to the "sermon" but to the account of woe in marriage:

> "Experience, though noon auctoritee
> Were in this world, is right ynogh for me
> To speke of wo that is in mariage;
> For, lordynges, sith I twelve yeer was of age,
> Thonked be God that is eterne on lyve,
> Housbondes at chirche dore I have had fyve. . . ."

The Wife's rejoinder to the Pardoner's interruption, in its turn, involves repetition and elaboration of these ideas. This rejoinder is not intended to introduce such a story as the Lover's Gift Regained or the fairy tale of the loathly hag, neither of which it fits; rather it is clearly designed to introduce the various materials forming the remainder of the Wife's Prologue, for it presupposes several husbands, tribulation, personal experience, and examples (169-79):

> "Abyde!" quod she, "my tale is nat bigonne.
> Nay, thou shalt drynken of another tonne,
> Er that I go, shal savoure wors than ale.
> And whan that I have toold thee forth my tale
> Of tribulacion in mariage,
> Of which I am expert in al myn age,
> This is to seyn, myself have been the whippe,—
> Than maystow chese wheither thou wolt sippe
> Of thilke tonne that I shal abroche.

> Be war of it, er thou to ny approche;
> For I shal telle ensamples mo than ten."

Thus upon examination, lines 1-6 of the Prologue appear to be in a strange location; I suggest that they (or similar lines) were originally written to connect the Epilogue of the Man of Law's Tale with the account of marital tribulation and woe which they actually serve to introduce; and that only later were the "sermon," the Pardoner's interruption, and the Wife's rejoinder inserted between these six lines and the narrative of the five husbands.

Certain facts suggest that husbands four and five represent a later stage in the development of the Wife than do the first three. It is dramatically inappropriate for the Wife to draw upon the *Aureolus Liber* of Theophrastus for ammunition (as she does with the first three husbands) before it has been read to her by her fifth husband, Jankyn clerk; hence it seems likely that when using the "book of wikked wyves" for the Wife's account of her first three husbands, Chaucer had not yet thought of presenting the book as the favorite reading of the fifth husband and thus using it as a crucial factor in the story of Alice's struggle with him. Further, it is notable that when he is quoting from his "book of wikked wyves," Jankyn does not offer a single nugget from "Theofraste," though he quotes from "Valerie," "Seint Jerome," "the Parables of Salomon," and "Ovides Art." Apparently Chaucer had already exhausted the treasures of "Theofraste" when presenting the tribulations of the first three husbands. Another piece of evidence which suggests that Chaucer had written the account of the first three husbands before he conceived the idea of the fourth and fifth is the presence of "oure apprentice Janekyn" in the former section. Chaucer has the Wife say (303-307):

And yet of oure apprentice Janekyn,
For his crispe heer, shynynge as gold so fyn,
And for he squiereth me bothe up and doun,
Yet hastow caught a fals suspecioun.
I wol hym noght, thogh thou were deed tomorwe!

Chaucer has been paraphrasing the following passage from Theophrastus: "Honoranda nutrix ejus, et gerula, servus patrinus, et alumnus, et formosus assecla, et procurator calamistratus. . . ." The marginal gloss "Et procurator calamistratus et cetera" opposite line 303 in the Ellesmere manuscript,[6] shows that Chaucer was expanding Theophrastus in the description of "oure apprentice Janekyn." In this passage Chaucer presented a triangle made up of Alice, one of her three old husbands, and the "apprentice Janekyn," which is matched by the later triangle consisting of Alice, her fourth husband, and "Jankyn clerk"; and in each triangle the death of the husband is presented as facilitating a *rapprochement* between Alice and a "Jankyn." Since the first triangle is based on Theophrastus, it is more likely that the second was based on the first than vice versa; a development from the simple situation (presented in five lines) to the complex narrative (presented at length, with wooing, funeral, and so on) is what we should expect rather than the opposite. In short, the trivial mention of the "apprentice Janekyn" could hardly have been caused by "Jankyn clerk" but could most naturally have led to him under the influence of the "book of wikked wyves."

Thus I conclude that in enlarging and developing the original portrait of the Wife of Bath, Chaucer first took the step of separating the Epilogue of the Man of Law's Tale, and the Wife's tale of the Lover's Gift Regained, and reconnecting them by means of lines very similar to lines 1-6 of her Prologue and the account of her browbeating those indistinguishable husbands, "goode men, and riche, and olde" (whether three or five in number, there is no telling). If he did this, the original phrasing was lost with the subsequent addition of the two young "badde" husbands; but the introduction of the final total of five seems fairly smooth in the text just as we have it if the three passages are juxtaposed:

> My joly body schal a tale telle,
> And I schal clynken you so mery a belle,
> That I schal waken al this compaignie.
> But it schal not ben of philosophie,
> Ne phislyas, ne termes queinte of lawe.
> Ther is but litel Latyn in my mawe!
> Experience, though noon auctoritee
> Were in this world, is right ynogh for me
> To speke of wo that is in mariage;
> For, lordynges, sith I twelve yeer was of age,
> Thonked be God that is eterne on lyve,
> Housbondes at chirche dore I have had fyve.
> I shal seye sooth, tho housbondes that I hadde,
> As thre of hem were goode, and two were badde.

Like the Wife originally presented by Chaucer, the Wife depicted in the section on the good, old, rich husbands, is concerned (as already noted) with money, clothing, dances, deceit, and her *bele chose;* but in these Theophrastian passages telling how she browbeat her husbands, her personality is given a tone of woe not found in the General Prologue, the Epilogue of the Man of Law's Tale, or the tale of the Lover's Gift Regained. The account of the Wife's wielding the whip of matrimonial tribulation is thus the section of her Prologue which is closest to Chaucer's first conception of her, and is at the same time the first natural step in the development of that portrait, creating a total effect that is

strikingly new and different. In fact this extensive autobiographical passage constitutes an innovation in the very
structure of the *Canterbury Tales.* From line 200 of her
Prologue through line 451, the Wife tells in detail how she
handled her old husbands, making them "swynke a-nyght,"
swearing and lying, accusing them of misbehavior in word
and deed. She refers to her prey now in the plural, now in
the singular; these rich, old husbands are undifferentiated
one from another; but their woes are vivid enough. Here
Chaucer effectively dramatizes material from the antimatrimonial treatises by having the Wife accuse these wretched
creatures of saying about her the very things that Theophrastus had said about wives. Thus spirited words and actions
are assigned to her, and she takes on a dramatic energy not
found hitherto in the *Canterbury Tales* or in the poet's
traditional predecessors.

This new Wife of Bath, who makes her husbands lead **lives**
of woe, was inspired largely by the *Aureolus Liber* of Theophrastus and by the reworking of this tract by Eustache
Deschamps in the *Miroir de Mariage.* In the *Miroir* the old
woman was presented as addicted to pilgrimages and punctil-
ious about precedence at offerings; hence it may have been at
this time that Chaucer's figure (that is, the portrait of the
Wife in the General Prologue) took on these characteristics.
In the *Miroir,* too, is the delicate touch of the widow who
buries her husband inexpensively and at his funeral has an
eye out for his successor—motifs by means of which Chaucer
was to fuse the adventures of husbands four and five.

With the introduction of individualized portraits for the
fourth and fifth husbands, new sources and a new tone are
again introduced: there is still woe in marriage, but now the
tables are turned on Alice, and the husbands seize the whip.
The fourth made her jealous by his "revelous" escapades

("he hadde a paramour"); and the fifth tormented her with
his book and beat her with his fist. These victories, however,
were only seeming, only temporary, for in the end she had her
revenge. The fourth she made fry "in his owene grece," buried
in an inexpensive fashion, and mourned for not at all, but
instead forgot in favor of her fifth husband, whom she
had already courted. The fifth she finally worsted in their
climactic brawl, making him agree to give her "soveraynetee"
through the rest of their married life.

The creation of this fifth husband, "joly" Jankyn clerk, was
clearly due to Chaucer's intimate acquaintance with the collection of controversial antimatrimonial tracts already discussed. In the narrative Chaucer brings the tracts to life by
making the "book of wikked wyves" a *dramatis persona*.
Jankyn had brought this volume down from Oxford, where
the influence of *Valerius ad Rufinum* is attested by at least
three fourteenth-century commentaries, two of them in several versions and many manuscripts.[7] It was his favorite
fireside reading. He would read sniggering to himself, or
aloud to Alice, or he would recount stories and sayings to
her in his own words: for example, about Eve, Delilah, and
Xantippe, and then about Latumyus and his "blissed tree."
After various stories of "wikked wyves," he read proverbs,
and finally (782-85)

> He seyde, "a womman cast hir shame away,
> Whan she cast of hir smok"; and forthermo,
> "A fair womman, but she be chaast also,
> Is lyk a gold ryng in a sowes nose."

This was the last straw; the formidable Alice took matters
into her own hands: she tore three leaves from the volume and
struck Jankyn such a blow on the cheek that he rolled back-
wards into the fire; he up and smote her on the head,

and she landed, as if dead, on the floor. Pathetically she asked him to kiss her before she died—and when he knelt down over her, she hit him square on the cheek with her "fest." At long last they reached an accord and drew up a treaty: she won governance of house and land, and of his tongue; and he, in turn, agreed to burn the book. Alice says, "After that day we hadden never debaat."

In the story of the fourth and fifth husbands there appear several details which occur also in the portrait of the Wife in the General Prologue, but are not found in the Epilogue of the Man of Law's Tale or in the tale of the Lover's Gift Regained, and hence were probably not in the earliest Prologue portrait of the Wife. It seems likely, then, that when these two husbands were created, the portrait of the Wife in the General Prologue was completed by the inclusion of at least some of the following details: deafness (I 446; III 634, 636, 668), attendance at religious observances (I 449-50; III 555-58), coverchiefs (I 453; III 590), scarlet array (I 456; III 559), pilgrimages (I 463-66; III 557), Jerusalem (I 463; III 495), and the fact that she was "gat-tothed" (I 468; III 603). In addition, revision around the time when the fourth and fifth husbands were being set down is suggested by three lines in particular (I 460-62):

> Housbondes at chirche dore she hadde fyve,
> Withouten oother compaignye in youthe,—
> But therof nedeth nat to speke as nowthe.

At this point mention should be made of the Merchant's Tale, for it must have been written (for its original teller, whether Merchant, Monk, or Friar) after the narrative of the five husbands but presumably before the "sermon," and before the tale of the monk and the merchant's wife (the Lover's Gift Regained) was taken from the Wife. The Merchant's

Tale reveals indebtedness to Jankyn's "book of wikked wyves" (Valerius, Theophrastus, and excerpts from Jerome) and also to the *Miroir de Mariage* of Eustache Deschamps, and parallels to the sections of the Wife's Prologue on the five husbands. Both in the allusions to the Wife (for example, "thise olde wydwes"; 1423) and in the actual mention of her (1685), the context has to do with the old experienced woman who has browbeaten her husbands and made marriage a miserable affair, whereas there is no hint of the Wife's "sermon." [8] Further, the Merchant's Tale seems partly intended as a retort to the Wife for her story of a rich old merchant who neglected his young wife and was cuckolded by a "yonge monk"; hence the Merchant's Tale was written presumably before that story was taken from the Wife—an event which I hope to show occurred at about the time her "sermon" was written.

The narrative of Alice and her fourth and fifth husbands offers the portrayal not only of a whip-wielding wife, but also of an experienced, man-hungry, lustful widow, scheming for another mate. With this total of five husbands, and this emphasis on unbridled, insatiable lust, comes the need for the Wife's defense of the sensual pleasures of marriage and of her right to marry many times, which is the business of her introductory argumentative "sermon" (lines 1-162). The excerpts from St. Jerome in Jankyn's "book of wikked wyves" may have reminded Chaucer of Jovinian's arguments in favor of many marriages, appearing earlier in Jerome's *Epistola adversus Iovinianum;* in any event, the Wife's defense of marriage and lust is based on this controversial tract. In making dramatic use of the *Epistola,* Chaucer allows the Wife to defend her own actions and beliefs by using Jovinian's arguments and his quotations from Scripture to controvert the orthodox position of Jerome. The Wife of Bath has been praised, in our time, for the modernity of her defense; but the modernist in this controversy is the fourth-century heretic Jovinian who, flying in the faces of St. Paul and monasticism, declared that virginity and marriage are equally worthy in the sight of God, and favored a married clergy. Chaucer, then, dramatizes portions of Jerome's tract by putting Jovinian's arguments into the Wife's mouth as answers to St. Jerome's arguments, which have been presented to her by unnamed "men" (26, 34, 66), "folk" (53), "clerkes" (125), or the like (9, 119).

The tone and wording (especially "my tale": 169, 172, 193) of the interchange between the Pardoner and the Wife (163-193), written as a transition from her "sermon" to her account of the five husbands, suggest that Chaucer had decided that this vigorous account offered a far better and more suitable tale for the Wife than the Lover's Gift Regained—and who would disagree? It is a brilliant narrative, full of conflicts, presented as garrulous autobiography, and hence far more vivid and exciting than the average tale told by a pilgrim; despite a superficial appearance of casual carelessness, the characters prove to be various and sometimes highly individualized, the plot intricate, and the action dramatic and well designed. In her rejoinder, promising "ensamples mo than ten" (179) to illustrate "tribulacion in mariage, Of which I am expert in al myn age" (173-74), the Wife clearly regards the account of her husbands as her "tale"; indeed, after it the Lover's Gift Regained would have been anticlimactic.

Various pieces of evidence combine to suggest that the creation of the "sermon" as the Wife of Bath's Prologue and the use of the account of the five husbands as the Wife of Bath's Tale were accompanied by three important changes in the structure of the *Canterbury Tales*. The Wife of Bath's contribution to the disport of the pilgrims was shifted from its position after the Man of Law's Tale of *Melibee,* and its Epilogue, to a new position after the Nuns' Priest's Tale. The Clerk's Tale, now framed by an especially prepared Prologue and ending, was made to follow the Wife of Bath's Tale and lead to the Merchant's Prologue (and Tale). Fragment VII was set up more or less as it now stands—particularly its latter half (*Melibee*-Monk-Nuns' Priest). One of the most important keys to these related moves is the cancellation of the Nuns' Priest's Epilogue and the original Clerk's endlink (IV 1212 ª⁻ᵍ) and their combination and rewriting and expansion to form the *Melibee*–Monk link (there is clear evidence that the Monk's Tale and the Nuns' Priest's Tale were linked already).[9]

Next it has already been suggested that whereas Alice's account of browbeating her old husbands is a merry tale which fits neatly between the Epilogue of the Man of Law's Tale and the tale of the Lover's Gift Regained, the argumentative "sermon," with its emphasis on learning and preaching, does not; indeed, the "sermon" sounds as if the subject of marriage were already under discussion, and in a number of passages appears to have been written expressly to counter certain satirical thrusts in the Nuns' Priest's Tale. The Nuns' Priest satirizes women, wives, and married life, and makes fun of a rooster for taking a woman's advice. In her "sermon" Alice of Bath defends "wyves" and "wyfhod" and marriage. Chauntecleer "hadde in his governaunce Sevene hennes for to doon al his plesaunce" (VII 2865-66), and the Nuns' Priest again and again makes fun of the rooster for having "sevene wyves." Alice, in turn, defends her right to have many marriages, to wed as often as her husbands die; she envies Solomon; and she claims power over each husband's "propre body" all her life. The Nuns' Priest makes fun of physical love and asserts that Chauntecleer does the work of Venus "Moore for delit than world to multiplye" (VII 3345); Alice praises and defends the "actes" of marriage and declares (III 28-29):

> God bad us for to wexe and multiplye;
> That gentil text kan I wel understonde.

Chauntecleer is teased for his uxoriousness; Alice points out that the Apostle "bad oure housbondes for to love us weel"; and adds, "Al this sentence me liketh every deel" (161-62). Chauntecleer presents his "auctours" and "ensamples olde"; the Wife is clearly proud of her ability to cite authorities and, looking towards the narrative of her five husbands, promises "ensamples mo than ten" (179), outdoing Chauntecleer. The placing of the Wife's "sermon" immediately after the Nuns' Priest's Tale of course meant the setting up of the more extensive sequence *Melibee*–Monk's Prologue and Tale– Nuns' Priest's Prologue and Tale–Wife of Bath's Prologue and Tale. The effects of this sequence were described by Lawrence, Tupper, Kenyon, and Hemingway, and have been summarized as follows: "Through this juxtaposition, the related problems of celibacy, women, marriage, wives, and 'sovereynetee,' start with Chaucer's own Dame Prudence, and Harry Bailey, and the antifeminist Monk, and then develop easily and naturally from the story of the vainglorious cock, whose multiplicity of wives is echoed by Alice of Bath's desire for many husbands, and whose flourishing of 'auctoritees' is matched by her public airing of her own 'experience.'" [10]

The Clerk's Tale was framed between the Clerk's Prologue, and his final words to the company and *Lenvoy de Chaucer*,[10a] in order to relate the Tale and its teller to the Wife of Bath, her "sermon," and her tale of the five husbands, and also to serve as introduction to the Merchant's Prologue and Tale. The Wife who is alluded to and named in this framework is clearly the woman who preaches heretical views on marriage, wields the whip of woe over five husbands, and wins complete "governaunce" in marriage. Chaucer allows her views and deeds, and the role and fate of her fifth husband, "joly" Jankyn, sometime clerk of Oxenford, to stir this fellow alumnus, the Clerk of the pilgrimage, to thoughtful retaliation and revenge. I believe that Chaucer originally designed these framing pieces to follow directly after the narrative of Jankyn clerk without intervention of the Lover's Gift Regained or of the Friar's and Summoner's Tales, because in this position richer overtones are offered by certain words of the Host and the Clerk. Having heard Alice's heretical prologue and having just learned how the "joly clerk, Jankyn" was beaten to a pulp, the Clerk is quiet, thoughtful, and sober. It is no wonder that the Host guesses that he studies "aboute som sophyme" (IV 5) and then asks him for "som myrie tale" (9); nor that the Clerk in turn admits that he is under the Host's "yerde" and "governance" (22, 23) and declares that Petrarch's "prohemye" (indeed shorter than Chaucer's rendering of it) was long and a "thyng impertinent" (52, 54). Then, mocking this "heresiarch" (as Kittredge brilliantly called the Wife), he wishes that God maintain "al hire secte . . . In heigh maistrie" (1171–72). In addition to the general appositeness to the Wife of the Clerk's words to the company and his mock encomium, there are specific parallels: her "maistrie" (IV 1172; III 314, 818) or "governaille" (IV 1192; III 219, 814); her causing jealousy (IV 1205; III 488); "doth hem no reverence" (IV 1201) and "Me neded nat do lenger diligence To wynne hir love, or doon hem reverence" (III 205-206); and best of all, the Clerk's saying (IV 1185-87):

> Ne lat no clerk have cause or diligence
> To write of yow a storie of swich mervaille
> As of Grisildis pacient and kynde. . . .

words which ironically echo Alice (III 688-90):

> For trusteth wel, it is an impossible
> That any clerk wol speke good of wyves,
> But if it be of hooly seintes lyves. . . .

and so on for twenty more lines. Finally, Alice's "myn entente is nat but for to pleye" (III 192) is picked up by the Host's "what man that is entred in a pley, He nedes moot unto the pley assente" (IV 10-11) and capped by the Clerk's "And lat us stynte of ernestful matere" (IV 1175).

Thus the writing of the Wife of Bath's "sermon" appears to have been involved in a complex of interrelated cancellations, shifts, and preparations of new arrangements and linkages. Together these developed and enlivened the personality of Alice and also extended her relationships with the other pilgrims. By now Chaucer was building up what has been called the "Marriage Group," though its extent in the structure of the *Canterbury Tales* and in complexity of theme is greater than this label implies.

Several pieces of evidence suggest that after the writing of the "sermon" came the short independent poem, *Lenvoy de Chaucer a Bukton,* concerning marriage. Here Chaucer declares that he promised "to expresse The sorwe and wo that is in mariage" (5-6) and commends to the nubile Bukton some outside reading (29-30):[11]

> The Wyf of Bathe I praye yow that ye rede
> Of this matere that we have on honde.

Further, *Lenvoy de Chaucer a Bukton* echoes lines found in the Wife's "sermon" and in the Wife's rejoinder to the Pardoner: "Bet ys to wedde than brenne in worse wise" (18) recalls "Bet is to be wedded than to brynne" (III 52); and "But thow shal have sorwe on thy flessh, thy lyf, And ben thy wives thral, as seyn these wise" (19-20) recalls III 154-57:

> An housbonde I wol have, I wol nat lette,
> Which shal be bothe my dettour and my thral,
> And have his tribulacion withal
> Upon his flessh, whil that I am his wyf.

Finally, the words "yf that hooly writ may nat suffyse, Experience shal the teche" (21-22) sums up the contrast basic to the entire structure of the Wife of Bath's Prologue and its division into "sermon" and personal narrative. Since *Lenvoy de Chaucer a Bukton* was written around 1396, presumably the entire Wife's Prologue had been written by this time—the "sermon" and the Pardoner's interruption and the Wife's rejoinder perhaps rather recently, so close are the parallels. Thus we are given a rough dating for the various changes related to the writing of the "sermon."

Only with the completion of the Prologue of the Wife of Bath, when her personality had become rather complex, did Chaucer, I believe, achieve his most brilliant stroke in his portraiture of the Wife by treating the "sermon" and the account of the five husbands as Prologue to a new tale, the fairy story of an "olde wyf" who became young and beautiful and faithful when the hero-knight, her unwilling husband, promised to obey her in all things—in short, yielded "sovereynetee" to her. Far from picturing woe in marriage, this tale emphasizes Alice's desire for a sixth husband. In retelling the old tale of the loathly hag and the hero's choice, the poet transformed the tale (as we know it through analogues)[12] in a number of ways, several of which stress the ideals, promote the aims, and enhance the personality of the Wife of Bath. Some innovations encourage the audience to identify the heroine of the tale with Alice, and the hero with any eligible candidate for the position of sixth husband. For example, only Chaucer leaves the hero nameless; again, the heroine is referred to as an "olde wyf" (1000, 1046, etc.); her loathliness is not described, in strong contrast to the vivid, almost nauseating olla-podrida of details offered in Gower's *Tale of Florent* and in the *Weddynge of Sir Gawen and Dame Ragnell;* and in her curtain lecture the "olde wyf" preaches, with as much illogic as Alice, on matters concerning which the Wife, in her Prologue, has already revealed sensitivity. Other innovations emphasize Alice's delight in lust, which is glorified from the start: the knight is a hero after Alice's own heart, for his crime is rape rather than murder or trespass; he is saved from the death penalty by "the queene and othere ladyes mo"; the "olde wyf" speeds him to altar and bed without pausing for bath or bridal array; she teases him about his reluctance "this firste nyght" (his "walwynge" is in sharp contrast to the "many a myrie fit" of Solomon's first nights in the Wife's Prologue); and in rewarding him at the end the "olde wyf" declares (1217-18):

> But nathelees, syn I knowe youre delit,
> I shal fulfille youre worldly appetit.

Next, certain innovations stress the theme of "sovereynetee": the knight plights his "trouthe" to do the next thing she requires without knowing what this will be; at court he does not try the wrong answers at all, but gives only the correct answer ("sovereynetee") and gives it immediately; and the answer satisfies every "wyf," "mayde," and "wydwe": all praise him.

Alice's desire to make marriage to her seem attractive brings about the greatest innovation of all, the "olde wyf's" curtain lecture on "gentillesse," poverty, old age, and loathliness. Alice's consciousness of low birth and her desire for social standing, have been made apparent in her struggles for precedence at offerings, and in her concern over her marital status; and to some degree in her unexpected moments of sensitivity concerning various proprieties[13] and in her marriage to Jankyn clerk. So the "olde wyf" preaches that gentle deeds and virtuous living, not high birth, make "gentillesse"— though what is gentle, what virtuous, she never divulges! The "olde wyf" next says (1177) that the knight had reproached her for poverty, even though he was not guilty of so mercenary a lapse (the "olde wyf" herself had said that she was poor—1063); her defense of poverty, however impressive (with quotations from Seneca, Juvenal, and Secundus Philosophus), serves only to gild the gold of Alice, who has managed to outlive three rich husbands. In answer to the knight's reproach that she is old and foul, the "olde wyf" says little except that "filthe and eelde" (1215-16)

> Been grete wardeyns upon chastitee.

These comments lead directly to her changing the childish problem of the analogues—whether to have her fair by day and foul by night, or the opposite—to the complex, sophisticated problem—whether to have her old and foul but faithful, or young and fair—a choice fitting Alice's complex desires and personality. The curtain lecture and the offered choice intensify the total effect of the audience's identification of Alice with the "olde wyf" and anticipate (while leading to) the climactic transformation scene, where, in return for yielding "sovereynetee," the knight is so rewarded that (1253)

> His herte bathed in a bath of blisse.

But the real transformation takes place in the listener's mind, a transformation more marvelous than any in fairyland, as Alice does her best to change all her disadvantages into advantages. Her old age, her low birth, and her homeliness, fade into her dreams of lost beauty and lost youth; her declaration under oath that her fifth husband's yielding the "sovereynetee" to her made all well (823-25)—

> God helpe me so, I was to hym as kynde
> As any wyf from Denmark unto Ynde,
> And also trewe, and so was he to me—

might suggest to the unwary that here in reality is the "parfit joye" so beautifully depicted in that tale of "manye hundred yeres ago" (1255-56):[14]

> And she obeyed hym in every thyng
> That myghte doon hym pleasance or likyng.

Along with (or soon after) the placing of the fairy tale of the knight and the "olde wyf" after the long Wife of Bath's Prologue, come the Friar's teasing interruption[15] (echoing and balancing somewhat the Pardoner's interruption), the start of the Friar–Summoner quarrel, and the Wife's teasing compliment to the Friar on his unique role as only extant incubus surviving from a lost world. Indeed, the interchange between Friar and Wife on the Canterbury road forms part of the motif of the knight's violation of the maiden in a "land fulfild of fayerye," and bridges the "straunge strem" between the fourteenth century and Arthour's kingdom of "manye hundred yeres ago" in such a way as to heighten the tone of reality which, for all our disbelief, permeates Alice's tale.

One statement in the opening thrust at the Friar may imply that the "olde wyf" of the tale is herself the queen of the fairies. In setting the tale, Alice says (860-61):

> The elf-queene, with hir joly compaignye,
> Daunced ful ofte in many a grene mede.

Later, when the knight leaves court in order to discover
"What thyng is it that wommen moost desiren," we read
(988-98):

> The day was come that homward moste he tourne,
> And in his wey it happed hym to ryde,
> In al this care, under a forest syde,
> Wher as he saugh upon a daunce go
> Of ladyes foure and twenty, and yet mo;
> Toward the whiche daunce he drow ful yerne,
> In hope that som wysdom sholde he lerne.
> But certeinly, er he cam fully there,
> Vanysshed was this daunce, he nyste where.
> No creature saugh he that bar lyf,
> Save on the grene he saugh sittynge a wyf. . . .

There can be little question about what we are intended to
believe, and the hint is all the more persuasive because indirect.

Thus the Friar's and Summoner's Tales came to form an
interlude between the Wife's Tale and those of the Clerk and
Merchant. We may wonder whether the Squire's Tale—had
it been completed for that "lovyere"—might not have achieved
a closer relationship to the Wife. In any event, the discussion
of marriage was eventually crowned by the Franklin, who
took up and gave a new turn to the Wife's themes of "gentillesse" and "sovereynetee," and presented a heroine who de-
sired to be like one of St. Jerome's good women who would
rather die than be defouled. Whereas Alice, in the preach-
ments of the "olde wyf," had failed to reveal the true nature
of "gentillesse," the Franklin, in his words to the Squire and
in his story of gentle deeds, more than made up for the omis-

sion. The Franklin's Tale completed what may be called the external developments in the portraiture of the Wife of Bath; there remain some internal developments still to be discussed.

Certain manuscripts of the *Canterbury Tales* contain in the Wife of Bath's Prologue five extra passages totalling thirty-two lines; it is generally agreed that these passages represent late additions by Chaucer to the text. His habit of inserting passages in his work is revealed also, for example, by the recurring insertion of *exempla* from St. Jerome's *Epistola adversus Iovinianum* in Dorigen's complaint in the Franklin's Tale (V 1367-1456) and his plans to add even more.[16] Hence it is reasonable to suspect that the Wife of Bath's Prologue, so much worked over by Chaucer, with so many *non sequiturs* and digressions, may for several years have undergone a process of growth through insertions not revealed by manuscript evidence.

A possible insertion may be detected in the Wife of Bath's Prologue where Chaucer briefly interrupts his paraphrase and expansion of Theophrastus and *Le Roman de la Rose* so as to offer sentiments derived ultimately from St. Isidore of Seville.[17] Theophrastus wrote: "Pulchra cito adamatur, foeda facile concupiscit." Chaucer's corresponding passage consists of four lines (253-56) based on the first clause and on *Roman de la Rose* 8587-96, six lines (257-62, italicized below) related to Isidore, and then two more lines (263-64) again based on the *Roman* 8595-96, and four lines (265-68) based on Theophrastus's second clause and on *Roman* 8597-8600.

> And if that she be fair, thou verray knave,
> Thou seyst that every holour wol hire have;
> She may no while in chastitee abyde,   255
> That is assailled upon ech a syde.
> *Thou seyst som folk desiren us for richesse,*

> *Somme for oure shap, and somme for oure fairnesse,*
> *And som for she kan outher synge or daunce,*
> *And som for gentillesse and daliaunce;*   260
> *Som for hir handes and hir armes smale:*
> *Thus goth al to the devel, by thy tale.*
> Thou seyst men may nat kepe a castel wal,
> It may so longe assailled been over al.
> And if that she be foul, thou seist that she
> Coveiteth every man that she may se,   266
> For as a spaynel she wol on hym lepe,
> Til that she fynde som man hire to chepe.

Clearly both the continuity of source material and the logical continuity have been broken by the insertion of the lines here italicized. This addition is of particular interest because it stresses "richesse," "fairnesse," and "gentillesse"—subjects discussed in the curtain lecture of the "olde wyf" in the fairy story which now forms the Wife of Bath's Tale. Similarly, one of the five late insertions about to be discussed ends with the couplet (625-26)

> I took no kep, so that he liked me,
> How poore he was, ne eek of what degree.

The mention of these qualities in the Prologue relates it to the curtain lecture of the "olde wyf," and helps the audience identify Alice with her and hence with the young and fair heroine of the ever-after perfect climax of the tale. This problem was evidently much in Chaucer's mind as he put the final touches on the Wife's Prologue.

Among the five passages which, according to manuscript evidence, were inserted late in the Wife of Bath's Prologue,[18] is one which is likewise related to Alice's efforts to attract a sixth husband; it is found in the early part of her Prologue between lines 44 and 45:[19]

Yblessed be God that I have wedded fyve!   44
Of whiche I have pyked out the beste,   44a
Bothe of here nether purs and of here cheste.
Diverse scoles maken parfyt clerkes,
And diverse practyk in many sondry werkes
Maketh the werkman parfyt sekirly;
Of fyve husbondes scoleiyng am I.   44f
Welcome the sixte, whan that evere he shal.   45

Another prominent concern of Chaucer during these final stages is the astrological background, which is emphasized by two of the five late insertions with which we are concerned. The Wife of Bath has vividly described the woe in marriage and has made clear her determination to have the "maistrie"; and she has emphasized her lust, her skill, and her desire for a sixth husband, and has pictured marriage as everlasting bliss. Now these two such opposite views towards marriage, together with the paradox of Alice's need both to love and to dominate, are finally reconciled by Chaucer through one of his most brilliant contributions to the portrait of the Wife, namely her birth under the influences of both Venus and Mars. This use of astrology is ably discussed by W. C. Curry,[20] whose evidence is found altogether in the following passage (593-631; the late insertions, 609-12 and 619-26, are here italicized):

To chirche was myn housbonde born a-morwe
With neighebores, that for hym maden sorwe;
And Jankyn, oure clerk, was oon of tho.   595
As help me God! whan that I saugh hym go
After the beere, me thoughte he hadde a paire
Of legges and of feet so clene and faire
That al myn herte I yaf unto his hoold.
He was, I trowe, a twenty wynter oold,   600
And I was fourty, if I shal seye sooth;

But yet I hadde alwey a coltes tooth.
Gat-tothed I was, and that bicam me weel;
I hadde the prente of seinte Venus seel.
As help me God! I was a lusty oon,   605
And faire, and riche, and yong, and wel bigon;
And trewely, as myne housbondes tolde me,
I hadde the beste *quoniam* myghte be.
For certes, I am al Venerien
In feelynge, and myn herte is Marcien.   610
Venus me yaf my lust, my likerousnesse,
And Mars yaf me my sturdy hardynesse;
Myn ascendent was Taur, and Mars therinne.
Allas! allas! that evere love was synne!
I folwed ay myn inclinacioun   615
By vertu of my constellacioun;
That made me I koude noght withdrawe
My chambre of Venus from a good felawe.
Yet have I Martes mark upon my face,
And also in another privee place.   620
For God so wys be my savacioun,
I ne loved nevere by no discrecioun,
But evere folwede myn appetit,
Al were he short, or long, or blak, or whit;
I took no kep, so that he liked me,   625
How poore he was, ne eek of what degree.
  What sholde I seye? but, at the monthes ende,
This joly clerk, Jankyn, that was so hende,
Hath wedded me with greet solempnytee;
And to hym yaf I al the lond and fee   630
That evere was me yeven therbifoore.

Clearly this theme of unification of the personality of the Wife
of Bath through astrology was not a part of Chaucer's original
intention, but a late addition to the portrait. Indeed, lines
605-608,[21] and even lines 613-18, may have been written at
some time after the narrative of the fourth and fifth husbands,

though 603 ("Gat-tothed I was") and the rest of that couplet must have been written at about the same time as the revision of the portrait in the General Prologue.

A fourth late passage, inserted between lines 574 and 585, permits Alice to enlarge upon her courtship of Jankyn clerk before she was widowed by the death of her fourth husband:

> I bar hym on honde he hadde enchanted me,— 575
> My dame taughte me that soutiltee.
> And eek I seyde I mette of hym al nyght,
> He wolde han slayn me as I lay upright,
> And al my bed was ful of verray blood;
> But yet I hope that he shal do me good, 580
> For blood bitokeneth gold, as me was taught.
> And al was fals; I dremed of it right naught,
> But as I folwed ay my dames loore,
> As wel of this as of othere thynges moore.

Alice's mention of her mother—twice, and here only—builds up the background of her "auncetrye" and "nortelrie." The mention of her dream is a delicate touch of insincerity. The blood and gold—the coupling of the themes of murder and money—prepare (by provident hindsight) for the murders of husbands by the "wikked wyves" of Jankyn's book and for Alice's theft of a leaf out of the book by accusing Jankyn of trying to murder her for her land (800-801).

The fifth insertion is a four-line expansion (717-20) of Jankyn clerk's comment on "Eva" (713-16; probably from *Valerius ad Rufinum*), which is thus made more antifeminist:

> Upon a nyght Jankyn, that was oure sire,
> Redde on his book, as he sat by the fire,
> Of Eva first, that for hir wikkednesse
> Was al mankynde broght to wrecchednesse,
> *For which that Jhesu Crist hymself was slayn,*
> *That boghte us with his herte blood agayn.*

Lo, heere expres of womman may ye fynde,
That womman was the los of al mankynde.

Thus Chaucer prepared a number of brief, enlivening insertions, each enriching the personality of Alice of Bath. Yet
this is not all. That the poet, had he lived longer, might have
made still further developments in the Wife's section of the
Canterbury Tales is shown by the presence in the Ellesmere
manuscript (and certain others) of glosses, almost certainly
auctorial, which suggests that Chaucer planned to expand
passages—two in the Wife's Prologue and one in her Tale—
by adding further materials from St. Jerome's *Epistola adversus Iovinianum* and Walter Map's *Valerius ad Rufinum*.
Into the discourse of the "olde wyf" on poverty apparently was
to go Jerome's example of Crates the Theban;[22] into Jankyn's
reading from his "book of wikked wyves" was to go the anecdote of Metellus and Mario from "Valerie";[23] and the interruption by the Pardoner (who in the General Prologue was depicted as *eunuchus ex nativitate*) is glossed with Jerome's
statement that Athenian priests castrate themselves by means
of potions of hemlock ("Ierophancias quoque Atheniencium
vxque hodie cicute sorbicione castrari").[24] Since the Pardoner
is here depicted as asking whether he ought to marry, and since
Alice here offers him "another tonne . . . shal savoure wors
than ale" (170-71), we well may wonder what she could have
had in mind for him.

The query unanswered, this account of the gradual development of Alice, Wife of Bath, comes to an end. By this time
her conflicting aims and desires, her approach to existence—
both realistic and romantic—and her variety of statements—
half of them in conflict with the truth—have been imaginatively combined by Chaucer with whims and foibles to create
a personality that is rich, deep, and convincing. In the *Canterbury Tales* Alice is successively matched against the Nuns'

Priest, the Pardoner, the teasing Friar, the idealistic Clerk, the disillusioned Merchant, the gentle Franklin, and the hen-pecked Herry Bailey, Host of the Tabard Inn of Southwerk— a total of seven completely various opponents. Further, Chaucer has given the Wife extension in space by having her tell of her life at Bath with husbands, gossip, apprentice, niece, at home, at church, and in the fields; and by sending her off on untold pilgrimages "to ferne halwes, kowthe in sondry londes"; and has given her extension in time, both by the story of her five husbands, and by little hints of her girlhood and youth and of possibilities for the future. The essential mystery of the Wife deepens as we are made aware of the cosmic background of the planets. When she tells her tale, successive shadowy egos loom behind her in deepening perspective: old Alice on the Canterbury road, the young Alice in her memory and "in the feeldes," the "olde wyf" of the tale, the heroine transformed to be young and fair, and the "elf-queene" who "daunced ful ofte in many a grene mede." In addition to these dimensions, Chaucer has given the Wife yet another by portraying her against the intellectual and emotional background of antimatrimonialism, a tradition so strong in the leading university of fourteenth-century England as to form a sort of contemporary Oxford movement: thus Alice becomes significant not merely for her magnificent in-dividuality, but also as a representative of a point of view— often labelled modern and Protestant by latter-day Chau-cerians—equally momentous in our day and in hers.

ROBERT A. PRATT,
University of Pennsylvania

[1] I follow F. N. Robinson, *The Works of Geoffrey Chaucer*, 2nd ed. (Boston, 1957). In general I have confined annotation to a minimum, and for passage after passage offer no footnote regarding sources, previous studies, and the like, when ample information is offered by Robinson, whose Notes should be consulted at almost every point.

[2] W. C. Curry, *Chaucer and the Mediaeval Sciences*, 2nd ed. (New York, 1960), p. 91.

[3] For discussion and references see *PMLA*, LXVI (1951):1145-46, 1154-57. I am chiefly dependent on R. F. Jones in *JEGP*, XXIV (1925): n. 29, pp. 524-25.

[4] See Jones, *op. cit.*, pp. 519-20. My elaboration of Jones, and certain later portions of this paper, are based on my study of medieval manuscripts related to Jankyn's "book of wikked wyves"—a project started by Karl Young; see the chapter on "Karl Young's Work on the Learning of Chaucer" in *A Memoir of Karl Young* (New Haven, 1946), especially pp. 53-54.

[5] The stories of the fourth and fifth husbands are interrelated in tone, plot, and source material. These are the two "badde" ones, the young, vigorous husbands who, for a time, succeed in wielding the whip—even though vanquished at the last. Their careers are interlocked, too; for the fourth lives chiefly to sharpen the scene of the Wife's "prehumous" wooing of Jankyn, and dies only to provide the enticing view of Jankyn's legs at the simple, frugal funeral and to free the Wife to marry yet again.

[6] See J. M. Manly and E. Rickert, *The Text of the Canterbury Tales* (Chicago, 1940), III:498; W. F. Bryan and G. Dempster, eds., *Sources and Analogues of Chaucer's Canterbury Tales* (Chicago, 1941), p. 211.

[7] See, for example, R. J. Dean in *Mediaeval and Renaissance Studies*, II (1950):128-50.

[8] Of the parallels between the Merchant's Tale and the Wife's "sermon," one (III 112, IV 1456: "by youre leve, that am nat I") is found also in *Melibee* (VII 1088); another (III 130; IV 1452, 2048: "yelde hire dette") is found also in the Parson's Tale (X 940), and is a commonplace based on I Cor. VII:3; the third is found in a late revision of the Wife's Prologue (see note 19, *infra*); I believe that none of these suggests any influence of the "sermon" on the Merchant's Tale.

[9] For these interrelated changes see G. Dempster in *PMLA*, LXVIII (1953): 1142-52. With these changes comes the creation of Herry Bailey's wife (see pp. 1151-54).

[10] See *PMLA*, LXVI (1951):1158-59 and note 34.

[10a] The title, *Lenvoy de Chaucer*, which is authoritative, has puzzled critics. I suggest that this envoy—found after the Clerk's Tale in certain manuscripts, existed originally as an independent piece, read by Chaucer to his audience as a *tour de force*, a sort of encore, after his reading of the story of Griselde; and that when the envoy was eventually given to the Clerk, its original title was carelessly allowed to remain and so was copied into the

text of the *Canterbury Tales*. The title offers striking parallelism with two other titles, *Lenvoy de Chaucer à Bukton* and *Lenvoy de Chaucer a Scogan*. Furthermore, certain passages—"I crie in open audience," "No wedded man so hardy be . . . ," and the apostrophes "O noble wyves" and "Ye arche-wyves"—seem better fitted for the poet's actual listeners than for the Canterbury road. Thus Chaucer, whose amusing side remarks are many, may have entertained himself and his sophisticated audience by reciting this brilliant piece as an auctorial comment on the story of Griselde. If so, it would represent a transition from a tale simply told by the Clerk to the tale finally integrated into the "Marriage Group."

[11] These lines echo a passage in the Merchant's Tale (IV 1685-87):

> The Wyf of Bathe, if ye han understonde,
> Of mariage, which ye have on honde,
> Declared hath ful wel in litel space.

Likewise "bewayle" and "wepe" (16) echo "wepying and waylyng" (IV 1213).

[12] See B. J. Whiting, chap. viii of *Sources and Analogues*.

[13] Yet her cry of "Fy!" for the tale of "Phasipha" may have been simply because of wholesome disgust rather than bourgeois moral indignation. It should, moreover, be recalled that, like the unnatural tale of Canacee and that of Antiochus (to which the Man of Law had said "Fy!"), the tale of "Pasiphe" had been told by the "moral Gower" (*Confessio Amantis*, V:5272-88).

[14] At the conclusion of the Wife's tale there is no explanation of enchantment by a stepmother as in the analogues.

[15] See Manly and Rickert, *op. cit.*, II:194-95. That the Friar's and Summoner's Tales may have been in existence (or at least started) when the Friar's interruption was designed, is suggested by the important role of St. Jerome's *Epistola adversus Iovinianum* in the Summoner's Tale.

[16] See Dempster in *MLN*, LII (1937):16-23; LIV (1939):137-38.

[17] See *MLN*, LXXIV (1959):293-94; *Sources and Analogues*, pp. 212-14, 218.

[18] See Manly and Rickert, *op. cit.*, II:191-94; III:454-55.

[19] The italicized passage is clearly related to a couplet in the Merchant's Tale, which may have helped inspire it (IV 1427-1428):

> For sondry scoles maken sotile clerkis;
> Womman of manye scoles half a clerk is.

[20] *Op. cit.*, chap. v.

[21] See Manly and Ricket, *op. cit.*, II:194.

[22] See Manly and Rickert, *op. cit.*, III:503.

[23] See Manly and Rickert, *op. cit.*, III:499; M. R. James, ed., *Walter Map: De Nugis Curialium* (Anecdota Oxoniensia, Mediaeval and Modern Series, Part XIV; Oxford, 1914), pp. 152-53, 267.

[24] See Manly and Rickert, *op. cit.*, III:498.

Chaucer's Retraction: A Review of Opinion

Interpretations of Chaucer's Retraction at the end of the *Canterbury Tales* have varied so widely in the past that it seems appropriate to ask whether there is a direction to the current of opinion and whether there is at present a concensus. The passage has always been considered significant. "The question of the authenticity of the passage is of importance, . . . since it presents to us the strange picture of Chaucer, under what seems to be the pressure of narrow tenets, apologizing for and condemning most of what he had labored for in literature." [1] The earlier scholars from the times of Hearne and Tyrwhitt could not reconcile the Retraction with their understanding of Chaucer as gained from the works themselves.[2] Either they refused to accept it at all, attributing it to the intrusion of a hypothetical monk, or they accepted it as genuine but due to senility or disease. Ward, for example, would have none of it: "As to the actual last words of the *Canterbury Tales* . . . it would be unbearable to have to accept them as genuine. . . . Those who will may believe that the monks, who were the landlords of Chaucer's house at Westminster, had in one way or the other obtained a controlling influence over his mind. Stranger things than this have happened; but one prefers to believe that the poet of the *Canterbury Tales* remained master of himself to the last." [3] Hales, perhaps influenced at the moment by his desire to establish the credit of Thomas Gascoigne, thought the passage "difficult to explain altogether away as Tyrwhitt and others have attempted to do." But he went on to identify asceticism

81

with mental decay: "Perhaps the poet's fixing his last abode
where he did, so close to the Abbey of Westminster . . . may
suggest that some ascetic tendency or turn marked his declining years. Such things have happened both before and since.
Men's judgments have decayed, and they have formed a
morbid estimate of their life and works." [4] Some of these early
opinions were obviously based upon emotional preferences,
but by the end of the nineteenth century judgments were becoming more cautious. Pollard accepted the Retraction as
"really the work of Chaucer's old age," [5] and Skeat not only
tried to reconcile it with Chaucer's life and work but even
found that "the poet had good cause to regret such Tales as
those of the Miller, the Reeve, and the Merchant." [6]

In 1905 Heinrich Spies subjected the passage to a more
detailed study than had hitherto been undertaken.[7] He divided
it into three parts, the first (1081-84) and the third (1090-92)
being separated by the middle section (1085-89), which is the
"retraccions" proper and which enumerates the works in the
two familiar categories. He then argued, basing his case
mainly upon Chaucer's predilection for reference to the person
of Jesus Christ and to penance and salvation, that the first
and third parts are undeniably Chaucer's in style and content.
But, he went on to say, if the first and third parts are read
consecutively without the middle, they form a grossly illogical
sequence. Therefore all three parts must be taken together;
and he concludes, "dass alle . . . drei Teile aus einer Feder
geflossen sind und dass nur Chaucer diese Feder geführt hat
—der gesamte Schlussabschnitt zeigt deutliche Spuren Chau-
cerscher Prägung."

He further dismissed as unimportant those discrepancies
which skeptics had pointed out between the works as named
in the Retraction and the canon as we know it today. The mis-
givings of others who found the passage uncharacteristic of

Chaucer he rejected as, for the most part, emotional, for he held that the Retraction is in accord with what we know of Chaucer's mind and temper. As to the time of composition, he offered, without proof, the theory that it was immediately after the final revision of the Parson's Tale, not immediately before Chaucer's death.

These views constituted a departure from the consensus of the time, which was immediately defended by Koch,[8] who replied that the Retraction cannot be reconciled with the image that Chaucer gives of himself in his poetry, and that the list of works is too inaccurate to be genuine. He supposed, therefore, that the list, if not the entire passage, is an interpolation made by a monk, probably of Westminster Abbey, who was Chaucer's confessor in his last hours and who simply executed Chaucer's desire as he understood it, without intending to perpetrate a fraud.

Some of Spies's most important points do, indeed, as Koch maintained, fall short of final proof, but most critics, relying upon the evidence of the manuscripts, have accepted the authenticity of the Retraction.[9] Tatlock called it certainly genuine[10] and later attempted to make it more comprehensible by relating it to a tradition which included St. Augustine, the Venerable Bede, Gerald de Barri, Jean de Meung, and, after Chaucer, Spenser (who lamented that his Hymns in the praise of love and beauty ministered overmuch to youthful passion), Herrick, Dryden, and others.[11] Nevertheless, its contents remained to him, as to other scholars of the highest repute, confusing and deplorable, for in the same article he adds that "Chaucer was no longer himself if he seriously would have liked to blot out entirely, on religious or moral grounds, *The Book of the Duchess,* the *Troilus,* the *House of Fame,* the *Legend of Good Women,* and the *Canterbury Tales . . ."* And Root, who later was to speak of the *Troilus* as evidence of a "serene Catholic temper," [12] found that in the Retraction "the poet's conscience was seized by the tenets of a narrow creed, which in the days of his strength he had known how to transmute into something better and truer." [13]

Professor Manly's references at different times to the Retraction illustrate particularly well the uncertainty in which even the most competent of scholars have found themselves concerning this passage. No one knew better than he the weight of the manuscript evidence, which (in his edition of the *Canterbury Tales* published in 1928) he said "is altogether in favor of the authenticity of the passage." [14] But his final judgment was that the manuscript tradition led no further than "the ancestor of the MSS. of the PsT," and that the authenticity remained unproved. [15]

He was impressed, on the one hand, by the fact that Chaucer's emotions were always deeply affected by certain expressions of religion, as he was by the supposed resemblance between the Retraction and the will of Sir Lewis Clifford. [16] Neither of these considerations, however, appears very weighty. In the first instance, though it is common enough today to think of religion as a simple emotional experience, for Chaucer it was also a matter of conviction, as the text of his works repeatedly shows. Any explanation, therefore, which ignores the rationale of this conviction will fall short of a solution. In the second instance, the resemblance between Chaucer's final statement and Clifford's will is superficial and points only to the fact that repentance was not unique in the Middle Ages. Since Clifford was known to be a supporter of Wyclif, his position was that of a heretic, which must in orthodox public opinion have been regarded as subversive. Chaucer's position was completely different.

On the other hand, Manly could not dismiss the apparent

inaccuracies in the list of works nor overcome his "unwilling-
ness to believe that even the tenderest conscience could have
felt that there was anything wrong in several of the poems
expressly mentioned as requiring forgiveness." [17] He fell back,
therefore, upon the theory of clerical influence, and remained
of that mind.[18]

The theory, then, of an interpolator, usually identified as a
monk of Westminster, who exercised an influence upon the
poet in the weakness of his last days, has had a long life,
but it is a theory which, upon examination, turns out to be
simply convenient and based upon the dubious assumption
that the Retraction was written *in extremis.*

Read from the beginning to end, the passage, though it has
the tone of finality suitable to the conclusion of a great
accomplishment, does not suggest the perturbation of one
unnerved by the fear of death. The poet's relations with a
confessor or spiritual adviser are beyond even speculation, but
it is reasonable to suppose that he would not have postponed
these relations to the end of his life and that his choice, therefore, would not have been determined by simple proximity
to the Abbey. Such an adviser may well have been unsympa-
thetic to humane literature; there is, however, no a priori
certainty that he would have been so. We have no evidence
that the poet's works were generally repugnant to the clergy
of his time or considered so scandalous in the public eye as
to require public penance, as some have interpreted the Retraction. His burial in the Abbey is not consistent with such
a supposition, nor is the lifelong veneration, openly and repeatedly expressed, of the Monk of Bury.[19] Moreover, Chaucer
undoubtedly had friends among the laity who were of a devout
and moral turn of mind and whose opinions could have raised
doubts with him about the propriety of some of his writings.
Among these was Gower, who expressed his disapproval and

whose devout temper led him to the shelter of a religious community. The fact (if it is a fact) that Gower's criticism resulted in an estrangement between them serves only to emphasize the importance which Chaucer attached to his opinion. Finally the apparent inaccuracy of the list of works does not prove the theory of an interpolator of any kind. In fact, references to works now unknown are not necessarily inaccuracies. Some of the shorter works were almost certainly lost.[20] The reference to the "book of the XV ladies" can be as reasonably explained by scribal transmission as by the hand of a misinformed interpolator.

It is not surprising, therefore, that recent critics have tended to accept the Retraction as authentic and to seek for an explanation in terms of literary criticism or of Chaucer's philosophy of life. Miss Hammond offered a theory of the first kind, which included a view of the structural importance of the Parson's Tale, but did not elaborate upon it. "The Recantation," she held, "seems to me neither a final nor a death-bed production, but a deliberately-planned conclusion, written while the *Canterbury Tales* was in the process of arrangement, possibly even before some of the Tales which 'sounen unto synne' had taken form." [21] This suggestion has been given detailed consideration in two more recent studies, which are directed mainly toward establishing a structural interpretation for the Parson's Tale, but which lead to quite different conclusions about the Retraction. Ralph Baldwin[22] argued for the close unity of the Parson's Tale with the structure of the whole of the *Canterbury Tales* and for the logical connection between the Parson's Tale and the Retraction. For the first he stated his case eloquently, if, indeed, he did not overstate it. "It is," he said, "most cunningly and artistically involved with the whole." [23] In brief, according to this interpretation, the Parson's Tale is a dramatic confrontation of the sins to which man is victim on his journey to the New Jerusalem and which are displayed by the Pilgrims on their symbolic journey to Canterbury. "Every one of the seven deadly sins has its perpetrators among the Pilgrims. It is against the blandishments and entanglements threatening their souls at that moment that the Parson assiduously, spiritually struggles. . . . If drama is basically a matter of conflict, then this is conflict of the gravest sort, because in context the Parson is battling . . . against the weaknesses and sins which have been displayed en route, which call for correction and repentance." [24]

One would like, in the interest of Chaucer's narrative art, to go along with this attractive interpretation. But Mr. Baldwin is equally sure of the function of the Retraction in the scheme of the whole. It "is no random appendage, but is indissolubly linked . . . with the problem both of character and of narrative art that the text presents at that juncture." [25] The nature of the connection is defined in these words: "That the [Parson's] tale and the scene it involves are not without drama is brought out most poignantly, because it even excites a public confession from Chaucer himself. . . . The Parson's Tale marks the culmination of the Pilgrimage, and Chaucer's immediate recantation is the denouement of the Pilgrim-drama." [26] Now this view of the Retraction would be easier to accept[27] if the closing passage consisted of the first and third parts, as Spies divided it; or if the works specifically revoked did not include much more than the *Canterbury Tales*. But, even more to the point, the sounder Mr. Baldwin's analysis is of the dramatic and moral significance of the Parson's Tale in the structure and texture of the whole work, the less understandable is a revocation of parts of the *Tales*.[28] What is necessary to the dramatic representation of man in his earthly pilgrimage to the New Jerusalem, including the role of sin and penance in such a drama, need not be cancelled out. The moral and artistic purpose of such material should be a sufficient guarantee of innocence.

Professor Lumiansky has also considered the Retraction in arguing persuasively for the importance of the Parson's Tale in the design of the *Canterbury Tales,* though on somewhat different grounds.[29] His strategy is to solve the anomaly of the Retraction by separating it altogether from the Canterbury Tales but retaining the Parson's Tale. To this end he invokes the support of Manly and Rickert, whom he quotes as follows: "The curious fact remains that in the Retraction there is not a hint of any sort that it is appended to the *Canterbury Tales.*" The entire context of the Manly–Rickert statement, however, should have been preserved, for only a few lines above we read, "Chaucer may have been responsible for both PsT and Rt and yet *they* may have no legitimate claim to a place in CT." [30] [Italics mine] Whatever we do with Fragment X(I), the Parson's Tale and the Retraction are explicitly linked in the manuscripts. If, therefore, as Professor Lumiansky so reasonably supposes, Chaucer made a careful placement of the Parson's Tale, possibly revised from earlier work on this material, at the conclusion of the Tales, we must accept the Retraction with it and assume that it was intended to be where it is.

A more common tendency today in accepting the Retraction is to try to reconcile it with Chaucer's concept of sin and repentance. Essentially this is a return to Skeat, who believed that the real meaning of the Retraction is that Chaucer was disclaiming those works which contributed nothing to the salvation of his soul, hoping that such things as were evil might be outbalanced by those that were good.[31] Professor Lawrence urged this point of view at greater length.[32] He believed, first, that the Retraction is completely authentic; second, that it represents a change of heart under the influence

of certain forces that he considered typically medieval, such
as the doctrine that a man must use his talents only in the
service of God, or the fear of ecclesiastical disapproval of
works dealing with sexual love; and third, that this change
of heart was the result of a religious crisis. "Illness or fear of
imminent death," he phrased it, "with the medieval fires of
hell glowing luridly in the distance, may have driven him
to make his peace with heaven, to disavow past literary 'sins,'
and to make such amends as were possible." [33]

In certain parts of his discussion, Lawrence approached
what I believe to be a reasonable explanation, though he
reveals in other places a regrettably patronizing attitude toward the fundamental assumptions implicit in Chaucer's final
statement. The force of this exception can best be sensed by
comparing Lawrence's words with those of Professor Donaldson, who has substantially the same understanding of the
passage, but is obviously more *en rapport* with its spirit:
"The poet was about to die and he feared for his soul. There
is no doubt that from the strictest point of view—that of a
medieval monk—much that he had written was sinful. Is it
not a Christian's duty to use the talents God had given him in
serving the glory of God, and had not Chaucer written much
that had no explicit Christian reference? . . . It had certainly
often occurred to Chaucer that there are other ways of cele-
brating God's glory than through direct praise of Him, but
at the close of the poet's life the voice of authority was on the
other side. Logical as ever, he did what was best for his
soul." [34]

Another kind of interpretation, which leaves unanswered
the question most disconcerting to modern readers, is characteristic of some specifically Catholic criticism. Canon Looten
sees in the Retraction the very natural scruples of a delicate
conscience which has reawakened after a long sleep. In the

light of eternity the dying poet becomes fully aware of his responsibilities; hence his remorse. This admirable behavior ("cette belle tenue morale") at the point of death is added reason why posterity should honor him.[35]

Besides assuming too much, this explanation does not tell us why *The Book of the Duchess, The House of Fame,* and *The Parliament of Foules* should trouble a reawakened conscience. The assumption of guilt it implies is, of course, due in part to the influence of Thomas Gascoigne's account of the death of Chaucer, in which the poet is quoted as regretting "illa quae male scripsi de malo et turpissimo amore hominem ad mulieres, et jam de homine in hominem continuabuntur." [36] Gascoigne was a learned and reputable chancellor of Oxford and also could have known Thomas Chaucer well enough to have had the facts from him, but his judgment was biased, as appears in his coupling the names of Judas and Chaucer as examples of belated repentance. For such reliability as it has, Gascoigne's quotation points only to the *Troilus* and the fabliaux. The latter, Lawrence believed, were less offensive to contemporary moral sense than to social decorum.

Like Canon Looten, however, Sister Madeleva believed otherwise, and went so far as to call the Retraction an exclusively moral document constituting public amends for "scandal or flagrant bad example." In supporting and developing this interpretation she seemed to see implied in the Retraction a double standard. "He was not now," she wrote, "concerned with the stuff of literature, but with the stuff of sanctity." [37] Perhaps this is one way to explain a difficult problem. Many readers of Chaucer, however, must feel dissatisfied with it, preferring to seek the assumptions upon which the poet could discharge his obligation to confront the realities of the human scene without at the same time appearing to embrace moral evil. We have no reason to believe that Chaucer wrote with less than complete integrity;[38] we have in his work, rather, every inducement to believe that, aware of the infinite variety and inconsistency of men, he conceived the high purpose of representing human life with a realism new to English literature. Without abandoning his belief in a universal order invisible to human eyes, he must have come to realize the impossibility of creating "a sinless literature of sinful man." When, therefore, he sincerely and generously presents the tragedy of heroic love or the comic aspects of ignoble lust, we incline to believe that with the instinct of genius he had discovered the limits within which a standard of propriety as well as of artistic realism could be met. But since he himself was obviously not convinced in the end that he had succeeded, we are left with the necessity to explain his uncertainties, but on better grounds than a reawakened conscience.

If there is anything like a general trend today on this subject, it is toward recognizing the Retraction as authentic, as the poet's final statement concerning his whole literary production, even though it is appended to the *Canterbury Tales,* and toward explaining it as a matter of conscience rather than of aesthetics. There is a difference of opinion as to whether it was written in the immediate expectation of death. There are also differences in attitude toward the convictions to which it gives voice, but in this respect there seems to be a strong leaning toward sympathetic comprehension such as that of Professor French in the *Chaucer Handbook.* "A more fanatic piety, hardly content to 'revoke' the offending works, would have committed the mad sin of consigning them to the flames; but Geoffrey Chaucer who was better instructed in 'what is behovely' and necessary to 'verray, parfit Penitence,' let his account stand as he had written it, very sure that 'the benigne grace of him that is king of kinges and preest over alle preestes' could strike a just balance between the evil and the good." [39]

There remains, of course, the incongruity between the Retraction and the apparent innocence of most, if not all, of what was revoked, but here also it is possible to find an explanation in the poet's anxiety arising from the conflict of two ideals unsatisfactorily resolved: that of the ascetic, who renounces worldly interests for the one thing necessary, and that of the poet of humanistic bent, who cannot escape involvement with humanity. That Chaucer was long aware of the conflict is traceable in the *Parliament of Foules* and fully evident from the conclusion of the *Troilus*. This explanation has been glanced at several times. Tatlock, for example, long ago referred to the "enormously strong pull of the whole spiritual teaching of the Middle Ages toward the ascetic attitude to worldly pleasure, which often has become stronger in a man as he has aged. . . ." [40] This ascetic tendency leaned essentially toward withdrawal and renunciation. It had its deepest roots in the ancient struggle of Christianity against Greek and Roman paganism and thus from very early times became an essential part of the monastic ideal. Since monasticism played so large a part in the Christianization of Western Europe and remained so prominent an element in its culture, its traditions naturally exerted a heavy and widespread influence in Christian thought, becoming to some extent the inheritance of all Christians. Thus the old suspicion of humanistic literature remained alive. In theory, therefore, though certainly not always in practice, the book was a means of personal sanctification and a weapon in the warfare against sin and ignorance. [41]

It is not necessary, however, to stigmatize this spiritual idealism as "narrow" or "pietistic" in order to recognize that it has limitations when applied rigidly to secular pursuits. Obviously it gave less than due consideration to the necessities and the true value of lay involvement. With the gradual emergence of the lay professional classes a review of what was proper and conducive to virtue, among those who were concerned at the highest intellectual levels with the serious affairs of this world, became a clear but neglected imperative. Especially desirable was an unbiased evaluation of the humanistic uses of literature which Chaucer had come to perceive.

Today it is somewhat easier than in the fourteenth century to recognize that the aims of the scholar and the artist are intrinsically important because they are, by one avenue or another, an approach to truth. The literary artist is reasonably secure in his high purpose of presenting the realities of this world without being held responsible for the state of things. Chaucer, however, was in a less secure position. We may surmise from the attitude of Gower and the substance of Gascoigne's report that Chaucer's doubts as to the propriety of his work were first awakened by unfriendly criticism of his vivid, realistic, and sometimes coarse presentation of the physical aspects of love, to which the English public was perhaps especially sensitive; and that these doubts, once aroused, suggested a total reappraisal of his work, and led at least to the renunciation of all his worldly achievements. Despite this reversal of values, the fact remains that part of the genius of Chaucer was his far-sighted intimation of new and greatly enlarged possibilities for the literary artist. What he lacked was a theory to sustain him.

It is instructive to recall at this point Petrarch's letter to Boccaccio, who was at the time alarmed over the status of his humanistic studies *sub specie aeternitatis*, about which he had recently been warned by a zealous Carthusian monk. "Nay, I answer, when he bids you pluck sin from your heart, he speaks well and prudently. But why forsake letters. . . . All history is full of examples of good men who have loved learning, and though many unlettered men have attained to holiness, no man was ever debarred from holiness by letters." [42]

Chaucer, in his dilemma, lacking the philosophical independence of Petrarch and his sympathetic friendship as well, chose the course of prudence. Fortunately, as has been said, it was a temperate course. The works remain.

JAMES D. GORDON,
University of Pennsylvania

[1] J. E. Wells, *Manual of Writings in Middle English* (New York, 1926), p. 747.

[2] For a brief review of these earlier opinions see E. P. Hammond, *Chaucer: A Bibliographical Manual* (New York, 1908), pp. 321-22; Heinrich Spies, "Chaucers Retractio," *Festschrift Adolf Tobler* (Braunschweig: Berliner Gesellschaft für das Studium Neuerer Sprachen, 1905), pp. 383-94.

[3] A. W. Ward, *Chaucer* (London, 1879), pp. 141-42.

[4] John W. Hales, *Folia Literaria* (New York, 1893) pp. 111-12. See also the same author's article in DNB.

[5] *Globe Chaucer* (London, 1898), p. xxxi.

[6] *Oxford Chaucer* (Oxford, 1894), III:503-04.

[7] *Festschrift Adolf Tobler*, pp. 383-94.

[8] *English Studies*, XXXVII (1907):227-29.

[9] The Retraction is contained "in practically all of the MSS. that have the whole of the Ps T." Manly and Rickert, *Text of the Canterbury Tales* (Chicago, 1940, II:471.

[10] *Development and Chronology*, p. 25n.

[11] J. S. P. Tatlock, "Chaucer's Retractions," *PMLA*, XXVIII (1913):521-29.

[12] *The Book of Troilus and Criseyde* (Princeton, 1926), p. l.

[13] *The Poetry of Chaucer* (Boston, 1906), p. 288.

[14] P. 657.

[15] *Text of the Canterbury Tales*, II:471.

[16] *Canterbury Tales*, p. 657; *Text of the Canterbury Tales*, II:471-72. Lewis Clifford's will was first brought to notice by Kittredge, *MP*, I (1903-04):13. Manly (*Canterbury Tales*, p. 657), printed the pertinent section.

[17] *Canterbury Tales*, p. 656. But note that the logic of these words, literally applied, would eliminate even the interpolator.

[18] *Canterbury Tales*, p. 658; *Text of the Canterbury Tales*, II:472; IV:527.

[19] Unfortunately data on the history of the manuscripts of the *Tales* are too scanty or too late to furnish a good estimate of the attitude of churchmen. We know, however, for what the facts are worth, that in the fifteenth century one manuscript (Harl. 7333) was copied and edited by the Austin Canons of St. Mary de Pratis. One was supposed to have belonged the monastery of Canterbury. Another seems to have been the property of Henry Dene, Archbishop of Canterbury. Still another belonged to John Leche, serious-minded vicar of Saffron Walden. See Manly and Rickert, *Text of the Canterbury Tales*, I:32-33, 214-18, 424, 426, 540-44.

[20] Cotton MS. Otho A XVIII, now lost, but listed in Thomas Smith, *Cat. Librl. Bibl. Cott.* (1696), p. 69, contained "A Ballade made by Geoffrey Chaucer upon his death bed lying in his anguish."

[21] E. P. Hammond, "Book of the Twenty-five Ladies," *MLN*, XLVIII (1933):514-16.

[22] *The Unity of the Canterbury Tales*, Anglistica, V (Copenhagen, 1955).

[23] *Ibid.*, p. 89.

[24] *Ibid.*, p. 104.

[25] *Ibid.*, p. 86.

[26] *Ibid.*, p. 99.

[27] It is, however, stretching the facts somewhat to establish a parallel between the "Confession of Mouth" in the Parson's Tale (318) and the Retraction, for the former refers surely to auricular confession.

[28] Baldwin anticipates this objection by proposing a double standard (p. 107); but see below, p. 90.

[29] R. M. Lumiansky, "Chaucer's Retraction and the Degree of Completeness of the *Canterbury Tales*," *Tulane Studies in English*, VI (1956):5-13.

[30] Lumiansky, *op. cit.*, p. 12; *Text of the Canterbury Tales*, II:472.

[31] *Oxford Chaucer*, III:503.

[32] W. W. Lawrence, *Chaucer and the Canterbury Tales* (New York, 1950), pp. 82-85, 152-59.

[33] *Ibid.*, p. 154.

[34] E. T. Donaldson, *Chaucer's Poetry* (New York, 1958), p. 949.

[35] Le Chanoine Looten, *Chaucer, ses Modèles, ses Sources, sa Religion* (Lille, 1931), p. 243.

[36] J. W. Hales, *Folia Literaria* (New York, 1893), pp. 110-11; Manly, *Canterbury Tales*, p. 657. It is worth pointing out that if these words are really Chaucer's, they show that he was less disturbed by the "medieval fires of hell glowing luridly in the distance" than by a generous concern for the well-being of us who were to read his works.

[37] Sister Madeleva, *A Lost Language* (New York, 1951), pp. 108-10. See also Baldwin, *op. cit.*, p. 107.

[38] However, Father Herbert Thurston, S.J., makes a harsher judgment in condemning Boccaccio and Chaucer together. These and their emulators (whoever they may be) "knew quite well that they were at heart insincere, that a good deal of what they wrote, by proclaiming the divinity of Venus and by satirizing with grievous exaggeration the moral transgressions and the cupidity of the clergy, was doing the devil's work." Both, however, "had the grace in the end to admit that they had acted in bad faith." ("The Conversion of Boccaccio and Chaucer," *Studies: An Irish Quarterly Review of Letters, Philosophy, and Science*, XXV (1936):215-25.)

[39] P. 338.

[40] *PMLA*, XXVIII (1913):528.

[41] The conventional attitude is nicely illustrated in the invitation extended by the citizens of Florence to Boccaccio: "Whereas divers citizens of Florence, being minded as well for themselves as for others, their fellow-citizens, as for their posterity, to follow after virtue, are desirous of being instructed in the book of Dante, wherefrom, both to the shunning of vice and the acquisition of virtue, no less than in the ornaments of eloquence, even the unlearned may receive instruction; the said citizens humbly pray . . ." Edward Hutton, *Giovanni Boccaccio, a Biographical Study* (London, 1910), p. 250.

[42] Hutton, *op. cit.*, pp. 199-201.

From Gorgias to Troilus

To complete my topic I should add "by way of Boethius," for it happens that through the ordinary activities of student and teacher I have come to have both knowledge and interest in three works that seem to me to be related to one another— the *Gorgias* of Plato, *The Consolation of Philosophy* of Boethius, and the *Troilus and Criseyde* of Chaucer, the last-mentioned supplemented by familiarity with Chaucer's other works. My knowledge and interest have come to me, as I said, by ordinary necessity. I have no reason to think my knowledge adequate in every particular, but I think it genuine as far as it goes. I have paid little attention to sources, influences, texts or technical aesthetics, although I have not been indifferent to these things in so far as they fostered my interest and increased my understanding. Frankly, there are scores of books and articles that I do not know or even refer to, but I overcome my diffidence by a desire to find out whether just to know literary works, to realize their qualities and admire them may not be a matter beyond the range of scholarship and, in a measure, the basis of elucidation. Certainly such an equipment fills most human needs and avoids that avoidance of literature in consequence of which some specialists may be said to know all about a given work except the work itself. This is old-fashioned, and belongs as I do to the days when English scholars were trained in the classics, modern foreign languages, history, and philosophy, and in science itself.

In the university I had a course in the Dialogues of Plato and was greatly interested in the *Gorgias*. Indeed, I recall my good fortune in that, when I appeared for examination in compliance with a possibly forgotten requirement of "a reading knowledge of Greek" for the Doctor's degree, I was assigned for translation a passage from *Gorgias*. I hope it was that about Zeus's reform of the judiciary of Hades in which Rhadamanthus was made the judge of those who came from Asia and Aeacus of those who came from Europe, and in which Minos was chief justice,[1] but I do not remember. In my time no stress was put on the political bearings of *Gorgias* as is done by modern interpreters, and I am sure that for a long time I was unaware of Nietzsche's espousal of the doctrines of Callicles.[2] *Gorgias* was personal to Socrates, who seemed to foresee his own impending destruction, and it was appealing. He brought up what must be one of the oldest metaphysical problems that confronted thinking humanity: why is the just and innocent man, when confronted by an evil society, powerless and endangered? Why is it unsafe to dissent from folly, falsehood, and selfishness? Plato finds the answer in his concept of happiness, which makes Socrates say that an evil-doer is happier when he encounters punishment than when he escapes. He might have said that happiness resides in the welfare of society, the service of righteousness, or in the state and practice of the good, but Plato leaves the matter in the form of a paradox and contents himself with showing that even orators or rhetoricians are bound by truth and morality. We may leave this commonplace of all the Dialogues with the remark that, although it has been attacked and worried by the logic of critical philosophy, it still lives on in the minds of men. The same is true of Plato's solution, namely, that full justice in rewards and punishments must await a life after death. One would not forget, however, the relative primitivity of Plato's thought, but recognize in him the concept that, compared with the life of the spirit, worldly life as such is dross.

Years ago I read *De Consolatione Philosophiae,* and it won my admiration from the start. No book has more of the simplicity of greatness, none has more perfect unity in its presentation of humanity caught in the meshes of injustice, ruined, doomed, and imprisoned, and yet still a thoughtful being determined not to curse God and die. During my years of teaching Chaucer I have read the *Consolation* many times and at some time saw that, particularly in the great fourth and fifth books, the work of Boethius runs parallel in the region of reflection to the *Gorgias* of Plato. I am not greatly interested in parallels as such except parallels of that sort.[3]

The language of the following summary reflects that of I. T. (Michael Walpole) as reproduced in *The Consolation of Philosophy,* edited by E. K. Rand and H. L. Stewart (London, 1936): Boethius begins by expressing his grief. The gentle lady Philosophy appears and speaks at first severely to the Muses who stand about his bed, indeed calls them harlots, and says that his case belongs to her. Boethius then recognizes Philosophy as his nurse and listens while she tells him of the victory of Socrates over "Epicures, Stoics and others," the point being that Philosophy will not desert him. She says his case is not singular—Anaxagoras was driven into exile, Socrates was poisoned, and Zeno tortured. Boethius defends himself: "Never did any man draw me from right to wrong." He has been falsely accused, and yet that "very day their accusation went for current." He has been condemned to death merely for bearing the senate too much good will— goods, dignities, and good name, all gone. Philosophy admits the hardships, but declares that Boethius is "turmoiled with the multitude of affections, grief and anger drawing thee to diverse parts"—the first note of the mastery of self. He has said that "in the sight of God that the wicked should be able to compass whatsoever they contrive against the innocent, is altogether monstrous," and the charge stands. Boethius is moreover mistaken in thinking that wicked men are powerful and happy; also in thinking that the government of the world is subject to chance instead of "divine reason." The first book ends with the metrum that begins:

> When stars are shrouded
> With dusky night,
> They yield no light
> Being so clouded.

The second book deals with the blind goddess Fortune and argues her out of existence by means of a master concept of Providence. Philosophy has attended to Boethius's education, and he has not lost the self that he has achieved. Misfortunes are common enough; they apply to things that do not matter. Certainly Boethius does not expect to find constancy in human affairs. The felicity of mortal men is placed within themselves, but "the souls of men are in no wise mortal," and Fortune "will never make those things thine which by the appointment of Nature belong not to thee. . . . In other living creatures the ignorance of themselves is nature, but in men it is vice. . . . And if sometime, which is very seldom, good men be preferred to honours, what other things can give contentment in them but the honesty of those which have them?" Their only satisfaction is in their own honesty; indeed, if dignities and power had any natural good in them, they would never be bestowed on bad men. "Whereas, if thou weighest attentively the infinite spaces of eternity, what cause hast thou to rejoice at the prolonging of thy name?" Moreover, when Fortune is opposite, she is more profitable to men than when she is favorable. The second book, having thus taken the bull by the horns, comes to an end.

In the third book Boethius asks Philosophy to say "wherein

true happiness consists." Not in wealth, not in display, not in power or authority, says Philosophy, and men seek after the greatest good like a drunken man who knows not the way home. The end of pleasure is sadness, and these ways to happiness are only bypaths, "which can never bring any man thither whither they promise to lead him." Dignities ought to make men honorable and reasonable, not jealous, conspiratorial, and tyrannical. The truth is that perfect goodness is true happiness. There cannot be two chief goods, "the one different from the other," so the sum, origin, and cause of all that is sought after is rightly thought to be goodness. Nature is not to be blamed for resistance to the "darksome minds of men." The third book thus arrives at a clear statement, and the question is not whether it is Plantonic, Aristotelian, Eleatic, or Christian, but whether it is true.

The fourth book begins with this statement by Boethius: "But this is the chief cause of my sorrow, that, since the governor of all things is so good, there can either be any evil at all, or that it pass unpunished," and with this the fourth book, as also the fifth, enter the field of *Gorgias*. There is still nowhere else to go. How are we to believe our eyes and at the same time believe in "the immense impotency of wicked men?" Shall we say with Boethius, "I would to God they were not potent" or with Philosophy, "Since therefore He that can only do good, can do all things, and they who can do evil are less potent?" Who is ready to say that in the vaster field of experience the doctrine of Philosophy does not seem to work or that it is at least not worth trying? The doctrine is announced again in these terms: "Some things which are placed under Providence are above the course of Fate." On a still lower level it may be stated: Is it better to be justly punished for evil deeds than to escape?

The fifth book proceeds on a high level of abstraction to

discuss the nature of fate or chance, and this is followed by the famous passage on what we should call the relation between foreknowledge and predestination. Boethius does not accept the solution that is usually attributed to him: "Nothing is therefore come to pass because Providence did foresee it, but rather contrariwise, because it shall be, it could not be unknown to Providence, and in this manner the necessity passes over to the other side. . . . Besides, it is manifest that every firm proof must be drawn from intrinsic and necessary causes and not from signs and other far-fetched arguments. . . . Wherefore, since every judgment comprehendeth those things which are subject to it, according to its own nature, and God hath always an everlasting and [a] present state, His knowledge also surpassing all motions of times, remaineth in the simplicity of His presence, and comprehending the infinite spaces of that which is past and to come, considereth all things in His simple knowledge as though they were now in doing. (In Plato's words "God is everlasting and the world perpetual.") . . . For there be two necessities: the one simple, as that it is necessary for man to be mortal; the other conditional, as if thou knowest that any man is walking, he must needs walk."

Thus in these simple terms Boethius changed the frame of reference and supplied the world for ages with a solution that it sometimes understood. It may be that Gibbon had this fifth book in mind when he made his often-repeated remark that the *Consolation* was "a golden volume not unworthy of the leisure of Plato or Tully." Specialized scholars may think that they know these things and that such things have no present importance. In both of these opinions they may be wrong, since they may not have observed that such simple Platonic abstractions recur inevitably in every thinking mind, recur not always in their primary forms.

Perhaps no one can say that Chaucer entered habitually into the intricacies of Boethius's philosophical thought. That he did so at times I think there is no question, for it is everywhere said, and rightly, that Chaucer's works are permeated with Boethius. The actual quantity of borrowings is great. They have been carefully collected and to some extent interpreted.[4] We shall not repeat them here, but content ourselves with certain observations of our own.

In the first instance it looks as if *The Consolation of Philosophy* had been a source of poetical inspiration to Chaucer. For example, there are the lovely sententious lyrics—*Fortune, Gentillesse, The Former Age, Lack of Steadfastness* and *Truth,* some of which are borrowed outright or nearly so. A stanza in *Anelide and Arcite* (ll.8-14) recalls the *Consolation* II, prosa 7; another such is in the Man of Law's Tale, ll.813-19 (I, met. 5), and elsewhere often in the form of gentle bits of wisdom. They are scattered throughout the works of Chaucer. Such is the discursus on Gentleness in the Wife of Bath's Tale, which recalls *Consolation* II, prosa 1, and III, prosa 6. Line 741 of the General Prologue is from III, prosa 18:

> The wordes moote be cosyn to the dede.

Typical is the Squire's Tale, ll.607-9:

> I trowe he hadde thilke text in mynde
> That "alle thyng repeirynge to his kynde,
> Gladdeth hymself"; thus seyn, as I gesse.

And even more so are lines 610-17 of the same tale:

> Men louen of propre kynde newefangelnesse,
> As briddes doon that men in cages fede,
> For though thou night and day take of hem hede,
> And strawe hir cage faire and softe as silk,
> And geve hem sugre, hony, breed and milk,

> Yet right anon as that his dore is uppe,
> He with his feet wol spurne adoun his cuppe,
> And to the wode he wole, and wormes ete.

Both passages are derived from III, metrum 2.

There are also of course a good many bits of sly humor that rest on Boethius: for example in the Knight's Tale, lines 1261-4:

> We faren as he thet dronke is as a mous,
> A dronke man woot wel he hath an hous,
> But he noot which the righte wey is thider;
> And to a dronke man the wey is slider.

This comes straight from III, prosa 2. The masterpiece in this kind is perhaps in the Nun's Priest's Tale, lines 4424-40, in which Chaucer pretends to be at a loss to tell whether Chauntecleer's unfortunte flight from the beams into the yard on an unlucky day was a matter of "symple necessete" or of "necessite condicioneel."

Chronology is doubtful, but it is at least possible that Chaucer's special study of *The Consolation of Philosophy* reached a climax in *Troilus and Criseyde*, for at least that poem and "Boece" are mentioned together in *Chaucer's Wordes unto Adam, his owne Scriveyn*. Certainly Boethius bulks larger in *Troilus and Criseyde* and enters more deeply into it than into any other work. What might be called the intensity of the influence cannot appear in even a selected list: Book I, ll.785-91 (III, met. 12), Tityus and the vultures in hell; ll.841-7 (met. 12), discursus on Fortune; ll.857-8 (I, pr. 4), wounds unwrapped for the leech to see. Book II, ll.622-3 (V, pr. 6), Necessity; ll.766-7 (I, met. 2), the cloud and the wind. Book III, ll.8-14 (II, met. 8), love and life; (see also Kn.T. l.2988); ll.617-20 (IV, pr. 6 and V, met. 1), "Fortune, executrice of wyrdes." Book IV is very full of Boethius, e.g.

ll.1-14 (II, pr. 1, met. 1), commonplaces of the uncertainty
of Fortune; ll.386-92 (II, pr. 2), further about the instability
of the blind goddess; ll.617-23 (IV, met. 6; cf. Kn.T., ll.1163-
8), manliness in the bearing of evil; ll.834-47 (II, pr. 4),
Criseyde's complaint against life; ll.953-1085 (V, pr. 2 and
3), predestination and free will. Book V of *Troilus and
Criseyde* makes in its narrative constant reference to foreknowledge and free will, Providence and Fortune and the im-
permanence of mundane existence, and the same thing may
be said still more truly of the fifth book of *The Consolation
of Philosophy.*

The *Consolation* enters of course deeply into the Knight's
Tale, as in lines 915-47 (II, pr. 2 *et passim*), the eldest lady's
speech; ll.1162-9 (III, met. 12), no law for lovers; ll.2028-30
(III, pr. 5), the sword of Damocles; ll.2987-3087 (I, met. 5,
I, met. 8 *et passim*), Theseus's great speech on the acceptance
of natural existence; also many incidental allusions. There is
no chronological guidance, but, since the use of Boethius in
the Knight's Tale seems more general and reflective there
than in *Troilus and Criseyde,* it may confirm the idea that
the Knight's Tale is the later of the two.

The relation of Chaucer to Boethius is not, however, a matter of direct quotation or unmistakable reference only. Boethius had entered into the texture of the literature of the
Middle Ages, and when an immediate source for some utter-
ance of Chaucer has been pointed out in the *Roman de la
Rose, De planctu naturae* of Alanus de Insulis, the *Teseide*
or other work of Boccaccio or the *Divina Commedia* of Dante,
there is no disposition to deny the truth of such discoveries,
but even so we are not through with Boethius, for it needs
to be remembered that the learning, the stock of ideas of the
Middle Ages, was a general pool that belonged to everybody.
It may be that Chaucer, saturated like other medieval writers

with Boethius as part of the general store of learning and wisdom, followed this or that source without forgetting Boethius. One can at least say that Chaucer reflects the philosophy of Boethius even when he is following an author who was also a follower of Boethius.

Let us take a striking instance in order to illustrate what I am attempting to express.

Three great stanzas in the fifth book of *Troilus and Criseyde,* lines 1807-27, are revisional and are regarded as certainly roughly translated from the *Teseide* of Boccaccio.[5] And yet the fact remains that, except in the *Gorgias* and *De Consolatione Philosophiae,* there is nowhere such a depiction in such convincing circumstances of the futility of earthly existence as Chaucer has added to his romance:

> And down from thennes faste he gan avyse
> This litel spot of erthe, that with the se
> Embraced is, and fully gan despise
> This wretched world, . . .
>
> And in hymself he lough right at the wo
> Of hem that wepten for his deth so faste.

It may be that the spirit of Boethius was in Chaucer's heart when he approached the highest levels of poetic feeling, whether in the Knight's Tale, the Man of Law's Tale, the Franklin's Tale, or elsewhere.

HARDIN CRAIG,
Columbia, Missouri

Notes

[1] Odysseus saw him on the bench "wielding a sceptre of gold and giving laws unto the dead."

[2] My study of the Dialogues goes little further than Jowett and of course is inadequate in that noble body of exposition itself, but I have not neglected Plato through the years. My reading has been casual but immediate. I should like to mention a recent book that has interested me: *Plato, Gorgias,* ed. E. R. Dodds (Oxford, 1959)—especially the Introduction (pp. 1-34) and Appendix pp. 387-97).

[3] Again, I lay no claims to specialized knowledge of Boethius. I have read a good deal about him in histories of philosophy and histories of literature simply because I wished to understand. Some years ago I read with much pleasure Howard R. Patch's *The Tradition of Boethius* (New York, 1935) and H. L. Stewart's *Boethius* (Edinburgh, 1891). I have also crossed the trail of Boethius in many works, such as those of C. H. Haskins, Lynn Thorndike, M. Manitius and H. O. Taylor.

[4] For lists, discussion, and references see B. L. Jefferson, *Chaucer and the Consolation of Philosophy* (Princeton, 1917) and Howard R. Patch, *The Tradition of Boethius, loc. cit.;* also notes and commentary in the editions of Chaucer's works by F. N. Robinson, John M. Manly, W. W. Skeat, and others, not forgetting Richard Morris in his edition of Chaucer's translation of *De Consolatione Philosophiae* published by the Early English Text Society (1868).

[5] See *The Book of Troilus and Criseyde,* ed. R. K. Root (Princeton, 1926), pp. lxxii, 559-60.

Scene-division in Chaucer's Troilus and Criseyde

In these days of constant revisionism in criticism and in history, there is often light to be gained by turning once again to our predecessors.[1] A case in point is a paper by Thomas R. Price, published in 1896: "Troilus and Criseyde, a Study in Chaucer's Method of Narrative Construction."[2] Price claimed to have analyzed the poem into fifty dramatic scenes, and his discussion of these scenes leads him to such conclusions as these:

[Chaucer] is dramatic, because, with intense realism of effect, he has made each spoken word of each character, and each action . . . however trivial in itself, spring as inevitable necessity . . . from the soul of each character that he has imagined. And, in the highest sense . . . Chaucer is dramatic, because, in tracing the emotional life of his chief characters, he has led that play of passion to its final expression in definite action, because he has created a definite dramatic problem and a definite dramatic solution, and because he has bound all the parts of the action together, with insurpassable dramatic skill, into a definite dramatic unity.

Though Price's buoyant tone is infectious, most of us will today tend to view his use of the word *drama* for a medieval romance of the Matter of Rome the Great as, at most, an audacious critical metaphor. There are other flaws in his argument. Instead of supplying the actual division into "scenes," he merely alludes to a numbered scene from time to time, and it is impossible to reconstruct his system in any detail. Moreover, his number fifty is too pat. Though we agree to plenty of conscious control on Chaucer's part, we can scarcely assent to such a formal miracle over intractable material. One might expect some variation in the number of scenes on the basis of slightly different methods of analysis, but the divergence between Price's fifty and my eighty-three scenes (for which I claim no final authority) is too great to give one assurance about his hidden scheme.[3] He has, in short, the reticences of a scholar-critic of his time, who is not quite sure of his canons. As obsessed as Brunetière and Manly with the "scientific" methods of a Darwinian theory of dramatic evolution, he considers Chaucer a genetic ancestor of Shakespeare's theater, which he is not. Such evolution as we might entertain, if any, would contain de Vriesian leaps as well as Darwinian gradual progression.

The dramatic metaphor is tempting, especially when we recall the well-known picture of Chaucer reading *Troilus* to the court of Richard II in MS. Cambridge Corpus Christi College 61,[4] which emphasizes Chaucer's role as performer as well as poet. Yet, however great might be his dramatic anticipations, one cannot assert that he technically knew drama as we know it or as the Renaissance knew it. Aristotle's *Poetics* were not available, even in Italy, until 1498,[5] and Horace and Cicero, whom Chaucer knew at least in part, were scarcely a substitute. The biblical drama which he knew at first hand, though dramatically sophisticated in places, was impotent to create in him the skilled sense of dialogue, visual image, and tempo which he instinctively betrays. Even the Wakefield Master had probably not yet appeared to help him. The "drama" of Chaucer is miles, even light-years, away from that of Shakespeare's *Troilus and Cressida*. The two works have not one scene in common, and Shakespeare's concern was only incidentally with the once noble love of two classic lovers—he was too occupied with Homeric travesty and the darkening of accepted values to reflect accurately the poem of passion and conviction which Chaucer had once achieved.[6]

Yet, though we must reject the central thesis or metaphor of Price's essay, we still find it instructive, not only as it reveals our own shifts in critical and historical awareness, but also as it provides for us a valuable technique for the comprehension of a massive poem the very size and complexity of which has frustrated critics who wish to view its design. We all agree with Professor Baugh about the skillful ordering of the poem, which is Chaucer's "greatest artistic achievement."[7] How, then, shall we make a modest attempt to grasp the poem in whole and in part in order to show this? There are many possibilities, among them Price's challenging method of "scene-division," which seems to have had little effect on subsequent criticism. This paper is an attempt to show how, without magniloquent claims to finality of demonstration or judgment, Price's principle may be modified, adapted, and applied to the poem in the nineteen-sixties.

As the appended analysis will show, I have divided the poem into some eighty-three scenes. In defining a "scene" it has seemed best to employ the French classical method, which marks a new scene not only with the shift of time and place but also with shift of person. Though we are not pressing the dramatic analogies too hard, the French division has a certain logic in that each new presence or absence signifies at least a minor *peripeteia*. Moreover, such a choice keeps us safely out of the realm of evolutionary hypothesis, since we should be much less tempted to consider Chaucer an ancestor of Molière or Racine than we should if Shakespeare were in question. But the major reason for the choice is its simple ease of application: the Elizabethan scene is a much harder thing to define without direct involvement of the conditions of the stage. Our formal analysis indicates "scenes" by Arabic, and auctorial comment—including third-person narrative—by Roman numerals: a device which will serve to emphasize the distinction between the author seeking the immediacy of dialogue and the author engaged in straight narrative, comment, or lyric invocation. A few scenes contain no dialogue: dreams, letters, and the highly visualized cosmic flight of Troilus in the epilogue seem to have closer kinship with the first-person character than with the omniscient author or his *persona*.

Price's formal fifty scenes seems to imply a conscious choice on the part of the author, as I have indicated, and one hard to defend. By contrast I claim for the device only a technique for critical discovery—a heuristic model or configuration. I hope it may prove to have many uses, but the remainder of this paper will discuss only four ways in which such critical shorthand helps us to grasp some of the complexity of this long and closely textured poem. It reveals to us, in short, the role of dialogue, the role of visual scene and image, the role of structural contrast, and the role of tempo and movement— all crucial elements in the demonstration of the poet's conscious or unconscious control of his "grete effect."

Let us turn first to dialogue. Mere statistics are our first discovery—about seven in eight lines of the poem turn out to be in direct discourse or its equivalent. Each scene deserves verbal analysis with attention to the wit of repartee and the interaction of character. There are many scenes which stand out: the sixth, with Pandarus accepting his task as confidant and raisonneur; the sixteenth, with Pandarus thrusting a letter into Criseyde's bosom (what we might call the farce of manners); the thirty-third, Troilus released from his "kanke-dort" by Criseyde's sympathetic and revealing words; the thirty-fifth, Pandarus's apologia; the forty-first, that consum-

mation scene on which Chaucer lavished all his art and
made a ritual out of a stolen night of joy; the fifty-first, with
the Trojan ladies in the role of Job's comforters;[8] the sixtieth,
where Troilus in despair gives Pandarus instructions for his
funeral; the sixty-fourth, Troilus's address to the shrine of
which the saint is out;[9] the seventy-fourth, Diomede's Machi-
avellian formal wooing of Criseyde; and the last scene, with
Troilus as *humanus christianus ex machina* ascending to
heaven, or wherever "Mercurye sorted him to dwelle."

There is one more brilliant scene, the seventh, in which
Pandarus comes leaping in to make his first vicarious verbal
assault on Criseyde, and finds one of her maidens reading
the *Roman de Thèbes* aloud. From this encounter we can
extract a taste of dialogue, public and witty, which reminds
us in its *non sequitur* somewhat of one of Henry James's con-
versations. Pandarus begins to speak in ambiguous terms:

> "Ye, nece, yee shal faren wel the bet,
> If God wol, al this yeer," quod Pandarus;
> "But I am sory that I have yow let
> To herken of youre book ye preysen thus.
> For Goddes love, what seith it? telle it us!
> Is it of love? O som good ye me leere!"
> "Uncle," quod she, "youre maistresse is nat here."

This is the essence of skilful dialogue—the audience knows
that Pandarus is holding back but ready to burst with news
that Criseyde has a royal lover, and it knows also that he
has just been sleeping off a "teene in love" from his own
shadowy mistress. That mistress, incidentally, must have been
an immortal tease to have daunted so comic and vital a spirit
as Pandarus. Hence his obliquity and Criseyde's wicked
verbal *touché* deeply engage us. But Pandarus is a worthy
dueller:

> "As evere thrive I," quod this Pandarus,
> Yet koude I telle a thyng to doon yow pleye."
> "Now, uncle deere," quod she, "telle it us
> For Goddes love; is than th'assege aweye?
> I am of Grekes so fered that I deye."

He continues to tempt her curiosity, but she keeps herself under control:

> Tho gan she wondren moore than biforn
> A thousand fold, and down her eyghen caste;
> For nevere, sith the tyme that she was born,
> To knowe thyng desired she so faste;
> "Now, uncle myn, I nyl yow nought displese,
> Nor axen more than may do yow disese."

The tension between her courtly breeding and her desire to know is handled in masterful fashion. We need not underline the wit, the swift psychological shifts, the dramatic ironies, and the appropriateness of such dialogue to the intrigue of the story.

But dialogue is not all that makes up a scene. Visual effect and image are a second element of importance, and Chaucer handles them with equal skill. One of the first is scene two, the Trojan Easter at the cathedral of Palladion, in which the two principals first see each other. Criseyde is there in her black widow's weeds:

> And yet she stood ful lowe and stille alone,
> Byhynden other folk, in litel brede,
> And neigh the dore, ay undre shames drede,
> Simple of atir and debonaire of chere,
> With ful assured lokyng and manere.

What a challenge for an actress to convey, were it converted into true drama—this paradox of Criseyde, courteously modest and humble, but with the defiance and dignity of a woman whose status is in doubt! Then Troilus enters, jesting at love, and asking for applause with wrinkled brow directed at his gay retinue of youths. Suddenly the God of Love shoots him with his bow, and that god is present alive to do it. Cupid is, in fact, the only supernatural figure active in the poem until the Mercury of the epilogue—a statement which will hold despite the use of the deities for local color, philosophical significance, or fatal atmosphere. These two "gods" the medieval poet can allow to act within the poem, since one of them is sanctioned by ages of literary convention and the other is, as psychopomp, much like the Christian guardian angel. Significantly enough, one of them acts when Troilus first falls into the love of an earthly mistress and the other when he rejects such love. But the center of the scene is still Criseyde. Troilus, not yet out of his adolescent rudeness, stares at the lady, and she turns her eyes aside as if to say "What! may I nat stonden here?" With such master strokes Chaucer first sketches in the beautiful and mysterious woman who, as Professor Baugh has said, forces us to "try without complete success to penetrate the mingling of impulses and the complex workings of her mind." [10]

There are many such effective "dramatic" images. In scene sixteen Criseyde refuses to accept Troilus's first letter to her. Pandarus is the man of action:

> "Refuse it naught," quod he, and hente hire faste,
> And in hire bosom the lettre down he thraste,
> And seyde hire, "Now cast it awey anon,
> That folk may seen and gauren on us tweye."
> Quod she, "I kan abyde til they be gon";
> And gan to smyle.

This ambiguous smile recalls the Pardoner's *gaude,* or Bluntschli's challenge to Raina in Shaw's *Arms and the Man,* where, after invading her bedroom, he keeps her from calling out for help by asking what people will think if they find a man in her private quarters. We must briefly skirt a number of similar visually striking scenes: Troilus in bed at Deiphebus's house waiting for his mistress, and the byplay when she comes to see him; Troilus lurking in a little closet waiting for Criseyde in the approach to the consummation scene; Pandarus's priest-like actions at the consummation scene itself, climaxed by his ritualistic words and actions:

> Quod Pandarus, "For aught I kan aspien,
> This light, nor I, ne serven here of nought.
> Light is nought good for sike folkes yen!
> But, for the love of God, syn ye be brought
> In thus good plit, lat now no hevy thought
> Ben hanging in the hertes of yow tweye"—
> And bar the candele to the chymeneye.

The mantel is surely an altar—with that gesture it is not hard to see the sacramental action of the priest Pandarus, who had betrothed the lovers in scene thirty-three, and who in this scene forty-one has symbolically married them one to another. Yet, as we discover from our search for a scene-division, Chaucer, so explicit on other occasions, never really says that Pandarus has left the room. In the preceding scene Criseyde's double-tongued uncle had promised her "I wol myself be with yow all this night." Chaucer has left the departure ambiguous: since Pandarus is present at the marriage climax in spirit in any event, what need to say that he left the room in body? The vividly realized sacramental action is enough.[11]

Finally we may mention other visually striking scenes in the last book, a book full of dust and ashes and disappointment for us and for the lovers, and often scanted because of its sorrow. Yet Chaucer's own sorrow did not lessen his art.

There is the hollow splendor of the procession at the beginning of Book V, when the prisoners are exchanged, and Troilus, struck dumb out of all diplomatic reason or courtesy, reveals by his silence the true state of affairs to his potential rival Diomede. There is also a remarkable panoramic sequence (scenes 64-70), in which Troilus, impatiently waiting for his Criseyde to return, addresses the various scenes of their love: the temple where he met her, a spot where she laughed, the moon which is a symbol to him of her return but to us a symbol of her fickleness, the wind coming from the Greek camp and from his lady, and, finest stroke of all, the first in the sequence, her empty palace:

> "O palais, whilom crowne of houses alle,
> Enlumyned with sone of alle blisse!
> O ryng, fro which the ruby is out falle,
> O cause of wo, that cause hast ben of lisse!
> Yet, syn I may no bet, fayn wolde I kisse
> Thy colde dores, dorste I for this route;
> And farwel shryne, of which the seynt is oute!"

That is enough to show that Book V, far from being a decline in artistic control, owes its dusty answer to calculated effect, to visual image at its best.

There is a third advantage in viewing *Troilus* through scene-division. This lies in structural contrast, the play of scene on scene as we have already watched the play of word on word in dialogue. In this use of contrast Chaucer anticipates certain similar triumphs in the *Canterbury Tales:* the theme of two lovers and a lady as viewed by both the courtly Knight and the churlish Miller; the theme of the Italian nobleman who marries a wife of his choice from humble circles, as treated both by the idealistic Clerk and the cynical Merchant; the theme of squire and lady in a garden as seen by both

Merchant and Franklin; the contrasting "tragedies" of Monk and Nun's Priest, and so on. Here we can watch it all in one finished poem.

A word about the word *structure*. I do not use it, as the examples from the *Tales* will show, to mean what some critics do—the mere story or argument of the poem, with a few political or psychological or moral themes to decorate it. *Troilus* is a "myth" of course—in Northrop Frye's sense of universal story. No lovers ever loved so deeply or so tragically; no courtly lover was ever so fastidious of his code or so genuinely worshipful of his lady; no fickle lady was ever so pathetic in her shifting "corage"; no confidant so skillful as Pandarus—not even in literature or in the archetypal consciousness. Nothing can be gained by reducing this story to all other stories, in spite of the dominant use of the father-image (Calkas, Hector, Troilus, Diomede, Pandarus), which tempts us and over-tempted Walton in his recent Troilus opera.[12] What I mean by structure is artistic configuration, the manipulation of plot and episode to enrich and deepen the bare details of a story, as the verbal texture enriches and deepens the juxtaposed scenes. On the whole I consider it to be conscious on the artist's part, whatever significant meanings might rise up unconsciously on the Road to Xanadu.

One set of such striking contrasts appears in scenes two to six: Troilus's youthful scorn of love and his unwitting *innamoramento* through the vengeful God of Love; the next scene, in which Troilus takes ironic farewell of his gay companions, still unaware of what has happened to him; the next, in which he sees the *eidolon* or vision of Criseyde; the next, in which he at last finds some consolation through Pandarus's offer of his witty aid. There is similar balanced contrast between scenes seven–eight and fifteen–sixteen, in each pair a public display of Pandarus's banter to Criseyde

followed by a private scene in which he works more inti-
mately upon her feelings. There is also in scene eight a brilliant reprise of scene six, in which we may contrast the
realistic first discovery of Troilus's love with Pandarus's ro-
manticized account of that discovery to Criseyde. Another
significant pair is scenes nine and twenty-one, in both of
which Criseyde views Troilus through a window. In the first
she sees him acclaimed by the Trojan public as he returns
from war, and she falls in love herself with the cry, "Who yaf
me drynke!" This is totally unarranged and yet effectual as
a stimulus. In the second, Pandarus has arranged to bring
Troilus to the window with his retinue; Criseyde turns her
lover off without a word or a concession. This time the meeting is arranged by human intervention, not by chance, but it
is ineffectual—an ironic comment on the assurance of Pandarus, who thinks himself responsible for everything that
happened before the Fate of Book IV steps in. And these
two window scenes foreshadow Troilus watching the arrival
of Criseyde on the night of the storm, almost a humanly
planned storm, but one which resolves the turmoil of the
lovers. There is, again, the skillful contrivance of the two
intrigue sequences, before the dinner at Deiphebus's palace,
with Pandarus's busy movements from hall to chamber, and
before the more eventful one at Pandarus's palace, where his
control, ambiguous storm aside, is much greater. I have already called the two climactic scenes the betrothal and the
marriage scenes.

Finally, there are the three apologias, those of Pandarus
(35), of Criseyde (75), and of Troilus (83). An apologia, as
I use the term, involves not only self-justification but also
self-revelation or discovery. There is always an ambiguity
of motive—a tension between character and audience, as
there is in those two notable confessions in the *Tales*, the

Wife of Bath's and the Pardoner's. Pandarus's apologia follows upon his success in arranging the first of the two dinners, and its sequel leads him to some sober afterthought and the revelation that even one who has become

> Bitwixen game and ernest, swich a meene
> As maken wommen unto men to comen

has the most rigorous and delicate views of the code of love. Criseyde in her analogous self-torment comes to a most lame and impotent conclusion, which leads Chaucer to the pathetic aside: "Men seyn—I not—that she yaf (Diomede) hire herte." And the hurt echoes through Criseyde's own words:

> O, rolled shal I ben on many a tonge!
> Thoroughout the world my belle shal be ronge!
> And wommen moost wol haten me of alle. . . .
> Al be I nat the first that dide amys,
> What helpeth that to don my blame awey?
> But syn I se ther is no bettre way,
> And that to late is now for me to rewe,
> To Diomede algate I wol be trewe.

These two apologias have been often so named, and their common elements, guilty defensiveness and a fear for what the world will say, perceived. But few have perceived in turn that the great epilogue to the poem is Troilus's apologia, masterfully integrated with the other two. Scene eighty-three is wholly visual. As Troilus rises in the stratosphere we have it thus:

> And in hymself he lough ryht at the wo
> Of hem that wepten for his deth so faste;
> And dampned al oure werk that foloweth so
> The blynde lust, the which that may nat laste
> And sholden al oure herte on heven caste.

> And forth he wente, shortly for to telle,
> Ther as Mercurye sorte hym to dwelle.

The ritual psychopomp, as I have said, releases him from the bonds which another god had laid upon him. Mercury leads him somewhere, which might be Dante's Purgatory or the Heaven of the penitent. But Chaucer is wary enough not to mention the Christian cosmos except obliquely, in the exalted words which follow to give us psychic and metaphysical distance from "payens corsed olde rites" and our close identification with the lovers. Such an analysis once more vindicates the epilogue, which has caused so much concern to secular moderns. The placing of the three apologias is one of the strongest structural effects in the poem. We need that of Pandarus at the beginning of the poem to bear with him; we accept Criseyde's late one as pure pathos after the event; and we need Troilus's only because heavenly values are different from those of earth—he really has little to apologize for on the human level. This *O altitudo* of the final scene also contrasts with that just preceding, in which Pandarus at last is empty of new devices for action, and is as speechless as Iago in a similar situation:

> What sholde I seyen? I hate, ywys, Criseyde;
> And God woot, I wol hate hire evermore! . . .
> And fro this world, almyghty God I preye,
> Delivere hire soon! I kan namore seye.

Two dreams likewise stand out for contrast. The first is Criseyde's dream, in Book II, of an eagle, the noble Troilus who tears out her heart and replaces it with his in violence of passion like Marvell's

> Let us tear our Pleasure with rough strife,
> Thorough the Iron gates of life.

The purport of this dream demands no interpretation. Against it we place Troilus's dream of a boar embracing Criseyde in Book V—to the audience the purport is clear, but we must watch the sad spectacle of the lover searching for a meaning he does not want to know. With almost Freudian insight Pandarus tells him the boar is her father; Cassandra tells him it is Diomede and he will not listen.

A fourth and final discovery forced on us by our scenic analysis is the role of tempo and its artistic manipulation. Shifts of tempo are of course not absent from straight narrative: in the *Canterbury Tales* one formula, the slow, rhetorical, learned, and leisurely opening followed by a swift middle of events and a pellmell end, is often repeated. The author knew how to command his audience's weakening span of attention through such structure of movement, and to climax his tales with such devices as the swift retribution on the Pardoner's three thieves who sought Death, or the barnyard chase of the Nun's Priest. *Troilus* opens with a similar shift. There is the slow and ceremonious litany for lovers, followed by a swift summary of the Trojan War which brings us *in medias res* in a fashion more Homeric than medieval:

> And biddeth ek for hem that ben at ese . . .
> To prey for hem that Loves servauntz be,
> And write hire wo, and lyve in charite,
> And for to have of hem compassioun,
> As though I were hire owne brother dere.

Then, suddenly:

> Now herkneth with a good entencioun,
> For now wil I gon streght to my matere,
> In which ye may the double sorwes here
> Of Troilus in lovynge of Criseyde,
> And how that she forsook hym ere she deyde.

Yt is wel wist how that the Grekes stronge
In armes, with a thousand shyppes, wente
To Troiewardes, and the cite longe
Assegeden. . . .

And soon he is describing, not the face that launched those
thousand ships, but one of "an hevenyssh perfit creature"
who launched a noble lover into woe and weal and woe again.

In the second book there is another skillful and significant
shift of tempo, this time more dramatic than narrative in
character. By the ninth scene Criseyde has already seen
Troilus as a conquering hero from her closet window, and
cried "Who yaf me drynke!" This speedy love Chaucer at
once checks by narrative and by the kind of auctorial intrusion we call romantic irony—he cannot risk it, she is a
courtly mistress and "sodeyne love" is the charge which future
ages will bring against her. So, after her visual love-potion,
we see move before us several scenes devoted solely to the
stimuli of love, the tempests and the portents of the mind. It
is as brilliantly juxtaposed as that sequence in which Conrad
shows us Lord Jim tormented into the fatal jump from the
deck of the *Patna*, which is against his whole ideal and proper
nature. The window scene and Chaucer's comment are followed by Criseyde's lengthy debate, rational and emotional,
concerning the relative joys of freedom and bondage in love.
Then follow in vigorous, incisively highlighted sequel certain lyric counterparts of the debate: Antigone's song of the
bliss of love, the song of the nightingale, a natural counterpart to the human lyric, and the dream of the eagle who is
Troilus. Chaucer thus protects Criseyde's name by a series
of psychologically sound episodes, all carefully controlled by
shifts in tempo.

Similar contrasts in speed of movement are Pandarus's
dashes back and forth in a swift series of scenes at Dei-

phebus's palace, as he arranges for the momentous meeting of the lovers, followed by a sober visit to Troilus's bedside; and the movement is further complicated by the fall of the curtain right in the middle of the crucial scene, at the end of Book II, as Troilus lies in suspense revolving all those words which he will say to his beloved—words which become the single reiteration "Mercy" when she finally appears. Again, the often criticized speech at the end of Book IV, Troilus on fatalism, is no blemish;[13] it slows the swift cumulation of events which follow upon the decision of the Greeks to exchange prisoners and to bring Criseyde back to her somewhat less than adequate father. The meditation of the tormented lover on the province of fate which no man, however assured he may be, has ever satisfactorily comprehended (not even Pandarus, the man of action, who is defeated at the end), prepares us for the climactic scene of the book, in which the lovers take final *private* leave of one another. The following scene, a public conveying of Criseyde to Diomede by Troilus, is a dry afterthought; Troilus, the soul of courtesy, speaks no courteous word. It is the proper prelude to that brilliant, wintry final book, crammed with scenes run off at double time and full of the misery, not of an author's failure, but of characters with whom one has too closely identified oneself, with whom one has too eagerly suspended disbelief and concluded that the transitory consummation, the joy of life's *summum bonum,* can be permanent. Irony fights us in this book all the way. There is much action, but not the right kind of action for our money. There is no poetic justice, no return of the loved one, not even a proper dying by Troilus at the hands of that charming villain Diomede who has replaced him as a lover. There is something of the speed and emptiness here which we find in the last scenes of *Hamlet* and

St. Joan. There is nowhere to go, only to heaven—a vague and unidentified heaven, as we have seen, but hopefully not the cold heaven of William Butler Yeats.

Hence, though we cannot follow the total critical position of Price's seventy-year-old essay, we can endorse with pleasure and discovery at least a modified form of his division of *Troilus* into scenes. Were we tempted to follow his dramatic metaphor into deep analogy, we might recall that Francis Fergusson has found the *Divine Comedy* full of the "histrionic sensibility" and of "our direct sense of the changing life of the psyche." [14] But it would take another demonstration than this one to show how *Troilus* might contain Fergusson's three prime requisites of drama—purpose, passion, and perception—the purpose of Troilus's quest of love, first earthly, then divine; the passion of the tortured lover before and after and during the exquisite peak of earthly love; the perception of worth in love and the fuller perception of its vanity. For this is an even bolder metaphor than that of Price. We may content ourselves with the simple conclusion that Chaucer's sense of scene shows itself in vivid dialogue, vivid visual image, intentional contrast between scene and scene, and the controlled and shifting tempo of verse and narrative.

ANALYSIS OF SCENES

(Arabic numerals precede the episodes, which are posited on dialogue [including monologue and letters], and on significant shifts in time, place and person. Very important scenes are starred. Roman numerals and remarks in parentheses describe invocation, digressions, and major narrative transitions.)

Book I

(i. Invocation to Thesiphone and bidding prayer for lovers) 1-56

(ii. The siege of Troy, Calkas's treason and desertion of Criseyde) 57-105

1. Criseyde obtains Hector's promise of protection. 106-133

(iii. Progress of the siege) 134-147

*2. April—feast in Palladion's temple. Troilus, scorning love, is punished by Cupid's arrow. 148-322

3. Troilus's palace. Still unaware of what has really happened, he leaves his followers with an ironic speech on love. 323-357

4. Chamber in palace. Troilus sees a vision of Criseyde and sings of love. 358-441

(iv. Progress of Troilus's love) 442-504

5. Troilus "complains" of his plight. 505-46

*6. Troilus's chamber. Pandarus takes on role as confidant. 547-1064

(v. Pandarus begins his work; Troilus's character expands with the joy of hope.) 1065-1092

Book II

(vi. Invocation to Clio) 1-49

(vii. May the third and fourth. Pandarus, himself nonplussed in love, gets up and goes to visit his niece.) 50-77

7. Criseyde's palace. A maiden is reading the *Roman de Thèbes* to Criseyde and two of her ladies. Pandarus banters her about her secluded life, and praises Hector and Troilus. The attendants leave the center of the stage. 78-216

*8. Same, two principals alone. Pandarus reveals Troilus's love and warns he will die; she agrees to be kind, and

Pandarus gives a highly idealized account of his discovery of Troilus's love. 217-597

*9. Criseyde's "closet." She sees Troilus through a window as he modestly refuses the public's acclaim. She falls in love with the dramatic words "Who yaf me drynke!" 598-665

(viii. All of this did not happen with indecorous speed.) 666-86

10. Same place, same time. Criseyde's soliloquy on the securities and dangers of love. 687-812

*11. Criseyde's garden. Criseyde and her ladies hear Antigone's naïve song on the blisses of love. 813-910

*12. Criseyde's chamber. In bed, she hears a nightingale sing of love, and dreams of her eagle lover. 911-31

*13. Troilus's palace, his chamber. Pandarus after much jest tells Troilus that he has secured Criseyde's "love of friendshipe" for him, and counsels him to write a letter. 932-1063

14. The same. Troilus gets up, writes the letter, and soliloquizes. 1064-92.

15. Next day. Criseyde's palace. Pandarus and Criseyde jest, and he asks for a private interview. 1093-1115

*16. Her garden. The two principals alone. She refuses the letter, but he thrusts it in her bosom. She accepts the gambit with a smile, but warns him she will write no letter. He agrees to write if she dictates the letter, and the scene ends with laughter. 1116-69

17. The dining hall. She leaves Pandarus with a brief word. 1170-71

(ix. She reads the letter in her chamber.) 1172-79

18. The dining hall. They jest and eat. 1180-84

19. After dinner. Pandarus draws her aside to the window, and convinces her she should write an answer. 1185-1214

20. Criseyde's closet. She writes and says she will be a sister to Troilus. 1215-25

*21. Her hall. She gives Pandarus the letter. Troilus with nine companions passes by the window, but she refuses at this time to speak to him. Pandarus leaves, confident. 1226-1302

22. Troilus's chamber. Pandarus gives Troilus the letter, which produces complex emotions in him. 1303-23

(x. Days pass, and Troilus writes more letters under Pandarus's tutelage.) 1324-51

23. Some time later. Pandarus promises to arrange a meeting with Criseyde at the palace of Deiphebus "ere houres twyes twelve." 1352-1401

24. Shortly later. Pandarus asks Deiphebus to help Criseyde, maligned by unnamed enemies, and he agrees to give a dinner. 1402-59

25. Criseyde's palace. Pandarus tells Criseyde of the malice of Poliphete, Antenor, and Aeneas, and says he has asked the aid of Deiphebus. 1460-84

(xi. Deiphebus invites Criseyde to dinner.) 1485-91

26. Pandarus instructs Troilus to pretend illness at the dinner, and Troilus says no pretense will be necessary. 1492-1536

(xii. Troilus returns home. That night he visits Deiphebus, who puts him to bed and asks him with fine dramatic irony to be a friend to Criseyde.) 1537-54

27. Dining hall of Deiphebus's palace, next morning just before noon. Helen, Criseyde and her ladies, and the others assemble. All praise the sick Troilus. 1555-96

28. The same, after dinner. Pandarus tells them of the enmity of Poliphete, and Helen and Pandarus suggest that she tell Troilus. 1597-1636

29. The sickroom. Pandarus tells Troilus that he has brought his "beere," and Troilus smiles. 1637-39

30. The dining hall. Pandarus returns and suggests that they visit Troilus in small groups. 1640-64

31. The sickroom. Helen, Deiphebus, and Pandarus urge Troilus to befriend Criseyde. He agrees and gives them a letter full of important state business. 1665-1701

(xiii. Helen and Deiphebus read the letter in an arbor for "the montance of an houre.") 1702-08

32. Pandarus returns to the dining hall, and escorts Criseyde to Troilus, urging her not to slay her lover. 1709-50

*33. Troilus lies in the sickroom "in a kankedort." 1751-57 . . .

Book III

(xiv. Invocation to Venus and Calliope) 1-49

*33 continued. In spite of his embarrassment Troilus makes love with "Mercy, mercy, swete herte!" She accepts him, and Pandarus, on his knees, prays to Cupid and Venus, and promises to arrange another meeting. 50-203

34. The same. Helen and Deiphebus return, Criseyde leaves, they praise her, then leave, and Pandarus stays. 204-26

*35. The same. Pandarus's apologia, and Troilus's promise of discretion and gratitude. They sleep. 227-420

(xv. I pass over many meetings and Pandarus's intrigues. "But to the grete effect." Pandarus plans an assignation in his own house.) 421-546

36. Criseyde's palace. Pandarus invites her to dinner, and she warns him to be careful. Rain is in the air. 547-94

37. Pandarus's palace. Criseyde comes with male and female retinue, while Troilus watches "Throughout a litel wyndow

in a stewe." After supper it rains, and Criseyde agrees to stay all night. 545-658

38. Pandarus escorts them to bed, Criseyde in his "litel closet," the women in a "myddel chaumbre," and Pandarus outside as "wardein." 659-93

39. The "stewe." Pandarus teases Troilus, and leads him to Criseyde through a trapdoor. 694-742

*40. Criseyde's chamber, Troilus in hiding. Pandarus tells the frightened Criseyde that Troilus is jealous of an imaginery Horaste. She agrees to see him, since Pandarus says "I wol myself be with yow all this nyght." 743-951

*41. Troilus materializes, on his knees. She blushes. Pandarus runs for a cushion. She kisses Troilus and bids him sit. Pandarus pretends to read a romance. Criseyde defends herself against the charge of jealousy, weeps while Troilus falls on his knees and faints, and Pandarus pushes him into bed. Criseyde revives him with kisses. Pandarus "bar the candele to the chymeneye." Troilus embraces Criseyde, and Pandarus "Leyde hym to slepe." (It is not said specifically that he leaves the room.) There follows a ceremonial consummation, with a brooch instead of a ring. 952-1414

42. Next morning. The lovers exchange dawn-songs and Troilus leaves. 1415-1528

(xvi. Troilus returns to bed in his own palace, as the two lovers dream about the other's virtues.) 1529-54

*43. Criseyde's chamber in Pandarus's palace. Pandarus comes in and jests, and she forgives him, as "God foryaf his deth." She leaves. 1555-82

44. Troilus's palace. Troilus and Pandarus talk of the blissful night, and Pandarus warns him to move cautiously. 1583-1666

45. Pandarus's palace, "soon after this." Another blissful night and sorrowful parting for the two lovers. 1667-1712

(xvii. There were many other nights like these, and Troilus's character rises in nobility and reputation.) 1713-36

*46. "Ful ofte" (a typical scene) Troilus would lead Pandarus into a garden and sing of the power of love. 1737-71

(xviii. Troilus is further ennobled. Chaucer rounds out the book with a further invocation to Venus and Cupid.) 1772-1820

Book IV

(xix. Invocation to Mars and the Three Furies, with a summary of what is to come) 1-28

(xx. The Greeks seek a truce for the exchange of prisoners.) 29-63

47. The Greek camp. Bishop Calkas "in consistorie" requests that Antenor and other Trojan heroes be exchanged for Criseyde, and the Greeks send messengers to Priam. 64-140

48. The Trojan "parlement." Troilus is silent, but Hector says "We usen here no wommen for to selle." The fickle people demand that they have their hero, Antenor, back, and the parliament so decides. 141-217

49. Troilus's palace. Troilus's despairing soliloquy. He faints. 218-342

*50. Pandarus rushes to his sorrowful friend, and his suggestions that Troilus either find another lady or abduct Criseyde are met with cold refusal. Pandarus promises to arrange a meeting. 344-658

*51. Criseyde's palace. Criseyde is visited by a group of sympathetic ladies, who congratulate her. She endures "thilke fooles sittynge hire aboute" and they go. 659-735

52. The same. She tears her hair and soliloquizes: "What is Criseyde worth, from Troilus?" 736-805

53. The same. Pandarus consoles her and arranges for Troilus's visit. 806-945

*54. A temple. Troilus in despair reveals his fatalistic temper in a long speech which uses only one side of the Boethian argument. Pandarus rebukes him and urges him to go to Criseyde. 946-1123

*55. Troilus goes to Criseyde. She faints and, believing she is dead, he is about to slay himself, but she awakens and restrains him. She promises to play on her father's greed and to return in ten days. He urges elopement, but she refuses. She urges him to be faithful, and he solemnly swears. Day comes and he departs in despair. 1124-1701

Book V

(xxi. Brief prologue, emphasizing "the fatal destyne") 1-14

*56. The field of truce, and the exchange of prisoners. Troilus is tempted to slay Diomede and abduct Criseyde, but he represses his impulse. He fails in the usual exchanges of courtesy and Diomede suspects something. Troilus returns to Troy. 15-91

57. On the road back to the Greek camp, Diomede offers himself as friend and servant, and Criseyde, little heeding his words, accepts. 92-188

58. The Greek camp. Calkas greets her. 189-195

59. Troilus's chamber. He goes to bed, sings an "ubi sunt" song, falls asleep and has nightmares. 196-273

*60. The same. Pandarus comes, and Troilus gives instructions for his funeral. Pandarus rebukes him for his folly in trusting dreams, and suggests that they pass the ten days of waiting at King Sarpedoun's country villa. 274-434

(xxii. Though Sarpedoun gives them a festive time, Troilus cannot get his mind off his lady.) 435-75

61. Sarpedoun's villa. On the fourth day Troilus wants to go home, but Pandarus urges him to stay a week. 476-97

62. The road back to Troy at end of the week. Troilus sings with joy and anticipation; Pandarus is skeptical inwardly. 498-511

(xxiii. Troilus's palace. After supper they go to bed.) 512-18

63. Troilus's palace, the next morning. Troilus tells Pandarus he wishes to go to Criseyde's palace. 519-25

*64. In front of Criseyde's palace. Troilus lyrically addresses the "shryne, of which the seynt is oute!" 526-55

*65. Panoramic scene, as Troilus rides by and addresses the various scenes of their love, the temple where he met her, a place where she laughed, another where she sang, another where she first took him "unto hire grace." To Cupid he says that men might well make a story of his sufferings. 556-602

66. The gates of Troy. He invokes the scene of their parting. 603-16

(xxiv. A day or so more passes, and he imagines that everyone is talking about him.) 617-30

67. He sings of the loss of his pole-star. 631-44

68. He addresses the moon, which will bring his lady when it is new again. 645-58

69. He fears the sun is delayed and each day too long. 659-65

70. On the walls of Troy he addresses the wind which comes from his lady. 666-79

(xxv. Pandarus seeks to console Troilus until the ninth night after the parting.) 680-86

71. The Greek camp. Criseyde, in despair, fears to ask her father for permission to return to Troy. 687-714

72. The same, later. She says she will steal away some time tomorrow. 715-65

(xxvi. But two months elapse without her doing anything.) 766-70

73. One night, Diomede decides to press his courtship. 771-98

*(xxvii. Three formal portraits of Diomede, Criseyde, and Troilus.) 799-840

74. Calkas's tent the tenth day after the parting. Diomede makes love to Criseyde, she hides her love for Troilus, and by evening she gives him a glove as favor. 841-1015

(xxviii. Criseyde sleeps, and the morning of the rendezvous with Troilus passes, as Diomede comes to her and "refte hire of the grete of al hire peyne." The story says she gave him Troilus's horse, a brooch, and a "pencil of hire sleve." It also says she wept when Diomede was wounded in battle by Troilus, and "Men seyn—I not—that she yaf hym hire herte.") 1016-50

*75. Her great sorrow as she finally decides to be false to Troilus. "To Diomede algate I wol be trewe." 1051-85

(xxix. But that was a long time afterwards, none knows how long.) 1086-99

76. The walls of Troy, morning. A flashback to the tenth day after parting. Troilus and Pandarus seek excuses for her delay. 1100-41

77. The same, evening. Troilus, eager, mistakes a travelling cart for Criseyde, while Pandarus keeps his skepticism to himself. The warden closes the gates and they must return home. 1142-81

78. The road home. Troilus says he has miscounted the days. 1182-91

(xxx. Next morning he returns to the walls. The sixth day past the date of rendezvous arrives and jealousy comes upon him.) 1192-1232

*79. He dreams a boar is embracing Criseyde. Pandarus says the dream means nothing, and urges him to write a letter, which he does. 1233-1421

(xxxi. She responds to the letter and says she will come back one of these days. But he grows more sure as time passes that she never will.) 1422-42

*80. Cassandra tells him the boar is Diomede, and in anger he calls her a sorceress and a liar. 1443-1537

(xxxii. More time passes. Achilles slays Hector. Troilus even imagines he might visit Criseyde, disguised as a pilgrim. He writes her often, and she finally answers.) 1538-89

*81. Her cold and accusing letter. 1590-1631

(xxxiii. He thinks the letter "strange," and when he recognizes his brooch on some "cote-armure" which Deiphebus has taken from Diomede, he knows she has betrayed him.) 1632-66

82. Troilus's palace. He tells Pandarus of the brooch and wishes he might fight with Diomede. Pandarus is at the end of his rope, and curses his niece. 1667-1743

*(xxxiv. Troilus continues to seek Diomede in battle, but Fortune willed that neither should die by the other's hand. Read Dares if you would know more. May all ladies beware of false men. Go little book, and kiss the steps of Virgil and his peers, and give me power to write a comedy.) 1744-99

*83. Troilus dies, and his spirit rises to the eighth sphere, whence he looks at this "litel spot of erthe" and laughs at the woe of those who weep for him, damns the blind lust of man, and then goes "Ther as Mercurye sorted hym to dwelle." 1800-27

*(xxxv. Such an end Troilus had for love! "O yonge, fresshe folkes, he or she," turn to the love of Christ. Behold the cursed rites of pagans and the form of ancient poetry. I

direct my book to moral Gower and philosophical Strode,
and pray to Jesus and the Trinity:

> So make us, Jesus, for thy mercy digne,
> For love of mayde and moder thyn benigne.)   1828-69

Francis Lee Utley,
The Ohio State University

[1] The scene-analysis will be familiar to many Chaucerians; it is a revised version prepared originally for a seminar at Columbia University in 1950, tested in mimeographed form in many subsequent classes, and distributed in that form to a number of my colleagues. The essay was originally delivered as a public lecture at Ohio State University and revised for presentation to the Chaucer Group of the Modern Language Association at Madison, Wisconsin, in 1957. It has had the benefit of some pointed criticism from my colleague, Morton Bloomfield, but he has been spared seeing it in its final form.

[2] *PMLA*, XI (1896):307-322.

[3] Price occasionally gives numbers which may facilitate comparison with the present analysis. His 1 = my 2, 36 = 54, 38 = 55, 39 = 56, 45 = 72, 50 = 83.

[4] Aage Brusendorff, *The Chaucer Tradition* (London and Copenhagen, 1925), pp. 19-23 and frontispiece.

[5] See Marvin T. Herrick, *The Poetics of Aristotle in England* (New Haven: Yale University Press, 1930), pp. 13-14 (his date moves forward the usually cited date of 1531, that of the Basel edition).

[6] See Robert K. Presson's analysis of the general indebtedness of play and poem in his *Shakespeare's Troilus and Cressida & The Legends of Troy* (Madison: University of Wisconsin Press, 1953), pp. 107-33. It is notable that in the twenty-three verbal borrowings which Presson lists only two are from the narrative portions of Chaucer's poems, and the rest are from what I have labeled "scenes." There are broad agreements, but no one-to-one equivalent. Shakespeare's I.i recalls scenes 13 and 23; I.ii scenes 7, 9, 21; III.i narrative digression xvi (Troilus's secrecy); III.ii is a poor shadow of the consummation scene, with echoes from 41, 44, 47, and 55; IV.ii combines 42, 43, xviii, 48, 55; IV.iv is 55 and 56; IV.i, in which Criseyde kisses all the Greek leaders, is of course completely alien to Chaucer (but compare Diomede's wooing 57); V.ii is derived from the post-Henryson tradition; V.iii may be the letter of 81, but it is remote; the scenes of battle between Diomedes and Troilus have no real equivalent in Chaucer (but compare V.iv and V.vii with 82); V.x with Troilus's rejection of Pandarus and Pandarus's madness is thoroughly alien to Chaucer. To turn to the other end of the tradition, we may say that Chaucer found the germs of dialogue in Boccaccio, and that there are some striking equivalents between Chaucer's 6-8, 13, 19, 41-42, 45, 48, 50, 54-55, 60-61, 74, 76-77, 80, 82, and the corresponding scenes in *Il Filostrato*. But the transformation is great.

[7] Albert C. Baugh, ed., *A Literary History of England* (New York and London: Appleton–Century–Crofts, 1948), p. 257.

[8] Price (p. 313) remarks that "there is here a pathos of social comedy that reminds us of the best scenes of the modern stage." He seems to have been the first to call it a "Trojan afternoon tea."

[9] The verbal texture is excellently probed by H. S. Bennett, *Chaucer and the Fifteenth Century* (Oxford University Press, 1947), pp. 91-92.

[10] Baugh, *op. cit.*, p. 256.

[11] Robert K. Root (ed., *The Book of Troilus and Criseyde* [Princeton University Press, 1926], p. 483) says flatly that when Pandarus "laid himself down to sleep" he went to his own bedroom. But he had given his own bedroom ("my litel closet") to Criseyde (III, 663). Thomas A. Kirby (*Chaucer's Troilus: A Study in Courtly Love* [Louisiana State University Press, 1940], p. 161) cautiously says no more than Chaucer did. Hamilton M. Smyser is perhaps surer than I am that Pandarus did go to sleep beside the hearth in the same room as the lovers—see his "The Domestic Background of *Troilus and Criseyde*," *Speculum*, XXXI (1956):309. Our modern sense of propriety would no doubt have been often shocked by the crowded conditions of medieval houses, or even of castles or "palaces." Compare the ruses Pandarus must employ to gain Criseyde's private ear in scenes 7 and 15. My own belief is that Chaucer was intentionally ambiguous; he can be explicit enough when he so desires.

[12] I know the opera only from Angel Record No. 35278. My impression is that Walton has made too much of this modernistic interpretation to obtain a proper invocation of the medieval romance. But we need make no apology for the Freudian phrase, for even Price (p. 316) saw the importance of Calkas's failure as a father, and made the natural comparison to the Gertrude–Hamlet situation. His conclusions, however, are more Darwinian than Freudian. For another modern reflection of Chaucer see Jean Giraudoux's *The Tiger at the Gates*. Giraudoux may well have found his atmosphere of fatality in Chaucer as well as in modern determinism, but he surely must be thinking of Chaucer's hero when he arranges the amusing scenes in which Paris eggs on Helen to make love to the rebellious adolescent Troilus, and the climactic one in which Troilus and Helen are seen embracing through the open gates of war in the last visual image of the play.

[13] Price (*op. cit.*, 311 and 314), unused as we are to Shaw's dramatic use of lengthy speeches, and writing too early to benefit from Patch's defense of the episode (*On Rereading Chaucer* [Harvard University Press, 1939], pp. 104-22), calls it the "chief artistic blemish on the poem." We read it differently today.

[14] *The Idea of a Theatre* (Garden City, N. Y.: Doubleday, 1953), p. 18.

Wyclif, Langland, Gower, and the Pearl Poet on the Subject of Aristocracy

No difference between medieval and modern life is more significant than that in the attitudes toward the nature and function of a social aristocracy. These attitudes find their way into any interpretation of political and social behavior, or of literary characterization and motivation. Students of literature have touched upon them in discussions of chivalry, of courtesy books, of the Elizabethan gentleman and gentlewoman, and of the common man. And there is a vast body of more or less pertinent scholarship in history and the social sciences. Yet most of the studies are dissatisfying because of their narrowness. Nothing is more difficult than trying to understand the popular sentiments of a former age, and investigating the sentiments which supported the existence of a hereditary aristocracy seems particularly involved. It leads at once into a bewildering interfusion of political, social, and legal theory, philosophy, and theology, all of which must be related to the actual events of the day. The following study is an attempt at a synthesis of some of these materials. It is based on two premises: first, that tracing an abstract concept like *gentillesse* or kingship presents a falsely oversimplified picture unless the prejudices and contradictions of an individual author are kept in mind; second, that it is only by juxtaposing the ideas of the individual thinkers in all their overlapping and ambiguity that the distinctive characteristics of either the individual or the period become evident. Wyclif, Langland, Gower, and the *Pearl* poet have been chosen for their intrinsic importance as well as because they represent fairly distinct points of view.

Support of the concept of a powerful warrior aristocracy by a writer in the fourteenth century implied his acceptance of a social system outdated by the whole drift of social and political life, not to mention events at Crécy and Poitiers.[1] In the place of this heroic feudal concept, medieval political theorists since John of Salisbury (*Policraticus,* 1159) had advanced the Roman concept of the commonwealth composed of a populace governed by a judicial (rather than military) king.[2] Men in the fourteenth century were about as consistent in their views of the functions of kings, knights, and common people as we are in our views of government, management, and labor. Yet out of the welter of contradictions, Wyclif seems to emerge as a clear supporter of the secular feudal aristocracy, even though this is completely at variance with his ecclesiastical doctrine. Langland, although he continued to be emotionally committed to the notion of hereditary aristocracy, could find no real function for its members in society. Gower espoused the cause of law, justice, and the common good. And while these were all wrestling with the problems of church and state and the lords and commons, the *Pearl* poet, removed from the city and unconcerned with its social developments, continued to maintain a mystical conception of hierarchy that was at the same time equality.

One of the central tenets of both Roman law and Christian theology had been the natural equality of all men, the former basing it upon reason and the latter upon the soul. Yet both Roman law and the Church had accepted slavery as a temporal reality, explaining it as the result of fortune or of original sin.[3] The "double-think" that made possible this contradiction between theory and practice is evident in the indifference St. Augustine expressed in *De Civitate Dei* to the actual mode of social organization: "For, as far as this life of mortals is concerned, which is spent and ended in a few days, what does it matter under whose government a dying man lives, if they who govern do not force him to impiety and iniquity?" [4] St. Augustine's view that since all government was the result of the fall, the question of what kind was merely a choice among evils, became a medieval commonplace.[5] The dichotomy between the spiritual ideal of equality and the temporal acceptance of inequality thus established made it possible for the Church to adapt itself to the Teutonic feudal system as it had to the Roman imperial, simply by asserting "Render unto Caesar the things which are Caesar's; and unto the God the things that are God's." [6] At the height of the struggle over investiture, Pope Innocent III told Philip Augustus and Richard I that he had no intention of judging feudal matters.[7]

Wyclif followed in this tradition. According to God's original plan, he argued, goods were intended to be possessed in common. In such a dispensation all of the natural possessors would have been lords: "omnis homo foret dominus dati usibilis." But man's fall altered the situation and made necessary civil dominion, individual possession, and the constraint of law.[8] The first argument led Wyclif to advocate the expropriation of Church properties and the abolishment of the ecclesiastical hierarchy, and the second made him a staunch advocate of the secular aristocracy. It is true that he asserted that only the virtuous are entitled to civil dominion, but his principal use for this qualification was to argue that the king was entitled to dispossess sinful clerics of their worldly possessions.[9] Like Chaucer and Gower, Wyclif insisted that nobility is due to virtue rather than birth.[10] But he made it abundantly clear that in this sinful world even bad masters are to be obeyed.[11]

For, to Wyclif, the aristocracy—good or bad—was the true governing body of the state, to whom "it bi-longþ here up-on erþe . . . , as vicars of the godhede, to do ponyschynge and rewarding to þe enemeyes and seruandis of god." [12] In accordance with feudal theory, Wyclif identified ownership with sovereignty.[13] The secular lords "moten haue . . . worldly signes";[14] they "schulden reule bi drede and powere, and so þei schulden be costli in fode and clothynge." [15] Clerical acquisition of wealth is to be feared because it may weaken the aristocracy "for þei [i.e., clerks] han grete lordschipis amorteised to hem, bi whiche lordschipis knyȝhtis schulden be susteyned to gouerne þe peple." [16] And when Wyclif appeals to his audience, particularly in the polemical English tracts, it is to the "secular lordis," to the "kyng and lordis," or to "knyghtes and comynes," [17] rather than to the king and commons.

One cannot help feeling that Wyclif's emphasis on the power of the lords had political overtones. Supported as he was in the 1370's by Gaunt and his faction, and confronted by the spectacle of the doting king, the dying prince, and the child Richard, Wyclif may well have felt that the security of the nation rested in the hands of a powerful aristocracy. But the drift of history was against him. The day of aristocratic rule in England was drawing to a close and that of a centralized monarchy was dawning.

Not, of course, that the authority of the king did not have abundant support in medieval tradition. Early Christian doctrine had been formed under the shadow of the declining Empire and its semi-divine emperor. St. Augustine's earthly city was conceived in terms of a monarchy, and his picture of the Christian prince was the original for many that followed.[18] The Holy Roman Empire claimed as its first support the doctrine of *De Civitate Dei.*[19] In *De Regno,* St. Thomas Aquinas had preferred the rule of a king to that of an aristocracy, and had described the king alone as God's vicar.[20] To the extent that he followed the antipapalist, imperial line,

Wyclif also tended to magnify the importance of the king,[21] but with him this appears to have been less a matter of principle than of tactics, that is of opposing the authority of the king to that of the pope. For example, the title of *De Officio Regis* suggests that that treatise is to be devoted to a definition of the duties of kingship. Yet in its opening lines Wyclif identified the function of the king with that of the knighthood: "Oportet ergo inprimis capere quod potestas *regum et militum* sit ex fide scripture." [22] Throughout the treatise, it is evident again and again that the king is regarded merely as a symbol of secular aristocracy.

We may summarize Wyclif's views on aristocracy in three points. First, his support of the powers and prerogatives of the secular aristocracy, side by side with his preaching of the ideals of the brotherhood of man and common possession of property, represents the traditional inconsistency of the Church's attitude toward lordship. Second, his view of the aristocracy represents the medieval concept of social status to which wealth and authority are subjoined as contrasted with the concept of status determined by wealth and authority. And, finally, his identification of the ruling functions of king and baronage perpetuated the feudal concept of the king merely as a sort of chairman of the board of directors, and of the knights as the actual rulers of the realm. All three of these are in contrast to views expressed in *Piers Plowman*.

Langland [23] showed little inclination either to justify the wealth of the knighthood or to find any political function for its members in society. The difference between the application of "Reddite quae sunt Caesaris Caesari" at the opening of *Piers Plowman* and *De Officio Regis*[24] points up the contrast between Wyclif's and Langland's treatments of the aristocracy. Wyclif used it in a traditional manner, to support the political argument that the clergy must render obedience to secular

lords in temporal matters, whereas Langland used it to introduce an economic discussion of the proper distribution of
wealth. Unlike Wyclif, who identified the aristocracy with
political power, Langland appears to identify it with wealth.[25]
The economics of knighthood is expressed at B.XI.285: "For
made neuere kynge no kny3te but he hadde catel to spende,/
As bifel for a kni3te, or fonde hym for his strengthe." Here we
seem to have status depending on riches, rather than vice
versa as in Wyclif. And unlike Wyclif, who confined his
praise of poverty and condemnation of riches largely to the
clergy, Langland followed the tradition of the sermons and
penitentials, praising poverty and warning against riches both
ecclesiastical and secular. "Of rychesse vpon richesse arisen
al vices" [26] is his warning to both bishops and earls. He compares the rich man to the foul peacock and the poor man to
a lark[27] and observes that "Kinghod and kni3thod . . . /
Helpith nou3t to heuene . . . / Ne richesse ne rentis, ne
realte of lordis." [28] References of this sort could be multiplied,
but in spite of his conventional warnings about the danger of
wealth and his reiterated praise of poverty, Langland makes
it clear that he subscribes to the principle of hereditary aristocracy. Actually, he supports the notion of heredity more
specifically than does Wyclif—or than do Chaucer and Gower.
We never find in *Piers Plowman* the "generositas virtus" cliché.
"Qualis pater, talis filius; bona arbor bonum fructum facit," [29]
Langland quotes to explain Mede's untrustworthiness. And
in the familiar passage condemning soapers and their sons who
buy knighthood and ecclesiastical office while "poure gentil
blod" is refused,[30] he expresses his sympathy for hereditary
gentility.

However, this is largely an emotional commitment. Although knights are allowed their traditional military role,
"trewely to take [i.e., arrest] and treweliche to fy3te," [31]

Langland found little use for them in civil life. His references suggest a system of government in which they play no part: for example, love is a "leder of the lordes folke of heuene,/ And a mene, as the maire is, bitwene the kyng and the comune," [32] and "Meires and maceres that menes ben bitwene/ The kynge and the comune, to kepe the lawes." [33] and "maires and men that kepen lawes." [34] When "comune" means the general populace, [35] we have no evidence of the author's view of the place of the knights, but the B version of the well-known lines "Thanne come there a kyng, knyȝthod hym ladde,/ Miȝt of the comunes made hym to regne" [36] and the ensuing passage, we find the same contrast between king, knighthood, and commons that is made between the "kyng, lordis, & comounte" (elsewhere *commouns*) in Wyclifite references, [37] and political power appears to be assigned to the common people. Some doubt is cast even upon the knights' effectiveness as protectors. Piers instructs the knights to protect "holikirke" against "wastoures" and wicked men and to hunt beasts and birds that destroy the crops. [38] In view of the game laws, hunting seems to me sheer rationalization. As to wicked men, when wasters later threaten to despoil Piers and he appeals to the knight to "kepe hym, as couenaunte was," all that the knight can do is to remonstrate weakly, and Piers must call upon Hunger for his real support. [39] The close association between the king and the knighthood in *Piers Plowman* is distinguished from that in Wyclif's works in that to Wyclif the king is still merely a member of the aristocracy, whereas all Langland's references show the king as all-important, and the knights, whom he can make and unmake, as simply part of the "comune." [40]

Society in *Piers Plowman* is thus conceived in Roman terms as a king and a populace regulated not by an aristocracy but rather by elected mayors and "men that kepen lawes"—

actually at one point referred to as "senatours." [41] The relation of the king to the law in the poem is ambiguous, for although as head of the state he can say "I am hed of lawe," he goes on "what I take of ȝow two, I take it atte techynge/ Of *spiritus iusticie,* for I iugge ȝow alle." [42] Furthermore,

> *Spiritus iusticie* spareth nouȝte to spille
> Hem that ben gulty, and forto correcte
> The kynge, ȝif he falle in gylte or in trespasse.[43]

Spiritus iusticie remains a fairly metaphysical concept in the poem, and is viewed as almost antithetical to law. All of the attention that the law and its functionaries receive is pejorative. The subject of the whole first vision, the marriage of Lady Mede, is legal corruption; and the solution offered is spiritual regeneration, not legal reform. At the end of the episode, the king frowns upon the lawyers and says:

> Thorȝ ȝoure lawe, ich leyue, ich lese menye escheytes.
> Mede and men of ȝoure craft muche treuthe letteth.
> Ac Reson shal rekene with ȝow, yf ich regne eny whyle.[44]

And in the end, Reason and Conscience are to govern the realm and administer the king's justice.

The fact that Wyclif and Langland were really interested in spiritual regeneration of the individual rather than in political solutions to the problems of order and justice probably accounts for the fact that neither made much of the concept through which the centralization of the monarchy and the development of legal machinery in succeeding centuries contributed to social and political levelling. This is the concept of the "common good," which is likewise inherited from Roman thought and blended with the Christian ideal of the natural equality of all men before the fall.[45] At the hands of the Lollards, it might be radical—"a favourite phrase of four-teenth century socialism, both in England and France"[46]—but it was used even more frequently as a synonym for the responsible state, in which each class performed its proper function.[47] The citations in the Oxford English Dictionary and Middle English Dictionary appear to attribute the earliest English use of the collocation to Chaucer, Trevisa, or Usk,[48] but the English thinker at the end of the fourteenth century who was most aware of its implications appears to have been John Gower.[49] The concept was directly related to the prob-lem of aristocratic privilege. As Ewart Lewis has remarked, "The emphasis which medieval writers placed upon the superiority of common good to private good was a response to the real medieval problem of persuading arrogant individual-ism to give way to community consciousness."[50] Gower ex-pected all classes to cooperate for the common good, and when he spoke of the justification for the knightly classes, this ideal is blended with that of the law:

> Primo milicia magno fit honore parata;
> Est tribus ex causis ipsa statuta prius.
> Ecclesie prima debet defendere iura,
> Et *commune bonum* causa secunda fouet;
> Tercia pupilli ius supportabit egeni,
> Et causam vidue consolidabit ope:
> Istis namque modis *lex vult* quod miles in armis
> Sit semper bellum promptus adire suum. . . .
> Non propter famam miles tamen arma gerebat,
> Set *pro iusticia* protulit acta sua.[51]

The emphasis upon law and the common good represents the most significant development in the attitude toward aristoc-racy. For in the end, as Holdsworth has observed, the very idea of the "normal person" is the creation of a common law:

Whether we give this or that class special status, it is, I think, clear that in the Middle Ages there were a number of persons who occupied special positions of their own. We should perhaps be guilty of an anachronism if we called them abnormal persons: for it may be doubted whether early law recognizes such a thing as a normal person. It recognizes rather various ranks and groups and classes, each occupying its own legal position in a loosely organized society. The very idea of a normal person is the creation of a common law which has strengthened the bonds of this society by administering an equal justice to all its members.[52]

The principal difference between medieval and modern social criticism is that the former begins with the conception that different classes have different codes and privileges, whereas the latter begins with the conception that all men have certain obligations in common. Since equality before the law is an outgrowth of the Roman and Christian tenets of the natural equality of all men, Gower's emphasis upon law as the basis for the common good is consonant with his conservative moralism. But just as Wyclif did not intend that his arguments for ecclesiastical socialism should alter the position or prerogatives of the secular aristocracy, and Langland could perceive the uselessness of hereditary aristocrats and still regret their being pushed around by the rising middle class, so Gower argued for law and justice without ever realizing that these very agencies would help destroy the social hierarchy he took so completely for granted. Yet the function of the aristocrats evidently raised questions even in his mind, for he concludes the discussion of knights in *Vox Clamantis*, Book V, by stating that the honor of knighthood is empty because it is without responsibility: "Milicie numerus crescit, decrescit et actus;/ Sic honor est vacuus, dum vacuatur onus." [53]

Gower's most extended discussion of lawyers and justice

comes, significantly, at the beginning of Book VI of the *Vox Clamantis,* which concludes with his first direct discussion of the responsibility of the king. He recognized the principal function of the king as judicial, and in the Christian tradition, he saw the common good as dependent upon the virtue of the king:

> Ergo videre queunt quotquot qui regna gubernant,
> Nostre pars sortis maxima spectat eis.
> Quicquid delirant reges, plectuntur Achiui,
> Nam caput infirmum membra dolere facit:
> Dux si perdat iter, errant de plebe sequentes.[54]

But the king is in turn subject to the law and therefore indirectly to the custodian of the law, the judge. Gower's diatribes against false and venal practitioners must be read against this high ideal.[55] He who pursues the law faithfully, "ad veras et sine fraude. . . . Vt psalmista canit, est vir magis ille beatus." [56] No such favorable view of the profession appears in *Piers Plowman.* Gower places an even greater value on the law itself:

> Pro transgressore fuerant leges situate,
> Quilibet vt merita posset habere sua. . .
> Gens sine lege quid est, aut lex sine iudice quid nam,
> Aut quid si iudex sit sine iusticia? [57]

This is Augustinian in its import. Law is made necessary by sin, but it is indispensable in any human society. The same thought is put in relation to the king at the beginning of the discussion of Justice in the *Confessio Amantis:*

> Propter transgressos leges statuuntur in orbe,
>   Ut viuant iusti Regis honore viri.
> Lex sine iusticia populum sub principis vmbra
>   Deuiat, vt rectum nemo videbit iter.

What is a lond wher men ben none?
What ben the men whiche are al one
Withoute a kinges governance?
What is a king in his ligance,
Wher that ther is no lawe in londe?
What is to take lawe on honde,
Bot if the jugges weren trewe? [58]

Pursuit of this line of reasoning would come near making the judges superior to the king—an organization which might bear some resemblance to the Platonic aristocracy of judges that Wyclif thought would make the best ruling body.[59] However, the responsibility Gower placed upon the king went far beyond anything Wyclif had envisaged. Not only is human sin the cause of law in the first place, but the king's individual sins have social and national, as well as purely individual, significance, and come eventually to be regarded by Gower as the chief reasons for the turmoil in England after 1382.[60] In all this, he was content merely to take the existence of the nobility for granted, never coming to their defense as had Wyclif and, to a lesser extent, Langland.

We have so far discerned three attitudes toward aristocracy, Wyclif's which actively supported a governing aristocracy, Langland's which found the aristocracy politically useless, and Gower's which would subject all society—king, knights, and commons—to the rule of law. We may conclude with a glance at an author whose apparent unconsciousness of social attitudes or doctrines itself offers a contrast to the acute awareness of the three we have been considering. The *Pearl* poet was a writer with predominantly theological interests, who wrote about and for the aristocracy. It is to be expected that we find in him no overt questioning of the social changes that troubled Langland and Gower. Yet beneath his detachment certain attitudes are discernible. It has recently been argued that the depiction of Arthur in *Gawain and the Green Knight* embodies an indirect comment on kingship,[61] and it may be worth noting that the passage detailing Arthur's character in *Gawain* which accuses him of childishness ("sumquat childgered")[62] is somewhat like that in which Gower scolds Richard in the *Vox*.[63] Yet this sort of reflection upon royalty by the *Pearl* poet, if such it really is, does not mean that the author questioned the aristocratic system. Just as Wyclif's support of the feudal aristocracy implied his acceptance of an outdated social system, the *Pearl* poet's choice of garden paradise or castle put his pieces in the context of the agrarian aristocracy. His settings may be contrasted with those in *Piers Plowman*. *Piers* opens in the Malvern Hills for the sake of convention, but it is almost at once transferred to London and returns to the country thereafter only for image or allusion. At the end of the Middle Ages, cities were being reborn, and with them the convention that "hell is a city." The choice of the rural setting of the *Pearl* gives us an even more direct evidence of the author's attitude, however. It must be remembered that he had two traditions to choose from, the Garden of Eden and a garden of love. In the Garden of Eden there were no lords and ladies and we have a nascent primitivism.[64] From this tradition emerge the legends of Adam and Eve and Wyclif's communism. In a garden of love, on the other hand, everyone is a lord or lady. In effect, the shining valley of the *Pearl*, with its courtly maiden and humbly suppliant lover, is a garden of love. And in it, the central exemplum of the master of the vineyard, for all its obvious allegorical intention, presents the notion of arbitrary authority in the familiar context of lord and laborer. Furthermore, *Pearl's* explanation of her state in paradise evidently recognizes grades in the hierarchy of heaven.[65] Yet this hierarchy is mystically resolved into equality and we face again the double standard of St. Augustine and Wyclif. The dreamer's question as to whether Pearl's "astate/ Is worþen to worschyp and wele" [66] reflects the crassness of secular society, as does his misunderstanding of her reply that she has been crowned queen.[67] This is the poet's artistic device for contrasting the dreamer's human obtuseness with Pearl's divine wisdom. The maiden's explanation is a mystical paradox:

> The court of the kyndom of God alyue
> Hatȝ a property in hytself beyng:
> Alle þat may þerinne aryue
> Of alle þe reme is quen oþer kyng.[68]

Here is equality on the highest level; and with it we have come full circle. For this seems very close to Wyclif's theory of natural dominion, that as divinely instituted there was no limit to the possible number of lords ("stat quotlibet ex equo super eodem dominabili dominare").[69] Like Wyclif's theory of a divinely instituted equality among men made impossible by man's sinful nature, Pearl's conception of a heavenly equality unintelligible to the mortal dreamer continues to mirror Augustinian dualism—the conception, that is, of a heavenly state of equality impossible of attainment in mortal society. As much as anything else, this willingness to apply a different standard to the organization of divine and temporal society sets the attitude toward aristocracy of Wyclif and the *Pearl* apart from those of later times, whereas it is an apparent willingness to apply the same standard to both which points the way to the future in the writings of Langland and Gower.

JOHN H. FISHER,
Indiana University

Notes

[1] Carl Stephenson, *Medieval Institutions,* ed. B. D. Lyon (1954) in three interesting essays (pp. 205-284) argues that there is evidence that the Teutonic social system was from earliest times divided into a ruling class of warriors and a laboring class of peasants. J. M. Lappenberg, *A History of England Under the Anglo-Saxon Kings,* trans. B. Thorpe (1854), II:375, 382, and *passim,* presents the more usual German concept of a society essentially equal on the Continent, in which a hereditary aristocracy of landed wealth developed after the tribes settled in England. A. T. Bayles, in E. Prestage, *Chivalry* (1928; pp. 193-94), advances the view that knighthood developed as a defense against the hierarchal pretensions of the priesthood and that the two became parallel lines of temporal advancement with the privilege of knighting and ordaining being jealously guarded by the secular and ecclesiastical bodies.

[2] In the *Policraticus* (ed. C. C. J. Webb [1909] and trans. John Dickinson [1927] and J. B. Pike [1938]) the interest is centered on the prince. John does not believe in absolute hereditary succession; the king may only hope to have his son succeed him if that son is worthy (see Lester K. Born, trans. and ed., *The Education of a Prince by Desiderius Erasmus* [1936], pp. 472 ff.). The profession of arms, so honorable among the Teutonic tribes, was not at all so among the Romans (Stephenson, p. 215 and refs.). St. Thomas Aquinas calls the king *gubernator* and compares his office to that of pilot, tradesman, teacher, etc., rather than to that of warrior (*De Regno* [trans. G. B. Phelan, (1949 ed.)], II. iii, par. 104); and he maintains that the desire for human glory takes away greatness from the soul (I. vii, par. 56). Fustel de Coulanges, *The Ancient City,* trans. Willard Small (Anchor Books, 1956), suggests that the notion of the commonwealth was introduced to replace the ideal of theocracy and religion (IV. ix, 317 ff.).

[3] St. Augustine's four points on slavery in the *De Civitate Dei* (Modern Library trans., 1950) are: (XIX:15) 1. men are by nature free; 2. slavery is the result of sin and war; 3. slaves should be subject to their masters "until all unrighteousness shall pass away"; 4. (XIX:16) masters should show consideration for their slaves. Seneca had laid great stress on the freedom of the soul and had explained bondage as the result of fortune. Cicero had inaugurated the conception of a slave as a person with rights— see R. W. and A. J. Carlyle, *A History of Mediaeval Political Theory* (1927 ed.), I:11, 22, and *passim.*

[4] *Civ. Dei,* V:17. Cf. G. Combes, *La Doctrine Politique de Saint Augustine* (1927), pp. 85-86, for discussion of Augustine's attitude toward civil government. His doctrine of live and let live resulted at least partly from the inferior position of the Church to civil government in his own day: see John N. Figgis, *The Political Aspects of St. Augustine's "City of God"* (1921), p. 75.

[5] For discussion of this "conventional" vs. the Aristotelian "natural" view

153

of government see Carlyle, I:13 ff., 118 ff.; III:5 ff. And for discussion of the concept of the natural equality of man underlying existing political inequality see Carlyle, I:88 ff., 111 ff.; Alan Gewirth, *Marsalius of Padua and Medieval Political Philosophy* (1951), pp. 191, 215 note.

⁶ Matthew XX:21.

⁷ Bede Jarrett, *Social Theories of the Middle Ages* (1926), p. 7.

⁸ *Tractatus de Civili Dominio,* Liber Primus, ed. R. L. Poole (Wyclif Society, 1885), I. xiv, pp. 98 ff.; xviii, pp. 126 ff.

⁹ Contrast the statements to the effect that the wicked can only possess in the lowest manner and that the lordship of the wicked is "usurpative falsum et pretensum" (*Civ. Dominio,* I. iii & iv)—made without any suggestion that wicked lords should be deprived of their holdings—with the insistence that if an ecclesiastical person or corporation habitually abused its property, it must be deprived of it (I. xxxvii). See also, in the English, T. Arnold, *Select English Works of Wyclif,* 3 v. (1869-71), III:88.

¹⁰ *Civ. Dominio,* I. xxxiii. The argument runs: "Omnes Christiani in radice Adam, Seth, et Noe sunt eque nobiles. . . . Ex istis colligitur quod omnis homo, ut virtuosior est, nobilior est; ut vicivior est, ignobilior est, et econtra" (p. 234). Cf. cap. i, p. 6, where righteousness is declared to be the one basis for lordship; Arnold, III:139-40, "gift of god is best titel, ȝe better þen heritage." E. R. Curtius, *European Literature and the Latin Middle Ages* (trans. Trask, 1953), has observed that "every period of enlightenment reaches the conclusion that noble descent is no guarantee of noble thought, that nobility is essentially a matter of possession of wealth, but that there is an intellectual nobility of good men that does not depend upon birth" (pp. 179-80 and refs.). G. M. Vogt has collected medieval references, *JEGP,* XXIV (1925):102-23. A. Brusendorff, *The Chaucer Tradition* (1925), pp. 254-58; J. L. Lowes, *MP,* XIII (1915):19-33; and W. P. Albrecht, *CE,* XII (1951):459, have discussed Chaucer's use of the idea. Gower refers to it several times, perhaps most strikingly in the *Mirour de l'Omme* 23389 ff. (Gower's *Works,* ed. G. C. Macaulay, 4 v. [1899-1901]). Also in *Mirour* 23331; *Vox Clamantis,* VI:1019; *Confessio Amantis,* IV:2205.

¹¹ *Tractatus de Officio Regis,* ed. Pollard and Sayle (Wyclif Society, 1887), pp. 8-9; cf. *The English Works of Wyclif Hitherto Unprinted,* ed. F. D. Matthew, EETS, OS, 74 (1880):226 ff.: God has ordained that servants should obey lords, even though both are the same in "kynd and feith"; Matthew, Introduction, xxxviii; and Arnold, II:295-96.

¹² Matthew, *op. cit.,* p. 362, in a text perhaps not by Wyclif, but "in substance purely Wyclifite."

¹³ See W. A. Dunning, *A History of Political Theories, Ancient and Medieval* (1923 ed.), p. 281. Dunning also discusses Wyclif's similarity to St. Augustine in attributing civil dominion to sin (pp. 261 ff.).

¹⁴ Matthew, *op cit.,* p. 471.

¹⁵ Arnold, III:158.

¹⁶ Matthew, *op. cit.,* pp. 116-17; cf. also p. 280. For a mild expostulation against luxury in secular lords, see Arnold, II:245. Wyclif was not insensible

of the danger of riches to the soul, but his admonition is generally directed toward the clergy. The first sermon in Arnold's collection is on the text of Luke XVI:19: "There was a riche man . . . ." Wyclif and his followers regularly referred to the Lollard preachers as "poor men" (Arnold, II:455 etc.). In his discussion of covetousness Wyclif blames the gentry particularly for conniving with the covetousness of the clergy. Merchants, lawyers, chapmen, and victuallers sin more in covetousness than "pore laborers" (Arnold, III:152-55).

[17] Matthew, p. 276 (secular lords); Matthew, p. 280 (kings and lords); Arnold, III:429 (knighthood and commons).

[18] *Civ. Dei*, V:24. For the influence of this portrait, see W. Berges, *Die Fürstenspiegel des hohen und späten Mittelalters*, Schriften des Reichsinst. für ält. deutsche Geschichtskunde, II (Leipzig, 1938). St. Augustine (*Civ. Dei*, XIX:17) finds a natural hierarchy with the soul, the father, and the king respectively superior. A complete society consists of a king, a court, ministers, and people; the king is not to be chosen from the oldest, richest, or bravest of the citizens, but rather he is the best (*Enarratio in Psalmam*, IX:8).

[19] Figgis, *op. cit.*, p. 84.

[20] *De Regno*, I. v, par. 36-40; vii, par. 53-57; viii, par. 62.

[21] For example, in *De Ecclesia* (Wyclif Society, 1885), XV:332 ff.

[22] *De Officio Regis*, p. 1.

[23] References to *Piers Plowman* are to the W. W. Skeat ed., 2 v. (1886). There seems to be sufficient unity in the attitude toward aristocracy in the three versions to ascribe them to a single point of view. Hence, although the B text is used generally, A and C are also quoted, and for convenience the author is referred to as Langland.

[24] *PP*, B.I.52. *De Officio Regis*, p. 1.

[25] The relationship between riches and aristocracy is a separate problem. Dunning (pp. 78 ff.) argues that in Greek theory, aristocracy was merely a matter of wealth. If this is true, it is so only relatively, since according to Greek theory the concept of citizen (patrician) was itself tantamount to aristocracy (de Coulanges, IV. i, pp. 224 ff.; Ernest Barker, *Greek Political Theory*, [1951 ed.] p. 31 note 4). G. F. Jones, "In early Germanic society, all freemen had the same rights. Nobility was due to ownership of allodial property," *MLQ*, XVI (1955):6 and refs. Stephenson held the opposite views: "The dooms do not justify the idea that [Anglo-Saxon] status ever depended on wealth" (p. 244 and refs.).

[26] *PP*, C.XIII.230.

[27] *PP*, B.XII.240.

[28] *PP*, A.XI.222.

[29] *PP*, B.II.27.

[30] *PP*, C.VI.78.

[31] *PP*, C.II.96.

[32] *PP*, B.I.157.

[33] *PP*, B.III.76.

[34] *PP*, B.III.94.

[35] E. T. Donaldson, *Piers Plowman: The C-Text* (1949), pp. 88 ff., explores the meaning of *comune*, which he finds to mean either the whole community or "the great body of common people socially considered" (p. 96), but never the Commons as a parliamentary unit (p. 105). With respect to his discussion of the plural form, *comunes*, it is worth observing that the Middle English Dictionary (Part C.4 [1960], p. 445) records the plural as meaning only the common people or the third estate.

[36] *PP*, B.Prol.112.

[37] Matthew, *op. cit.*, pp. 278 ff.

[38] *PP*, B.VI.28.

[39] *PP*, B.VI.161.

[40] This view differs from Donaldson's carefully argued conclusion. However, there is some contradiction between Donaldson's initial view that the term knighthood "is generally used in all texts in its military, chivalric sense, without political connotation" (p. 92), and the view he reaches concerning the change of *the comunes* to *the* (or *tho*) *men* in C, "C permits a chivalric knighthood to share with Kind Wit and Conscience . . . in drawing the blueprint for the kingdom" (p. 109). My own view would be that the political importance accorded knighthood in this and a few other passages (cf., B.Prol.116, B.III.313) is a reflection of the sentimental regard we have observed in "poure gentil blod." Langland felt that the knighthood *should* play some role in the community, but other than soldiering he did not see what.

[41] *PP*, C.IX.87.

[42] *PP*, B.XIX.466-76.

[43] *PP*, B.XIX.298.

[44] *PP*, C.V.168.

[45] Background on this concept may be found scattered throughout Ewart Lewis, *Medieval Political Ideas*, 2 v. (1954); see index. Langland uses it twice, both times rather casually, in the cat-belling exemplum, *PP*, B.Prol. 148, 169. I have not noted the term in Wyclif's writings.

[46] Hope Emily Allen, *Writings Ascribed to Richard Rolle* (1927), p. 176, note 1. Froissart's account of John Ball's combination of this idea with those of *generositas virtus* and natural dominion is the most familiar example of the radical application: see quotation and discussion in G. G. Coulton, *Medieval Panorama* (1938), p. 80.

[47] See M. E. Temple, "The Fifteenth Century Idea of the Responsible State," *Romanic Review*, IV (1915):402 ff.

[48] H. R. Patch, *JEGP*, XXIX (1930):382 ff., discusses Chaucer's use of the term. The OED and MED citations do not take account of the wide circulation of the term in England in French and Latin treatises.

[49] Gower's use of the term is frequent throughout his works. Cf. *Mirour*, 23178, 24345, 25501; *Vox*, V:6, VI:*549; *Confessio*, Prol.377, VII:1993.

[50] Lewis, *op. cit.*, I:214.

[51] *Vox Clamantis*, V:3. One of the central themes of the discussion of the knight in the *Mirour de l'Omme* 23750 ff. is his relation to *la loy civile* and *le commun droit*.

[52] William Holdsworth, *A History of English Law,* 9 v. (1953 ed.), III:457.

[53] *Vox Clamantis,* V:555.

[54] *Vox Clamantis,* VI:495.

[55] For the typicalness of Langland's and Gower's accusations, cf. John A. Yunck, "Lawyers and the Medieval Satirists," *American Bar Association Journal,* XLVI (1960):267-70.

[56] *Vox Clamantis,* VI:11.

[57] *Vox Clamantis,* VI:469, 481.

[58] *Confessio Amantis,* VII:2696.

[59] *De officio Regis,* XXVII:192, asserts that an "aristocratia" of judges forms the best government, even better than a king. Dunning (p. 262) sees Wyclif's aristocracy as a blending of Plato's guardians, Aristotle's aristocracy of virtue, and the judges of the Israelites.

[60] On the moral basis for Gower's conception of social order see Maria Wickert, *Studien zu John Gower* (1953):151 ff. For Gower on kingship, G. R. Coffman, *PMLA,* LXIX (1954):953-64.

[61] Hans Schnyder, "Aspects of Kingship in 'Sir Gawain and the Green Knight,'" *English Studies,* XL (1959):289-94.

[62] *GGK,* ll.86-89. *Gawain* references to J. R. R. Tolkien and E. V. Gordon, eds. (1925); *Pearl* to E. V. Gordon, ed. (1953).

[63] *Vox Clamantis,* VI:555.

[64] Seneca's Golden Age is the source of Boethius's primitivism and of Chaucer's "Former Age." Cf. George Boas, *Essays on Primitivism* (1948); Carlyle, I:114 ff.

[65] See discussion of this disputed point in Gordon's Introduction, xxiv.

[66] *Pearl,* l.393.

[67] *Pearl,* ll.481 ff.

[68] *Pearl,* l.445.

[69] *De Civ. Dominio,* I. xviii, p. 126. In *De Ecclesia* (XV:349) Wyclif accepts the notion of a hierarchy in heaven, but argues that it is no model for earth since clerks, "ciciores et criminosiores quam layci," have overthrown it.

Remarques sur le Prologue du Couronnement de Louis (v. 1-11)

Le *Couronnement de Louis* débute par un prologue ou, plus modestement, un préambule qu'on peut limiter aux onze premiers vers. Cette façon de commencer une chanson de geste n'a rien d'exceptionnel. Dans un article récent sur l'ensemble de la question, M. Manfreid Gsteiger[1] a remarqué justement que "la plupart des chansons de geste ont des préambules" et que celles qui commencent *ex abrupto* "sont extrêmement rares" (*Chanson de Roland, Guibert d'Andrenas,* les *Narbonnais,* le *Pèlerinage de Charlemagne*). Ces préambules sont en général très courts, et l'on peut dire que celui du *Couronnement,* avec ses onze vers—suivis d'ailleurs d'une quinzaine d'autres (v. 12-26) sur la grandeur du royaume de France et la haute mission de son roi—est l'un des plus importants, bien qu'il soit de moindre longueur que les préambules de *Girart de Roussillon* et des *Saisnes* de Jean Bodel. Il mérite à mon avis qu'on s'y arrête un peu.

Bien entendu, le trouvère s'adresse à son auditoire, qui est de "seigneurs" et de "barons," il nomme le héros de sa chanson, et il fait l'éloge de cette chanson en ajoutant des mots désobligeants à l'intention du "vilain jongleur" dans deux vers (4-5) qui vont me procurer l'essentiel de mon commentaire.

En effet les épithètes laudatives employées par le trouvère à son propre usage (*estoire vaillant,*[2] v. 2, *bone chançon, corteise et avenant,* v. 3, *chançon bien faite et avenante,* v. 11) n'appellent guère de remarques. Seul dans cette série l'adjectif *corteise* me paraît digne de quelque attention.[3] On peut se demander s'il ne convient pas de lui donner une signification littéraire et s'il n'a pas pour synonyme "bien faite" au vers 11 (on trouve symétriquement "chançon *corteise et avenant*" au vers 3 et "chançon *bien faite* et avenante" au vers 11). Rien du reste n'interdit d'attribuer à *chanson corteise* le sens de "chanson faite pour des barons et des seigneurs" ou, plus vaguement, celui de "chanson qui n'a rien de vilain, de grossier."

Les vers 4-5 nous retiendront plus longtemps, car leur interprétation ne va pas sans difficultés. En premier lieu ils posent un problème de critique textuelle qu'il importerait de tirer au clair. Precisons qu'à cet égard les éditions successives d'Ernest Langlois, celle de 1888 (*Société des Anciens Textes Français*) et celle de 1920 (*Classiques Français du Moyen Age*), ne nous apportent pas un secours suffisant. Chaque fois Langlois adopte un texte différent, qui chaque fois ne se trouve exactement dans aucun manuscrit. Dans les deux cas il n'indique les variantes que partiellement et s'abstient de nous dire comment il comprend un passage dont le sens n'est pas évident.

> Vilains juglere ne sai por quei se vant
> Nul mot n'en die tresque l'en li comant.
> (Ed. de 1888)

> Vilains joglere ne sai por quei se vant
> Nul mot en die tresque on li comant.
> (Ed. de 1920)

Voici comment se présente en réalité la tradition manuscrite pour les deux vers en cause:

A1 (B.N., fr. 774)   Vilains juglerres ne sai por quoi se vant
                       Nul mot a dire trusque l'an li comant.

A2 (B.N., fr. 1449)   Vilains juglerres ne sai por quoi s'en vant
                       Nul mot a dire trusque l'an li comant.

A3 (B.N., fr. 368)	Défaillant. Ne contient qu'un fragment du *Couronnement*.
A4 (Milan, Bibl. Triv., 1025)	Uns vain juglierres ne sai por quoi se vant Un mot a dire jus que l'en li comant.
B1 (Musée Britannique, Royal 20 D XI)	Les trois premières laisses sont supprimées et remplacées par une laisse qui rattache le *Couronnement* à la fin des *Narbonnais*.
B2 (B.N., fr. 24369/70)	Vilain jougleres ne sai por quoi se vant Nul mot n'en die dusque l'en li comant.
C (Boulogne-sur-Mer, Bibl. Municipale, 192)	Vilains jougleres ne sai por coi s'en vant Nul mot ne die des que on li comant.
D (B.N., fr. 1448)	Vilain jugleres ne cuit que ja s'en vent Un mot en die se ge ne li comment.

Si l'on considère la syntaxe, les manuscrits semblent se répartir en deux groupes:

a) *B2* et *C* doivent mettre une pause (point ou point-virgule) après *vant*, à la fin du vers 4, chaque vers représentant une phrase à lui seul:

B2   Vilain jougleres ne sai por quoi se vant;
     Nul mot n'en die dusque l'en li comant.

C   Vilains jougleres ne sai por coi s'en vant;
     Nul mot ne die des que on li comant.

Le sens se dégage ainsi avec assez de clarté: "Je ne connais pas de raisons pour qu'un jongleur vulgaire puisse se vanter à propos de cette chanson; qu'il n'en dise pas un mot jusqu'à ce que (*des que* dans *C* est un équivalent de *dus-que*), avant qu'on le lui commande." Ce qui est une manière de dire: "Que le jongleur vulgaire ne dise jamais un mot de cette chanson (car il n'en est pas digne)." E. R. Curtius a soutenu cette interprétation en donnant sa préférence au texte de la première édition de Langlois (1888), mais en le ponctuant à la fin du vers 4, car tel quel il n'offre apparemment aucun sens: "Aber was bedeutet Vers 5? Man musz nach *vant* ein Komma oder ein Semikolon setzen. Der gemeine Spielmann hat keine Ursache sich zu rühmen; er soll von diesen Dingen schweigen, "bis man es ihm befiehlt." (*Romanische Forschungen*, 62 [1950]:302). Mais Curtius laisse en suspens le problème de critique textuelle que nous signalions plus haut, car il ne tient aucun compte du groupe représenté par A1, A2, A4 et D.

b) Dans ce second groupe les vers 4 et 5 forment un tout, une unité syntaxique. Le premier hémistiche du vers 5, dans ses formes variées (*Nul mot a dire, Un mot a dire, Un mot en die*), ne peut dépendre que de *se vant* à la fin du vers précédent. Certes la construction *se vanter a,* peut-être dialectale, n'est pas courante, mais son authenticité est bien attestée à l'intérieur de la famille A et on ne peut faire autrement, me semble-t-il, que de la regarder comme parallèle et équivalente à *se vanter de.*[4] Par contre la construction de D (*se vanter* suivi du subjonctif sans que la conjonction *que* soit exprimée) n'a rien d'anormal, qu'elle soit primitive ou qu'elle constitue une amélioration de la leçon de A, de même sens assurément.

Autre remarque: alors que dans l'autre groupe (*B2, C*) le vers 5 est négatif (*Que le jongleur vulgaire ne dise pas un mot*), il est positif dans ce groupe-ci. En effet *nul* (A1, A2) sans *ne* n'a pas une valeur négative (les exemples contraires sont très rares) et son emploi s'explique tout simplement par la nuance de doute ou d'indétermination que comporte la phrase, dont le sens n'est en rien modifié par la substitution de *un* à *nul* dans *A*4 et *D*.

Dans ces conditions, le texte de *A*1, *A*2, *A*4 *et D* peut s'interpréter ainsi: "Je ne vois pas pour quelles raisons un jongleur vulgaire pourrait se vanter, se faire fort de dire un mot de cette chanson avant qu'on le lui commande" ("si je ne le lui commande," d'après la leçon de *D*, d'un ton plus impérieux).

Selon toute apparence, à mes yeux du moins, la leçon originale est représentée par le groupe *A*1, *A*2, *A*4 et *D*. La leçon de *B*2 et de *C* semble bien la correction d'un texte jugé obscur ou trop dur. Au surplus l'expression "ne sai por quoi se (s'en) vant" (remplacée en *D* par "ne cuit que ja s'en vent") gardée par *B*2 et *C* est un tour assez savant, plus ou moins calqué sur le latin et d'un style écrit plutôt qu'oral, semble-t-il.

On aura constaté que malgré la divergence de leurs leçons les deux groupes de manuscrits nous proposent à peu près la même interprétation. L'idée générale ne change pas. Il faut comprendre: "A un jongleur de basse catégorie, à un jongleur de carrefour on ne demandera jamais de réciter pareille chanson, car elle dépasse son entendement."

Lieu commun, affirmation banale, boniment de jongleur, sans plus? Peut-être. Pourtant le contexte semble autoriser à donner une interprétation plus positive de ces deux vers et à y déceler un accent personnel de dignité et de fierté. "On sent derrière ce préambule, comme le disait E. R. Curtius (*loc. cit.*), quelqu'un qui peut commander ou fait partie dans la maison où il se trouve d'une équipe habituée à donner des ordres." ("Man spürt hinter diesen Eingang jemanden, der befehlen kann oder in einer Schicht zu Hause ist, die ans Befehlen gewöhnt ist.")

A l'incapacité du jongleur "vilain" l'auteur du *Couronne-*

ment oppose la prérogative de son talent et de sa liberté d'inspiration (v. 4-6). Cette interprétation me paraît confirmée par l'emploi du mot "essemple" au vers 10:

> Seignor baron, plaireit vos d'un *essemple*
> D'une chançon bien faite et avenante?

Mot significatif, révélateur, dont l'importance n'a pas échappé à M. Manfreid Gsteiger: "Il arrive enfin, écrit-il,[5] que le préambule parle de la valeur intérieure du poème: celui-ci contient un 'sens' et il a la fonction d'un 'exemple': *A ceste estoire dire me plest entendre, Ou l'en puet molt sens et essenple prendre* . . . (*Aimeri de Narbonne,* v. 1-2; *Couronnement de Louis,* v. 10-11). Dans de telles allusions se manifeste vraisemblablement l'influence des arts poétiques médiévaux, lesquels recommandent l'emploi d'un exemple ou d'une sentence."

Influence possible, vraisemblable, je le pense aussi. Mais peut-être convient-il de préciser la valeur du mot *essemple* plus que ne l'a fait M. Gsteiger.

On doit, me semble-t-il, l'interpréter à peu près au sens du latin médiéval *exemplum:* anecdote, événement, récit d'où se dégage un enseignement religieux et moral. Si *essemple, esemple* ne signifie souvent en ancien français que "nouvelle, récit," le sens que nous lui attribuons ici se rencontre ailleurs, notamment au vers 3979 de la *Chanson de Roland,* où Charlemagne parle ainsi de l'instruction religieuse qu'a reçue sa captive Bramimonde:

> En ma maisun ad une caitive franche.
> Tant ad oït e sermuns e essamples
> Creire voelt Deu, chrestientet demandet.

J. Bédier traduit *essamples* par "paraboles." [6] Plus exactement sans doute, au *Glossaire* de l'édition,[7] L. Foulet définit le mot: "récit qui met en scène des personnages empruntés à l'histoire ou à la vie contemporaine en vue de tirer des faits un enseignement moral." C'est avec la même valeur à mon avis que le mot est employé au vers 10 du *Couronnement*.

Dans l'*Altfranzösisches Wörterbuch* de Tobler-Lommatzsch, *essemple* est défini "Erzählung, Kunde, Bericht"—ce qui est insuffisant. Outre les vers 10-11 du *Couronnement* le Tobler-Lommatzsch cite le vers 1561 de la même chanson: *A cest essemple que je t'oi ci conter* (interprété: "nach diesen deinen Worten zu schliessen").[8] Je crois qu'à cet endroit encore il convient d'attribuer à *essemple* un sens plus riche et plus précis. Guillaume, s'adressant au portier qui, faute de le reconnaître, n'a pas voulu lui ouvrir les portes de Tours, doit faire allusion aux vers 1541-43 où ce partisan de la royauté légitime vient de regretter l'absence du lignage d'Aymeri, en le prenant comme un modèle pour tous les vaillants chevaliers, en lui donnant une valeur exemplaire:

> "Ou sont alé li vaillant chevalier
> Et li lignages Aimeri le guerrier,
> Qui si soleient lor dreit seignor aidier?"

Ainsi Guillaume peut lui répliquer aux vers 1557-62:

> "Amis, bels frere," dist Guillelmes li ber,
> "Estoltement m'as ton ostel veé;
> Mais se saveies de quel terre sui nez
> Et de quel gent et de quel parenté,
> A cest essemple que je t'oi ci conter,
> Molt l'overreies volentiers et de gré."

Le *Couronnement de Louis* est un "essemple" parce qu'il doit servir à illustrer une doctrine politique et qu'il constitue un "miroir" (E. R. Curtius), une "somme" de la royauté. Le préambule de cette chanson de geste contient plus qu'une affirmation banale et traditionnelle, un "boniment de jongleur."

L'auteur y manifeste sa personnalité avec un peu d'éclat. A l'annonce du sujet il joint une petite profession de foi littéraire, morale et politique.

Je verrais volontiers en lui "un écrivain de métier." [9] Je pense notamment que la composition du *Couronnement*, si épisodique soit-elle, n'en correspond pas moins à un dessein lucide, réfléchi et qu'on peut aller plus loin encore que ne l'a fait Bédier dans la défense de son unité, comme j'espère le montrer au tome II de mon étude sur le cycle de Guillaume d'Orange. J'ajoute que cette vue ne me paraît pas incompatible avec la technique "orale" de l'épopée [10] (on peut *écrire* une oeuvre destinée à la récitation) et que je n'en tire aucune conséquence de portée générale sur l'origine des chansons de geste.

JEAN FRAPPIER,
Sorbonne

Notes

[1] "Note sur les préambules des chansons de geste", dans *Cahiers de Civilisation Médiévale, Xe-XIIe siècles*, II, n°2 (avril-juin 1959), p. 213-20.

[2] Sujet de haute valeur, l'*éstoire* étant la "matière" d'où est tirée la chanson.

[3] Il est très rare en effet qu'on qualifie de "courtoise" une chanson de geste. Peut-être même s'agit-il d'un cas unique.

[4] La construction *se vanter a* s'explique et apparaît régulière, compte tenu des observations que voici. Dans son édition de *Buevon de Conmarchis* d'Adenet le Roi (*Les oeuvres d'Adenet le Roi*, t. II, Bruges, 1953), A. Henry remarque à propos du vers 929 (*Qui li promet a rendre sa terre et son pays*): "*a* introduisant un infinitif objet est fréquent chez Adenet, comme, en général, chez les écrivains du Nord." Sans doute vaut-il mieux ne pas déceler une influence dialectale dans le texte de la vulgate (mss. de la famille A), mais certains auteurs ont pu avoir des préférences. De son côté E. Gamillscheg (*Historische französische Syntax*, p. 467) signale que les verbes renvoyant à l'avenir (*jurer, asseürer, chercher, promettre*, etc.) peuvent introduire l'infinitif qui depend d'eux avec la préposition *à*. Il cite en exemple les vers 3709/10 du *Roland: O est Rollanz li catanie, Qui jurat mei cume sa per a prendre?* Autre remarque intéressante de Gamillscheg (*ibid.*, p. 468): *à* s'emploie même avec les verbes qui régissent l'infinitif pur quand le verbe principal et l'infinitif sont séparés par un membre de phrase; dans ce cas *à* a pour fonction d'isoler réciproquement le verbe et l'infinitif.

[5] *Loc. cit.*, p. 220.

[6] *La Chanson de Roland*, publiée d'après le manuscrit d'Oxford et traduite par Joseph Bédier (Paris: Piazza, 47e éd., 1924), p. 300-301.

[7] *La Chanson de Roland commentée par Joseph Bédier* (Paris: Piazza, 1927), p. 385.

[8] Telle est d'ailleurs l'interprétation d'E. Langlois dans une note de son édition des *Classiques français du Moyen Age*, p. 156: "A en juger par ce que je viens de t'entendre dire."

[9] Voir Maurice Delbouille, *Les chansons de geste et le livre* dans *La technique littéraire des chansons de geste* (Colloque international tenu à l'Université de Liège du 4 au 6 septembre 1957; Bibliothèque de la Faculté de Philosophie et Lettres de l'Université de Liége, fascicule CL, 1959), p. 295-407.

[10] Voir Jean Rychner, *La chanson de geste, Essai sur l'art épique des jongleurs* (Société de publications romanes et françaises, LIII; Genève, Droz, et Lille, Giard, 1955).

The Enfances of Tristan and English Tradition

The two major branches of the Tristan legend represented by the romances of Eilhart and Thomas preserve versions of the hero's *enfances* that differ widely in length and in substance. In Eilhart's brief account,[1] Tristan was born to the sister of King Mark of Cornwall after her death in childbirth on the voyage to her husband's home in Loenois. The child was cut from her body, and his father Rivalen named him Tristan to commemorate the sorrow that attended his birth. At the appropriate time Rivalen entrusted him to the care of Gorvenal, who instructed him in harping, running, leaping, wrestling, casting the stone, and wielding the lance and the sword. After Tristan had acquired these and other accomplishments, he obtained permission from his father to seek honor outside Loenis among those who were not Rivalen's vassals. Rivalen gladly provided a good ship, laden with costly stuffs and fine gold and silver; and Tristan, accompanied by his master Gorvenal, eight squires, and two noblemen, set sail for Cornwall. When they arrived, he asked his companions to conceal his identity as the son of the king's sister. King Mark received him cordially and accepted his offer of service.

In contrast, Thomas[2] recounts a long sequence of colorful adventures that befell Tristan during this period of his life. Thomas relates that both parents died almost simultaneously, the father first and the grief-stricken mother soon afterwards as her child was born. Tristan was thus left a helpless orphan in Brittany, his father's land, at the mercy of threatening

169

enemies. As in Eilhart's version, the child was named Tristan to suggest the French word *triste*. Roald the seneschal fostered the infant as his own child, protecting him against the enemies who would have destroyed him, educating him in all courtly accomplishments, and treating him so tenderly that his foster brothers became envious. One day, when merchants arrived in a ship from Norway, Tristan, at the request of his foster brothers, purchased falcons for them because only he knew how to converse with the visitors in their own language. Then he began a chess game with one of the Norwegians, and Roald left him on board with his tutor. But the merchants, noting his absorption in the game, decided to abduct and sell him. Tristan's tutor, set adrift by the pirates in a small boat, eventually reached home and reported Tristan's fate to Roald. Meanwhile, a mighty tempest arose that would not abate until the merchants realized that their abduction of Tristan had brought them misfortune. As soon as they vowed to release him, the storm ceased, and they set Tristan ashore in a strange land. Two pilgrims on their way to Tintagel invited him to accompany them. Encountering some hunters who had just captured their quarry, Tristan instructed them in the hunting customs of his own country, which all acknowledged to be superior to their own. The grateful huntsmen asked him to present the head of the stag to the king in accordance with the new usage. King Mark welcomed him after he heard the story. Later that evening, when Tristan displayed his remarkable skill in harping, King Mark was so enthralled by these rare accomplishments that he made the stranger a personal attendant. After many hardships, Roald made his way to Tintagel and revealed Tristan's history and lineage to Mark, who was overjoyed to find the beloved youth his own nephew. Tristan was knighted by his uncle, and accompanied by the faithful Roald returned to recover his patrimony from the duke who had seized it. He slew the usurper, routed the disloyal barons, and granted the realm to Roald and his sons as a token of gratitude before returning to serve King Mark.

The two versions have little in common: only the tragic birth, Tristan's skill in harping, his sea voyage to Cornwall, and his temporary concealment of his identity at King Mark's court. The most important difference arises from the double bereavement of Tristan at his birth, in Thomas's version. In Eilhart's, Rivalen is alive during Tristan's childhood and youth so that the hero does not suffer the perils of an orphaned heir beset by enemies, as in the other narrative. Eventually in Eilhart's story, after the death of Rivalen many years later, Tristan returns home to recover his patrimony.

It is easy to dispose of the story of Tristan's *enfances* as an unimportant variant of the "exile and return" formula,[3] but the literary problem is by no means so simple. Mrs. Bromwich[4] has noted that the outlines of the composite story resemble the *macgnimartha* pattern characteristic of the early exploits of such Celtic heroes as Cuchulainn, Finn, and Peredur. The hero is born posthumously and reared by his parents' friends in seclusion to protect him from enemies; later he makes his way to the home of his maternal uncle, where he attracts attention by amazing skill connected with hunting, receives arms, and ultimately returns to take vengeance upon his father's foes.

This pattern, however, is partially obscured in Thomas's version by the elaboration of incident, and almost obliterated in Eilhart's by the fact that the hero's father remains alive. Both versions in their present form have evidently been reworked by French-speaking Bretons and adapted to twelfth-century tastes. The location in Brittany and the Breton names Rivalen and Roald are significant.[5] Significant, too, for the influence of the French language, are the mother's name Blancheflor and the association of the hero's name with the French word *triste*.[6]

Although the *macgnimartha* framework is discernible in Thomas's version, it does not account for the expanded sequence of Tristan's adventures. Why were they introduced and where did they originate? A clue is offered by one of the notable features of Thomas's romance—its glorification of England. Mark is said to be king of all England, not merely of Cornwall; at the beginning of the romance, England is lavishly praised for its noble chivalry, mighty castles, and abundant riches;[7] and a passage near the end celebrates the superlative merits of London:

> Lundres est mult riche cité,
> Meliur n'ad en cristienté,
> Plus vailliante ne melz preisiee,
> Melz guarnie de gent aisiee.
> Mult aiment largesce e honur,
> Cunteinent sei par grant baldur.
> Le recovrer est d'Engleterre:
> Avant d'iloc ne l'estuet querre.[8]

These features, usually ascribed to Thomas's invention,[9] suggest a possible source for the incidents that embellish the *enfances*. An examination of other "exile and return" stories reveals that the Tristan legend has its closest affinities with a group popular in eastern England during the early twelfth century, when they could have been adapted to the Celtic *macgnimartha* pattern.

Long ago Deutschbein[10] pointed out the similarity between the childhood experiences of Tristan and Havelok the Dane. According to the two earliest extant versions of the Havelok story, the passage in Gaimar's *Estoire des Engleis* (ca. 1140-

1150)[11] and the French *Lai d'Haveloc* (ca. 1190-1220),[12] the child Havelok was protected from his enemies by a faithful baron named Grim, who brought him up as one of his own sons. After the king's death, Grim fled by ship with the queen, Havelok, and his own family; outlaws set upon them at sea, and killed the queen and all others except Grim, his wife and children, and Havelok. Landing at Grimsby in Lincolnshire, Grim established himself as a fisherman, but he and his wife devoted themselves to the care of Havelok, who early displayed exceptional physical strength and skill. Later he took service at a foreign court, and after many adventures with no resemblance to Tristan's, he recovered his kingdom.

Despite obvious differences, there is a marked parallel in the fostering of the two heroes. Both Roald and Grim are high-ranking, trusted associates of the royal father; both conceal the child's identity to protect him from enemies; both bring him up as one of their own children, though displaying a preference for him over their own. Both are also reduced to penury as a result of their devotion: Grim, after the capture of his treasure by the pirates, makes a precarious living as a fisherman; Roald is so impoverished by his prolonged travels overseas to Denmark, Norway, the Orkneys, and elsewhere in the search for Tristan that he arrives finally in Cornwall in tattered garments. Although the service of the hero in a foreign court, the revelation of his identity, and the recovery of his kingdom are commonplaces of the "exile and return" formula, the parallel between the foster fathers of Tristan and Havelok is too specific to be fortuitous, and together with the more general resemblances points to a relationship between the *enfances* of the two heroes.

Studies of the Havelok story have established that it is based upon Anglo-Scandinavian traditions current in the eleventh century.[13] Gaimar, living in Lincolnshire and writing at the behest of his patroness there, inserted into his history a form of the Havelok legend circulating in Lincolnshire and localized at Grimsby.[14] Whether or not the legend actually originated in the east of England,[15] it was surely a region in which Anglo-Danish tradition flourished. Just as Gaimar came upon his version in Lincolnshire, so a similar floating tradition may have reached a *conteur* travelling in England, who grafted it upon the Breton story of Tristan's childhood. The superfluous presence of Tristan's tutor in the abduction by the Norwegian merchants suggests such a development. In Eilhart it is Gorvenal alone who educates Tristan and accompanies him on the sea voyage to Cornwall; in the new story, although the foster father supersedes the tutor as the most important figure in the hero's youth, the temporary presence of the tutor on board the ship that eventually brings Tristan to Cornwall seems to be a vestige of the earlier tradition.

The merchants from Norway, the inclusion of Norway, Denmark, and the Orkneys in Roald's search, his encounter in Denmark with a pilgrim who informs him of Tristan's whereabouts, all support the view that this part of Tristan's *enfances* is indebted to Anglo-Scandinavian tradition. Further evidence that Anglo-Danish legend current in the east of England contributed to Tristan's early adventures appears in a curious story preserved in Matthew Paris's chronicle (1195-1204).[16] This story, a prelude to the martyrdom of St. Edmund (A.D.870), relates how Lothbroc, a member of Danish royalty, set out alone with his hawk in a small boat to hunt waterfowl. A sudden storm drove him out to sea, and after several nights of peril, he was cast upon the shores of Norfolk in East Anglia, near Reedham in the neighborhood of Yarmouth. The folk of the region found him alone with his hawk and took him to Edmund, king of East Anglia, as an example of miraculous survival. The king received him well, listened sympathetically to his story of the shipwreck, and granted his request to remain at court. Lothbroc attached himself to the king's huntsman Bern to have an opportunity to practice the art of hunting, in which he was expert. His superior skill in hunting and fowling delighted the king and the court, but it aroused the jealousy of Bern so that he murdered Lothbroc. The victim's faithful greyhound revealed the crime, and Bern was set adrift in Lothbroc's little boat. He landed in Denmark, told Lothbroc's sons that Edmund had murdered their father, and so instigated them to the revenge that culminated in the martyrdom of the king.

The outline of this tale parallels certain of Tristan's experiences. Hawks or falcons in both stories played an important part in the embarkation of the hero upon a tempest-tossed voyage: Lothbroc, with his hawk, sailed out alone in a small boat that was driven to the shores of England; Tristan boarded the merchants' vessel to purchase falcons and was driven by storms to Cornwall. Both Tristan and Lothbroc were received with kindness by the king when they were cast ashore, and both distinguished themselves by displaying superior skill in hunting. There is also a parallel in the experiences of Bern and Tristan's tutor: both were set adrift in a small boat and both landed in the castaway's home, where they reported his fate to his relatives or friends. The resemblance, to be sure, implies no close relationship, but it does suggest the sketch of the tale that was more fully elaborated in the Tristan legend. None of the other accounts of Ragnar Lothbroc, Scandinavian or English, contains this romantic story. It seems to be an independent tale attached to the Viking hero by Danish inhabitants of England,[17] from whom the monkish chroniclers obtained it. The localization in Norfolk, near Yarmouth, implies that the story was current in eastern England, in the same region where the Havelok legend also circulated. Norfolk, indeed, is said by Gaimar to be the kingdom of Havelok's bride.[18] All these facts suggest that Anglo-Scandinavian tradition contributed to the account of Tristan's fostering by Roald and his display of exceptional skill as a huntsman in a foreign court which he reached as a castaway.

These traditions, however, were combined with still another legend of a shipwrecked hero, the celebrated romance of Apollonius of Tyre, known in western Europe as early as the sixth century and continuously popular, as the large number of surviving Latin texts, vernacular adaptations, translations, and allusions testify.[19] Apollonius, fleeing the wrath of a king whose guilty secret he had discovered, set out in a ship. A fierce tempest wrecked it and destroyed all aboard except Apollonius, who was cast ashore at Cyrene. An old fisherman befriended him and advised him to seek his fortune in the city. He joined a throng going to the gymnasium to attend a competition called by the king, and Apollonius distinguished himself by his skill in ball-playing. His performance attracted the friendly interest of the king, who invited him to the palace. To cheer him after he had recited his woes, the king's daughter played the lyre. Only Apollonius remained silent when everyone else praised her performance, and in reply to the king's question, he took the lyre and performed so superlatively that all recognized his mastery of the musical arts. The king's daughter persuaded her father to permit the stranger to instruct her in music.

Like Tristan, Apollonius is cast ashore in a strange land after a tempest at sea; he utters a similar lament;[20] on the way to the royal court he displays such amazing skill in a sport that the interest of the king is aroused; later that evening in the palace he takes the lyre from the king's daughter and demonstrates his superiority in music as well. At a later point in Thomas's narrative, a king's daughter, Isolt of Ireland, like-wise persuades her father to allow Tristan, a newly arrived stranger, to instruct her in playing the harp.[21]

These precise and detailed correspondences are clear indi-cations of influence from the Apollonius story. It is not sur-prising that Apollonius's triumph in ball-playing should have been transformed into an activity more typical of medieval life. In *Jourdains de Blaivies,* for example, which borrowed a sequence of incidents from *Apollonius,*[22] the hero engages in a fencing contest with the king and thus displays his superi-ority. Since Tristan's skill as a hunter was traditional,[23] this feature would be a natural substitution for the ball-playing in the gymnasium, especially if the Apollonius story was attached to the Tristan legend after it had absorbed the Anglo-Scandi-navian tradition of the solitary castaway who wins favor in a foreign court by his unexcelled powers as a hunter and fowler. Although we cannot determine exactly when and where the Apollonius material entered the version that reached Thomas, signs point to the same period and the same region that con-tributed the other elements in the *enfances* of Tristan.

A translation of *Apollonius* into Old English prose in the eleventh century, before the Norman Conquest, shows that this story was familiar in England at the time when the Havelok legend was in the process of formation.[24] A Danish ballad of the thirteenth century[25] implies Danish acquaintance with the story at an early period. This version, emphasizing the shipwreck and the hero's playing of the lyre, also reveals affinities with the Old French *Jourdains de Blaivies.*[26] In the early twelfth century, therefore, when the *conteurs* were active, the narrative of the shipwreck of Apollonius, his en-counter with a kindly fisherman, his playing before the king, and his instruction of the princess in music could have been gathered from the people of English, Danish, or French stock who lived in eastern England, where the Havelok legend also circulated.

Resemblances between the stories of Havelok and Apollonius could have suggested their combination. Both heroes underwent an adventurous voyage: Apollonius was sheltered, fed, and clothed by a fisherman after the shipwreck; and Grim, Havelok's foster father, after the sea disaster, became a humble fisherman to provide for his family. Both heroes were also sent by their benefactors to the royal court, where their accomplishments were recognized. It would have been natural for a *conteur* to weave the two stories together and to use the results to fill the gaps in the Breton tradition of Tristan's early years. The simple voyage that conveyed Tristan from his homeland to Cornwall became the highly dramatic sequence of the abduction, the tempest, and the casting ashore; Tristan's traditional skills in hunting and playing the harp were imaginatively displayed by the use of the Apollonius legend, modified by Anglo-Scandinavian traditions. There is no evidence that any redactor of the Tristan legend derived this material from a Latin manuscript of *Apollonius;* on the contrary, the adaptation is most closely related to those freely handled vernacular versions, like *Jourdains de Blaivies* and the Danish ballad,[27] that are based on oral tradition.

There are other indications that the interweaving of the Havelok, Apollonius, and Tristan legends was the work of a Breton *conteur*. One is the Breton name of Tristan's foster father Roald. Another is the treatment of the tempest in Thomas's version, which strikingly resembles Breton beliefs about storms at sea and their connection with human guilt. The Norwegian merchants attribute their predicament to their sin in abducting Tristan, and upon their oath to release him, the storm subsides. Nothing like this occurs in the stories of Havelok, Apollonius, or Jourdain de Blaivies. The incident reflects, rather, an old belief, especially strong in Celtic lands[28] though not confined to them, that a tempest is caused by the presence of guilty human beings on board a ship, and that only atonement for the guilt will appease the fury of the sea and permit the ship to reach a haven.[29] An early Breton instance occurs in Marie de France's *Eliduc*,[30] when a mariner denounces Eliduc's entanglement with two wives as the cause of the tempest and demands that the second lady be thrown overboard. Later examples from Brittany illustrating the supposed connection of human sin with storms at sea were collected by Sébillot.[31] None of these examples, to be sure, reproduces exactly the situation found in the Tristan story. Usually the person thought to be responsible for the disaster is supposed to be thrown overboard, as in *Eliduc*; but since the merchants themselves were guilty in the abduction of Tristan, they atoned for their sin by releasing their victim as soon as the ship touched land. It may be worth noting that in *Eliduc*, too, the motif is handled with similar freedom: Eliduc throws the mariner overboard instead of his beloved lady, and although the storm does not abate, the ship is steered safely to land.

It seems likely that it was a Breton *conteur* who combined the various traditions in the tempest episode. If his source contained only a bare outline somewhat like Eilhart's, he could have developed it by drawing upon Anglo-Scandinavian tales attached by others to Havelok and Ragnar Lothbroc, and upon the legend of Apollonius. All of this story material was current in eastern England in the early twelfth century and easily accessible to a Breton who sought his livelihood there.

Another element in Thomas's version that points to English influence is the detailed description of the hunting ritual that Tristan teaches to Mark's huntsmen. The exhibition of Tristan's skill, as Remigereau has shown,[32] consists of four little scenes, each illustrating a particular technical term: *défaire, fourchie, droits, curée.* This excursus into cynegetics confirms the English provenance of this part of the story. Since hunting as a sport and French hunting techniques were introduced into England by the Normans,[33] the subject would still have the interest of novelty to an English audience at the time when the amplified version of Tristan's *enfances* was composed.

To sum up: if the Celtic *macgnimartha* tradition was attached to Tristan in the earliest insular versions of the story,[34] it underwent considerable modification when the legend was reshaped in Brittany. The original Breton story of the *enfances* probably included only the tragic birth of the hero, his training by foster father or tutor in playing the harp and in physical skills, his voyage from his homeland to Cornwall, his reception by King Mark, the revelation of their family relationship, and the regaining of his patrimony. This is substantially Eilhart's version although the traditional pattern is hardly recognizable because of the postponement of the father's death and the recovery of the hero's inheritance until almost the end of the romance. Thomas's account is clearer because the death of both parents leaves the infant Tristan in the same precarious plight as his Celtic forebears. A Breton *conteur* familiar with Lincolnshire and Norfolk seems to have enriched the story with Anglo-Scandinavian traditions of Havelok's fostering by the faithful Grim. The introduction of this material emphasized the foster father rather than the tutor and provided stronger motivation for the concealment of Tristan's identity than we find in Eilhart's version. The impoverishment of the devoted Roald, corresponding to Grim's fate, is brilliantly employed in the recognition scene that leads to the disclosure of Tristan's relationship to King Mark. The sea voyage, uneventful in Eilhart, is transformed

into the vivid adventure of the abduction and its conse-
quences. The Apollonius legend contributed not only the
tempest but also the exhibition before King Mark of Tristan's
accomplishments in sport and music after his arrival as an
unknown castaway. The traditional skill of Tristan as a
hunter ws assimilated to an Anglo-Scandinavian story current
in Norfolk about an unknown castaway who won favor in an
alien court by his expert hunting and fowling, feats that
replaced the ball-playing of Apollonius. Possibly, too, the attack of the pirates upon the ship in which Grim fled with the
young Havelok furnished some suggestions for the abduction
of Tristan by the Norwegian pirates. But the tempest, an
important element in the stories of Apollonius and Lothbroc,
was modified by the Breton superstition that human guilt was
the cause of tempests at sea. This modification accounts plaus-
ibly for Tristan's arrival as a castaway.

The adaptation of these diverse stories to the basic plot
of the *enfances* reveals a literary intelligence of a high order.
Whoever blended these elements had an instinct for the dramatic that governed his selection of narrative material. Instead
of merely listing Tristan's accomplishments, he presented them
in a series of vividly dramatic scenes—the purchase of the
falcons, the chess game, the mastery of the art of hunting, the
musical performance before a foreign court. By use of the
Breton superstition about the storm, he was able to motivate
an action that in the analogous stories of Apollonius and Lothbroc is pure chance.

It is most unlikely that Thomas himself composed this
sequence of incidents, if only because his interest lies so
plainly in the refinements of psychological analysis rather
than in plot construction.[35] Nothing that we know of Thomas
indicates any connection with the region in Lincolnshire and
Norfolk that provided the narrative substance of the *enfances*.

All the signs, moreover, point to a period earlier than Thomas's for the incorporation of Anglo-Scandinavian traditions in the legend. When Thomas wrote, towards the end of the twelfth century, interest had shifted from plot to characterization, with the emphasis upon sentiment and psychological realism. Thomas's romance represents an effort to idealize and rationalize the old legend to satisfy the sophisticated tastes of the Angevin court without drastic changes or additions to his source.[36]

The English contribution to the *enfances* raises an interesting question about the eulogy of England and its inhabitants in Thomas's romance. Were these passages, or suggestions for them, already in his source? The complimentary references to England and London, as well as the description of the hunting ritual and the extension of Mark's kingdom to the whole land, could have been introduced to please an Anglo-Norman audience by the same *conteur* who developed the story of the *enfances* from traditions current in the east of England. The question, of course, remains unanswered in the present state of our knowledge, but it is best to be cautious in drawing conclusions about Thomas himself from the eulogistic passages about England in his text.

The elaborated version of the *enfances* in Thomas's version may not, as Bédier observed,[37] perceptibly advance the main action, but it is not mere padding. The unknown artist, by developing the latent suggestions in the original outline, brings the story to life in a swiftly paced, varied, and dramatic narrative that is its own justification.

HELAINE NEWSTEAD,
Hunter College

Notes

[1] Eilhart von Oberge, [*Tristrant*], ed. F. Lichtenstein (Strassburg, 1877), vss. 75-350.

[2] Thomas, *Le Roman de Tristan*, ed. J. Bédier (Paris, 1902), I:22-71; *Die nordische und die englische Version der Tristan-Sage*, ed. E. Kölbing (Heilbronn, 1878), I, chap. xiv-xxv.

[3] For some references see Bédier, II:197; M. Deutschbein, *Studien zur Sagengeschichte Englands* (Cöthen, 1906), pp. 120-31, 171; L. A. Hibbard, *Medieval Romance in England* (New York, 1924), p. 111.

[4] R. Bromwich, *Trans. Hon. Society of Cymmrodorion* 1953, p. 45.

[5] Bédier, II:122; R. S. Loomis, *MLN*, XXXIX (1924):326 ff.; H. Newstead, in *Arthurian Literature in the Middle Ages*, ed. R. S. Loomis (Oxford, 1959), p. 126; H. Zimmer, *ZFSL*, XIII(1891):5. Eilhart's Loenois as the home of Tristan's father probably represents a Breton tradition. The historic original of Tristan was a Pictish king who ruled in Scotland north of the Firth of Forth. When the insular legend migrated to Brittany, the Breton name Rivalen was substituted for the Welsh Tallwch (from Pictish Talorc) as the name of Tristan's father, and his kingdom identified with Lothian (Loenois), a region of other legendary associations but not the kingdom of the original Pictish dynasty.

[6] Bédier, II:125. Thomas makes the association with *triste* explicit. The name Tristan is ultimately derived from the Pictish name Drust: Zimmer, *ZFSL*, XIII:65-72; Bédier, II:105-108; Newstead, *op. cit.*, p. 125.

[7] Bédier, I:4 ff.; Kölbing, I:6.

[8] Bédier, I: vss. 2651-58; B. Wind, *Les Fragments du Tristan de Thomas* (Leiden, 1950), vss. 1379-86.

[9] Wind, pp. 11 ff.; F. Whitehead, in *Arthurian Literature in the Middle Ages*, ed. Loomis, p. 141.

[10] *Studien zur Sagengeschichte Englands*, pp. 121-23.

[11] *Le Lai d'Haveloc and Gaimar's Haveloc Episode*, ed. A. Bell (Manchester, 1925), pp. 6-19, 60-79, 143-75; Geffrei Gaimar, *L'Estorie des Engles*, ed. T. D. Hardy, C. T. Martin (Rolls Series, Vol. 91, 1888), Part I, 11-34, 290 ff. On Havelok, see Hibbard, pp. 103-113; A. Bugge, *Viking Society for Northern Research, Saga Book*, VI(1910):275-95.

[12] Bell, pp. 19-59, 176-220.

[13] Hibbard, *op. cit.*, 108; Bugge, *Saga Book* VI:285 ff.; H. G. Leach, *Angevin Britain and Scandinavia* (Cambridge, Mass., 1921), p. 327; R. M. Wilson, *Early Middle English Literature*, 2nd ed. (London, 1951), 221-24; Bell, pp. 60-70. Bell's opinion (p. 48) that Gaimar in his account of the murder of Edmund Ironside derived his reference to "l'arc Qui ne faut" from the Tristan legend seems to be without foundation, as M. D. Legge, *Medium Aevum*, XXV(1956):79-83, has shown.

[14] Bell, *Medium Aevum*, VII(1938):184-88; *Lai d'Haveloc*, p. 72. Bell, pp. 59 ff., concludes that the author of the *lai* also drew upon local Lincolnshire tradition for the embellishment of Gaimar's account.

[15] Bugge, *Saga Book*, VI:261, 281, argues that its point of origin was Cumberland. Cf. Hibbard, pp. 109 ff.

[16] Matthew Paris, *Chronica Majora*, ed. H. S. Luard (Rolls Series, 1872), I:393-95. On the date see p. xxxii.

[17] Leach, *Angevin Britain*, pp. 317-20; I. P. McKeehan, *University of Colorado Studies*, XV(1925):1:13-74.

[18] Bell, *Lai d'Haveloc*, p. 145, vss. 31 ff.

[19] Elimar Klebs, *Die Erzählung von Apollonius aus Tyrus* (Berlin, 1899); A. B. Smyth, *Shakespeare's Pericles and Apollonius of Tyre* (Philadelphia, 1898); S. Singer, *Apollonius von Tyrus, Untersuchungen über das Fortleben des antiken Romans in spätern Zeiten* (Halle, 1895); Hibbard, pp. 164-73. The correspondences between Tristan and Apollonius have been pointed out by C. Voretzsch, *Epishche Studien*, I (Halle, 1900), pp. 144-46; Bédier, I:94 n.1; Hibbard, p. 166 n.4.

[20] Cf. Bédier, I:39 ff. and *Historia Apollonii Regis Tyri*, ed. A. Riese (Leipzig, 1893), chap. xii.

[21] Bédier, I:94.

[22] *Amis et Amiles und Jourdains de Blaivies*, ed. K. Hofmann (Erlangen, 1892), vss. 1212-3516. The earliest MS. of the text dates from the first half of the thirteenth century (*ibid.*, viii; Hibbard, p. 167), and the *chanson de geste* is commonly dated in the same period (Klebs, p. 413). Jourdain's foster parents flee with him. When Saracen pirates attack them, Jourdain leaps overboard, and clinging to a plank, is cast ashore and befriended by a fisherman. As in Tristan, there is no actual shipwreck, but both heroes are castaways. Singer, pp. 16 ff., points out the influence of the Charlemagne legend upon Jourdain's early history.

[23] G. Schoepperle, *Tristan and Isolt* (Frankfurt, London, 1913), II:289 ff., 396; Bromwich, *op. cit.*, pp. 32, 45.

[24] Klebs, p. 459. The Old English version was edited by J. Zupitza, *Archiv*, XCVII(1896):17-35. Cf. Hibbard, p. 165 n.2.

[25] Singer, p. 31; S. Grundtvig, *Danmarks gamle folkeviser*, II:466; Klebs, p. 379.

[26] Hibbard, p. 168.

[27] Klebs, pp. 379, 413.

[28] Marie de France, *Lais*, ed. A. Ewert (Oxford, 1944), p. 187.

[29] Bédier, I:38 n.1; Marie de France, *Lais*, ed. K. Warnke, 3rd ed. (Halle, 1925), pp. clxx-clxxiv.

[30] Marie de France, *Lais*, ed. Ewert, vss. 830 ff.

[31] P. Sébillot, *Le Folk-Lore de France* (Paris, 1905), II:14 ff. For other instances see *Lais*, ed. Warnke, above, n. 29. Cf. also E. Löseth, *Le Roman en prose de Tristan* (Paris, 1890), p. 4: Sadoc kills his brother for violating his wife Chelinde and flees with her by ship. When a storm bursts, an old man informs the sailors that the tempest is due to the presence on board of someone guilty of a crime. One sailor by sorcery discovers Sadoc's guilt and throws him overboard.

[32] F. Remigereau, *Romania*, LVIII(1932):218-37.

[33] E. A. Freeman, *History of the Norman Conquest* (*Oxford*, 1871),

IV:608-15; V:163 ff., 455-60; J. C. Fox, *The Royal Forests of England* (London, 1905), pp. 4 ff., 25, 52 f. On the hunting practices, see *La Chace dou Cerf* (thirteenth century), in *Nouveau Recueil de Contes, etc.*, ed. A. Jubinal (Paris, 1839), I:154-72, especially pp. 166-69; *The Art of Hunting*, ed. Alice Dryden (Northampton, 1908), pp. 16 ff.; *The Master of Game*, ed. W. A. and F. Baillie-Grohman (London, 1909), pp. 174 ff.; H. L. Savage, *JEGP*, XLVII(1948):48 ff.

[34] Cf. R. Bromwich, *op. cit.*, pp. 32-60; H. Newstead, *op. cit.*, pp. 122-29.

[35] F. Whitehead, *op. cit.*, 141-43; P. Le Gentil, *R Ph*, VII(1953-1954):118-29.

[36] Whitehead; Le Gentil; Wind, pp. 10-16; P. Jonin, *Les Personnages féminins dans les romans français de Tristan au XIIe siècle* (Aix-en-Provence, 1958), pp. 34-55, 249-335, 373-450.

[37] Bédier, II:198.

The Antecedents of Sir Orfeo

Sir Orfeo is the best of the Middle English Breton lays and one of the loveliest and most charming of all Middle English romances. No one will question that it is worthy of study, especially if the study seeks to establish in greater detail the relationship between it and its antecedents, and to draw some critical conclusions from that relationship. Such is the task I have set myself in these pages.

In origin *Sir Orfeo* is classical, stemming from Ovid and Virgil, passing through Boethius and Alfred's elaboration of Boethius,[1] mingling with Celtic story and myth to issue transformed as a Breton lay, thence done into French, and thence finally into English. It bears marks of all these influences, blended into the successful unity of the Middle English romance.

The most obvious classical influence is in the title and the names: Sir Orfeo, Heurodis, Traciens. In broad outlines the story is like its ultimate origin in Ovid and Virgil: Orfeo's loss of his wife to the Otherworld, his inconsolable grief at the loss, his visit to the Otherworld to seek her, the description of the Otherworld as a place of the dead, Orfeo's captivation of all those below by his harping, his request that she be returned to him and his winning her back through his music.

Yet the story has been so transformed by the later influences that even in some of the broad outlines *Sir Orfeo* is strikingly unlike its classical antecedents. Instead of dying from a snake-bite on the heel, as in Ovid and Virgil, Heurodis is spirited away by the fairy king. Orfeo's inconsolable grief, briefly stated by Ovid and Virgil, is developed into a willful ten-year self-exile from human society. His visit to the Otherworld does not originate in a grief-induced search for Heurodis, but in his accidentally seeing her in a group of ladies whom he follows. There is no mention of the numerous specific denizens of Hades whom he charms in the classical versions; instead, we are merely told that his playing captivates all in the fairy king's palace. In place of his frank revelation of who he is and what he wants, as in Ovid, Orfeo hides his identity, elicits through his music a regal rash promise that he may have whatever he desires, then when the king demurs at his choice of Heurodis wins her by an appeal to the king's sense of honor. The most striking difference of all is the substitution of a happy ending for the classical unhappy one—a change effected simply by the omission of the violated condition that the hero must not look back or he will lose what he has won. And finally, the whole concluding episode of Orfeo's recovery of his kingdom is not found in the classical originals.

The sources of these changes and of other lesser changes in the tale make a fascinating study, and, in large part, though by no means entirely and not with complete agreement, they have been worked out.[2] One source which has not been sufficiently stressed, I feel, is King Alfred's adaptation of the tale in his very free translation of Boethius's *De Consolatione Philosophiae*. It is in Alfred's expansions of Boethius's telling of the tale that interesting parallels occur. Since in his translation of King Alfred's version W. J. Sedgefield puts into italics the passages which do not occur in the Latin original, I have thought it helpful to cite the account from his translation.[3]

Once on a time it came to pass that a harp-player lived *in the country called* Thracia, *which was in the kingdom of the Crecas (Greeks). The harper was so good, it was quite unheard of. His name was Orfeus, and he had a wife without her equal, named Eurudice. Now men came to say of the harper* that he could play the harp so that the forest swayed, and the rocks quivered for

the sweet sound, *and wild beasts would run up and stand still
as if they were tame, so still that men or hounds might come near
them, and they fled not. The harper's wife died, men say, and her
soul was taken to hell. Then the harpman became so sad that he
could not live in the midst of other men, but was off to the forest,
and sate upon the hills both day and night,* weeping, and playing
on his harp so that the woods trembled and the rivers stood still,
and hart shunned not lion, nor hare hound, *nor did any beast feel
rage or fear towards any other for gladness of the music.* And when
it seemed to the harper that nothing in this world brought joy to him
*he thought he would seek out the gods of hell and essay to win
them over with his harp, and pray them to give him back his wife.
When he came thither, the hound of hell, men say, came towards
him, whose name was Ceruerus and who had three heads; and he
began to welcome him with his tail, and play with him on account
of his harp-playing.* There was likewise there a most *dreadful*
gateward *whose name was Caron; he had also* three heads, *and
was very, very old. Then the harper fell to beseeching him that
he would shield him while he was in that place, and bring him
back again unharmed. And he promised him to do so, being overjoyed at the rare music. Then he went on farther* until he met
the *fell* goddesses *that men of the people call Parcae, saying that
they know no respect for any man,* but punish each according to
his deeds; *and they are said to rule each man's fate. And he began
to implore their kindness;* and they fell to weeping with him.
*Again he went on, and all the dwellers in hell ran to meet him,
and fetched him to their king; and all began to speak with him
and join in his prayer.* And the ever-moving wheel, that Ixion *king
of the Leuitas (Lapithae) was bound to for his guilt,* stood still
for his harping, and King Tantalus, *that was in this world greedy
beyond measure, and whom that same sin of greed followed there,*
had rest, and the vulture, it is said, left off tearing the liver of *King*
Ticcius (Tityus), *whom he had thus been punishing. And all the
dwellers in hell had rest from their tortures whilst he was harping
before the king. Now when he had played a long, long time,* the
king of hell's folk cried out, saying "Let us give the good man

his wife, for he hath won her with his harping." Then he bade him be sure never to look back once he was on his way thence; *if he looked back, he said, he should forfeit his wife.* But love may hardly, nay, cannot be denied! Alas and well-a-day! Orpheus led his wife along with him, until he came to the border of *light and* darkness, and his wife was close behind. *He had but stepped into the light* when he looked back towards his wife, and immediately she was lost to him.

It is interesting to compare the opening of the story in the versions of Ovid, Virgil, Boethius, and Alfred. Ovid's story in the *Metamorphoses* begins with Hymen's coming inauspiciously to Orpheus's wedding, and passes thence immediately to the bride's death from the serpent-bite upon her ankle. In Virgil's *Georgics,* the story opens in nearly the same way with Orpheus's anguish at losing his wife by the snake-bite. Boethius (after the opening *sententiae* which must be disregarded for our purposes) also begins with the grief of the Thracian poet and passes immediately to the skill of his mourning song which charms woods, and rivers, and beasts. Alfred, however, begins by introducing his hero: a harp-player who lived in Thrace, exceedingly skillful, whose name was Orpheus. Then he introduces Orpheus's wife, Eurudice, a peerless woman. Similarly at the beginning of *Sir Orfeo,* Orfeo is introduced, with emphasis upon his exceeding skill as a harper, and we are told that he lived in Thrace. Then Heurodis is introduced, pre-eminent in beauty, love, and goodness. *Sir Orfeo* and Alfred's version begin in identical fashion.

Orpheus's skill in charming wild beasts with his playing is found in all three pre-Alfredian versions (in Ovid, he charms beasts, trees of all kinds, the very shade under trees, and stones; in Virgil, tigers and oak trees; in Boethius, forests, rocks, rivers, and animals); but in Ovid and Virgil there is little concerning the beasts beyond the bare statement; in

Boethius, there is some slight development in that the hart comes unafraid of the lion and the hare of the hound. Alfred, however, repeatedly dwells upon the beasts, expanding at every mention with graphic detail: wild beasts running up and standing as if they were tame, unafraid of men or dogs; and again—no beast feeling anger or fear, but only gladness because of the music; and again—Cerberus coming to welcome the harp-player, with wagging tail. The result is that in Alfred's version the effect of the music on the wild beasts is dominant; and interestingly, this is the one feature of Orfeo's playing that is stressed too; there is no mention of trees, and shade, and stones, and rivers; only

> Þat alle þe wilde bestes þat þer beþ
> For ioie abouten him þai teþ,
> & alle þe foules þat þer were
> Come & sete on ich a brere,
> To here his harping a-fine.   (273-77.)[4]

It is noteworthy, too, that the emotion which the wild beasts feel is "ioie"; only in Alfred's version is the gladness ("mergðe") of the animals mentioned, and in Alfred's version joy is the effect which the playing has upon Charon, too ("he waes oflyst").

A most colorful addition to the bare outline of the classical versions is the ten-year period of self-exile in which Orfeo, overcome with inconsolable grief, forsakes all human association, specifically all womankind, abandons his kingdom and all the comforts of life, and goes to dwell alone in the forest with wild beasts. There is nothing comparable at this point in the classical versions: Orpheus's grief quickly sends him to the Otherworld to try to regain his spouse. To be sure, after he loses her a second time by looking back, he lingers disconsolate on the hither shore of Styx, denied a second passage by

Charon, bewailing his cruel fate—for seven days, foodless and unkempt, says Ovid; for seven months, says Virgil. But this is not the willful abandonment of all society by a man so grief-stricken that he cannot longer dwell with others.[5] Notice, however, the exact parallel in Alfred's expansion:

The harper's wife died, men say, and her soul was taken to hell. Then the harpman became so sad that he could not live in the midst of other men, but was off to the forest and sat upon the hills both day and night.[6]

This modification of the story due to Alfred's influence will turn out to be of the utmost structural importance to the medieval romance, as we shall see later.

Alfred's expansions of Boethius's retelling of the classical tale, then, seem to account for the opening of *Sir Orfeo*, with its introduction of the main characters, for the passage describing the joyful effect of Orfeo's harping upon the wild beasts, and above all for the introduction into the tale of the long period of self-exile. On the force of these parallels, perhaps it is not too much to suggest that the classical version which the original Breton poet knew, and which he blended with Celtic myth to create the original Breton lay, was Alfred's translation of Boethius, or some closely related telling of the tale. No classical detail which could have influenced *Sir Orfeo* is present in Ovid and Virgil and Boethius that is not also present in Alfred's translation of Boethius;[7] and in addition the parallels cited above are uniquely present in Alfred.

Celtic influences account for most of the remaining differences between the classical versions and *Sir Orfeo;* indeed, these influences are so strong that the dominant mood of the whole is Celtic. One Celtic version which made its contribution was that found in Walter Map's *De Nugis Curialium,* Distinctio IV, cap. 8, which runs as follows:

There was once a knight of Lesser Britain who, having lost his wife, and grieved for her a long time after her death, came upon her by night in a large company of women, in a valley situated in a region devoid of inhabitants. He was seized with astonishment and fear: seeing her alive again whom he had buried, he could not believe his eyes, and wondered what the fairies might be up to (*dubius quod a fatis agatur*). He resolved to carry her off by force, in order to have the happiness that her capture would bring him if she were real, or to avoid the imputation of cowardice in holding back (if he were being deceived by an illusion). He accordingly seized and carried her off, and lived happily with her for many years, as agreeably and as naturally as before; and she presented him with sons, of whom there are descendants in great number at the present time, and who were known as "the sons borne by the woman who had died." This departure from the course of nature would be incredible and monstrous, if assured evidences of its truth were not still in existence.[8]

First of all, we may observe that this account, written about 1182, already blends classical and Celtic elements. Classical is the fact that the wife really died of natural causes; for the Celtic Otherworld was the land of the living and characteristically the human visitant was alive.[9] Classical also is the allusion to the husband's long period of mourning. Interestingly, both these features of the classical tale are more likely to have their source in Alfred's version than in Ovid or Virgil; for Alfred merely states that "the harper's wife died, men say, and her soul was taken to hell" ("Ða saedon hi þaet ðaes hearperes wif sceolde acwelan, ond hire saule mon sceolde laedan to helle"), whereas Ovid and Virgil are specific about the cause of death—from snake-bite. Similarly, Map's account briefly states the fact of death without citing the cause. And, as I demonstrated earlier, it is Alfred's version which stresses the long period of the husband's grief beyond anything found in the earlier versions.

Celtic are the uninhabited valley suggesting the Otherworld, the allusion to the fairies, the large company of women
among whom the departed wife was found, and the identification of the husband as "a certain knight of Lesser Britain"
("miles quidam Britannie minoris").

It is not difficult to see how Map's story of the *Filii Mortue,*
already a blend of classical and Celtic, influenced the poet
who was himself blending classical and Celtic sources to produce the Breton *Lai d'Orphey.*[10] Like the classical story—as,
let us say, in Alfred's version—the *Filii Mortue* was a tale
which told of the death of a beloved wife, of the husband's
ensuing long grief, of his finding his lost wife in an Otherworld, and of his winning her back to himself. All these elements common to Alfred and Map, merged and modified, went
into the Breton lay and thence into *Sir Orfeo.* Others, from
Map alone, importantly modified the classical account: the
husband's coming upon his departed wife, not as the result
of an intentional trip to the Outerworld to seek her out, but
by pure chance during his long period of mourning; his
coming upon her in a large group of ladies; his awareness of
fairies at work in all this and the suggestion that it is occurring
in a Celtic Otherworld; his emotions when he determines to
try to win her back—desire for the happiness of having her
again and self-esteem which leads him to scorn the danger in
attempting to recover her;[11] and his complete success and
subsequent happiness through a long life with her.

These contributions from Map's story altered the classical
tale considerably, both in tone and conduct of the plot; but
they were not so important as certain other changes effected
by another Celtic tale—the *Wooing of Etain (Tochmarc
Etaine*).[12] According to this tale (in part), Eochaid Airem,
king of Ireland, marries Etain, who is so beautiful that men
speak of her as out of the fairy mounds. Midir, a fairy prince

(who was Etain's husband in a previous existence) approaches her and asks her to come with him; but she refuses, saying that she will not leave the king unles Midir obtains her from him. Midir challenges the king to a series of chess games for high stakes, and loses them all. Then they play a final game, the stake, at Midir's suggestion, being whatever the winner shall demand. This time the king loses, and Midir demands the right to embrace Etain. The king perforce agrees, but stipulates a month's delay. Against the appointed day he gathers the armies of Ireland and stations them in rings outside his palace, and inside it, too, to prevent Midir from coming; but mysteriously Midir appears in the center of the palace, during the banqueting. He approaches Etain and sings to her of the beauty and delight of his fairy realm, inviting her to come with him. Then turning to the king, he demands what he has won and, when the king is reluctant, reminds him of the sacredness of a promise. The king finally permits Midir to put his arms around Etain, and Midir thereupon carries her off through the smoke-hole in the roof. The king and his armies dig up all the fairy mounds in Ireland, seeking Etain for nine years; and when they are close to finding her, Midir sends out sixty women, all exactly like Etain. Eventually Etain makes herself known, and the king carries her away in triumph to his palace.

A Celtic bard aware of this story, of the classical tale, and of Map's narrative would find such basic similarities that he might naturally blend them together into one. For the *Wooing of Etain*, like the other tales, tells of a mortal who loses his wife to the Otherworld, is without her over a long period, finally enters the Otherworld, finds her there, and wins her back. Certain elements in Map's account, though different from the classical tale, would also blend with their parallels in the Irish legend of Etain: the fairy atmosphere, the Celtic Otherworld, the large company of women among whom the wife was found, the seizing her by force, and the complete success in winning her back, for a happy ending of all. And once the similar elements had brought the tales together in the imagination of the poet, it is easy to see how other features of the *Wooing of Etain,* not present in the other two narratives, would pass into the plot of the Breton lay. One of the most striking of these is the substitution of the abduction of Heurodis for her death as the means by which she is transported to the Otherworld.[13] Midir's song of the beauties of the Otherworld may have suggested Heurodis's dream. Also attributable to the Irish legend are the preliminary visit of the fairy king in the dream, the setting of a date for the abduction, the stationing of armed men to protect the queen, the mysterious ravishing away, nobody knew whither, and possibly the period of about a decade before the reunion. The Irish legend also suggested the means by which Orfeo tricked the fairy king into yielding Heurodis: the rash, blind promise, and the appeal to a sense of honor to fulfill it, though of course in the *Wooing of Etain* it is the mortal who must hold to his promise in an episode leading to the loss of the wife, whereas in *Sir Orfeo* it is the fairy who must hold to his promise in an episode leading to the recovery of the wife. Finally, a new feature which the *Wooing of Etain* suggested is that Orfeo is a king and Heurodis a queen—an important development for its influence upon the structure of the poem, as we shall see later.

No doubt ancillary Celtic influences affected our Breton bard, aside from those to be found in the *Filii Mortue* and the *Wooing of Etain.* The Celtic belief in the marvelous power of minstrelsy, the honor accorded to harpers, the representation of a harper as a king, the winning of a woman through minstrelsy, the tradition of the wild man of the woods, as in accounts of Merlin Silvestris, the fairy army of knights, the fairy hunt, the fairy dance, sleeping under a tree as putting one under fairy power,[14] passage into a rock or hill as entrance to the Otherworld, the specific splendors and beauties of the Otherworld itself, the peculiarly Celtic quality of the fairies and their king—mysterious, reverend, of human size but of more than human power and beauty:[15] all these Celtic features blended with those in the *Filii Mortue* and the *Wooing of Etain* to modify the classical story and transform it into the Breton lay.

It is highly likely that the Breton lay was translated into French with little change. The French influence, as Kittredge observes, was "rather pervasive than striking," [16] possibly perceptible in the titles "Sir" and "Dame," the masculine singular adjectival form "Traciens" for "Thrace" (47, 50), the retention of French "griis" ("grey") at the end of a line, perhaps to preserve a rhyme with "biis" (241-42), the retained Old French phrase "en exile" (493), and the mention of flying buttresses (361-62), more French than English.[17]

It is difficult to determine how much the English author of *Sir Orfeo* contributed to the story. There is no doubt that the pervading high artistry of the poem is his, for that artistry depends upon a simultaneous awareness of all parts of the story, all details of description, all traits of character, and how they all fit together economically and effectively to create the unity of the poem. Ascribable to the English poet are the refreshing ignorance of classical mythology and geography (King Pluto and King Juno, Thrace as the ancient name of Winchester), the representation of Orfeo as an English king, and Orfeo's order for summoning a parliament to appoint a new king after his death—reflecting English polity and suggesting, as Mrs. Loomis has observed, a date shortly after 1327, when an English parliament replaced

Edward II by Edward III. Descriptive details, as of the winter landscape, are also no doubt the English poet's own, as, very likely, are the moral concepts of marital and feudal loyalty.[18] But in all the essentials of the story itself, it is highly likely that the English poet merely followed the French, as the French had followed the Breton.

There is only one important plot element that seems not sufficiently accounted for by the classical versions, the *Filii Mortue,* the *Wooing of Etain,* and the subsidiary Celtic influences. That is the all-important final episode in which Orfeo regains his kingdom. All the antecedent versions end with the episode in which the hero regains his wife. No one has paid much attention to accounting for the unique presence of this final episode in the tale. Who added it to the tale? The Breton poet or the English?

Attention to the genesis of the story, as we have been attempting it above, suggests an answer to the question. The Breton poet, influenced by the Celtic association of harping with kingship and by the fact that the hero of the *Wooing of Etain* was a king, made Orfeo a king; at the same time, influenced by Alfred's version, he sent his hero into a decade-long self-exile from the society of men. The combination of these two elements—a king into self-exile—led to the new motif of the abandonment of the kingdom. This in turn meant that the story could not be complete until Orfeo had regained his kingdom; hence, the necessity for the final episode. And since these influences must have operated first on the Breton bard, who first combined them, he must first have seen the need for completing the story by the regaining of the kingdom. The working out of the episode by the return-and-recognition motif—so well known from the *Odyssey* to King Horn —was a natural development inherent in the story.[19]

Despite the general critical praise accorded *Sir Orfeo,* this concluding episode has drawn its share of critical blame. The charge has been made that it is tacked on, superfluous, anti-climactic; that it violates artistic unity and destroys the structural integrity of the poem. The proper climax should have been the rescue and return home of Heurodis, and the double climax obscures what should have been made prominent. The poem would be much better minus the whole section.[20]

I believe that a more favorable critical view is implicit in the account of the origin of the concluding episode which I have given above. It will become explicit if we examine the structure of the poem, which may best be presented as follows:

Prologue. (Ll. 1-56:56 lines.)
I. Loss of Heurodis. (Ll. 57-194:138 lines.)
II. Loss of the kingdom. (Ll. 195-280:86 lines.)
III. Orfeo's fairy experiences, culminating in recovery of Heurodis. (Ll. 281-476:196 lines.)
IV. Orfeo's human experiences, culminating in recovery of the kingdom. (Ll. 477-605:128 lines.)

It should be clear, first of all, that the two simultaneous modifications of the classical story, namely, kingship (Celtic) and self-exile (Alfredian classical), led to a new loss on Orfeo's part—loss of his kingdom as well as loss of his wife, both losses occasioned by the same catastrophe, one leading naturally to the other. This is important, for it transforms the classical story into something quite different: it is a story now of a double loss. And what is important is that the poem is carefully organized and carefully developed to exploit all the values in both these losses. Each loss is displayed for itself, fully and poignantly, as artistic preparation for the correspondent recovery at the end of the story. Just as the loss of Heurodis naturally led to the loss of the kingdom, so the winning back of Heurodis must be followed by the winning back of the kingdom. Indeed, were the concluding episode lacking, the story would be sadly incomplete and the reader would feel quite unsatisfied. Both motifs are satisfyingly combined in the concluding lines of the story (587-96).

To perceive this unity, it is helpful to examine the poet's account of the loss of the kingdom (II above) and relate it to the other parts of the poem. The king, overcome with inconsolable grief, in a speech to his lords declares his abandonment of his kingdom and all society, appoints the steward, and gives directions for a successor. And all the lords kneel before him weeping, praying him not to go. (Compare in the concluding episode [IV] his climactic speech of about the same length, after which all his lords again kneel before him, this time rejoicing and acclaiming him.) Then he forsakes the kingdom, despite their prayers, and goes into the hardships of the wilderness. There follows one of the most elaborate and most effective of the rhetorical passages in the poem (234-80), in which a whole series of contrasts develops the sufferings which the king, accustomed to luxury, underwent. The effect is pathos—pity for a *king* in the *wilderness*. All this, of course, points by contrast toward the final episode when he comes back to his regal comforts in a happy ending. This whole second section, with all its elaboration, is lacking in the classical account, for no *king* is involved in that account.[21] And if the poem were to be without the concluding episode of the recovery of the kingdom (IV), all this stress upon the deprivations suffered by a king used to luxury and companionship (II) should, of course, have been omitted by the poet. Both sections (II, IV)—the loss and recovery of the kingdom— fit together, each looking forward or back to the other, just as the two sections dealing with the loss and recovery of Heurodis (I, III) fit together. Indeed, even the proportional development in the two pairs of sections is the same: the loss of the kingdom (II:86 lines) is to the recovery of the kingdom (IV:128 lines) as the loss of Heurodis (I:138 lines) is to the recovery of Heurodis (III:196 lines).

The dominating technique of suspense employed by our author also serves to bind all parts of the tale together. The story consists of a series of situations developed by uncertainty and interest as to how the situation will end—in a word, by suspense. (I) What caused Heurodis's horrible dismay at the dream? Will Orfeo be able to keep Heurodis from the fairies? (II) What will befall Orfeo's kingdom? What will befall Orfeo himself in the wilderness? [22] (III) What will befall Orfeo in fairyland? Will Orfeo be able to win Heurodis back? (IV) What will befall Orfeo on his return to human society? Will Orfeo be able to win the kingdom back? The final question, therefore, is merely one in a series; and each question in the series leads naturally and inevitably to the next.

Finally, the two climactic episodes—recovery of Heurodis and recovery of the kingdom—are bound together by an unusual series of parallels which it is interesting to draw critical attention to. (1) Both climactic episodes are laid in a royal court. (2) In both Orfeo comes to court in the guise of a minstrel. (3) In both his appearance in old and ragged clothing plays a part.[23] (4) In both he is seeking something from the ruler, who has power to grant or withhold what he is seeking. (5) In both he has a right to the thing which he seeks. (6) In both he plays his harp for the ruler, and the playing leads to the climactic incident. (7) In both he employs a strategy of misrepresentation, or at least a withholding of the whole truth, and it is through the exercise of his wit that he proceeds. (8) In both the reader knows the true situation, but the ruler does not. (9) In both he succeeds in winning what he is seeking. (10) In the first episode, at the beginning he possesses both wife and kingdom; in the second, at the end he once again possesses them both.

To be sure, the fact that in two episodes the same technique is employed—suspense—or that striking parallels obtain between them, does not establish an artistic unity embracing them both. That must be established on other grounds involving the conduct and effect of all elements in the tale, as I have sought to establish it earlier by demonstrating the relationship among all the story's parts. But the pervasive similarity of technique and parallel development does contribute in a minor way to the over-all effect of unity, and so supports the basic considerations of organic structure which I urged earlier. The tale is a unified whole, and the final episode is an essential and integral part of the whole. And I hope I have done something in these pages, by studying the antecedents of the tale and relating them to the artistic performance of our Middle English poet, to support the structural integrity of his work and enforce the general critical opinion that

Gode is the lay, swete is the note.

Sir Orfeo remains one of the most charming and most successful of all our Middle English romances.

J. BURKE SEVERS,
Lehigh University

Notes

[1] Ovid, *Metamorphoses*, X, XI; Virgil, *Georgics*, IV; Boethius, *De Consolatione Philosophiae*, III, metre 12; King Alfred's translation of Boethius, chap. xxxv, sect. 6.

[2] G. L. Kittredge, "Sir Orfeo," *American Journal of Philology*, VII (1886): 176-202; G. Schoepperle, *Tristan and Isolt* (London, Frankfort, 1913), II:541-44; L. A. Hibbard, *Medieval Romance in England* (New York, 1924), 195-99; R. S. Loomis, "Sir Orfeo and Walter Map's *De Nugis*," *MLN*, LI (1936):28-30; C. Davies, "Notes on the Sources of 'Sir Orfeo,'" *MLR*, XXI (1936): 354-57; G. V. Smithers, "Story-Patterns in Some Breton Lays," *Medium Aevum*, XXII (1953):61-92, esp. 85-88; A. J. Bliss (ed.), *Sir Orfeo* (Oxford, 1954), Introduction; and three important reviews of Bliss, to wit, by M. L. Samuels in *Medium Aevum*, XXIV (1955):56-60; by H. M. Smyser in *Speculum*, XXXI (1956):134-37; and by L. H. Loomis in *JEGP*, LX (1956):290-92. For a sketchy chronological account of the versions of the Orpheus story and the chief allusions to him, see J. Wirl, "Orpheus in der Englischen Literatur" (*Wiener Beiträge zur Englischen Philologie*, XL, 1913).

[3] W. J. Sedgefield, *King Alfred's Version of the Consolations of Boethius, Done into Modern English* (Oxford, 1900), pp. 116-18. The Old English runs as follows:

Hit gelamp gio ðaette an hearpere waes on ðaere ðiode ðe Ðracia hatte, sio waes on Greca rice; se hearpere waes swiðe ungefraeglice good, ðaes nama waes Orfeus; he haefde an swiðe aenlic wif, sio waes haten Eurudice. Ða ongon mon secgan be ðam hearpere, þaet he meahte hearpian þaet se wudu wagode, ond þa stanas hi styredon for ðy swege, ond wildu dior ðaer woldon to irnan ond stondan swilce hi tamu waeren, swa stille, ðeah him men oððe hundas wið eoden, ðaet hi hi na ne onscunedon. Ða saedon hi þaet ðaes hearperes wif sceolde acwelan, ond hire saule mon sceolde laedan to helle. Ða sceolde se hearpere weor ðan swa sarig, þaet he ne meahte ongemong oðrum monnum bion, ac teah to wuda, ond saet on ðaem muntum, aegðer ge daeges ge nihtes, weop ond hearpode, ðaet ða wudas bifedon, ond ða ea stodon, ond nan heort ne onscunede naenne leon, ne nan hara naenne hund, ne nan neat nyste naenne andan ne naenne ege to oðrum, for ðaere mergðe ðaes sones. Ða ðaem hearpere ða ðuhte ðaet hine nanes ðinges ne lyste on ðisse worulde, ða ðohte heðaet he wold gesecan helle godu, ond onginnan him oleccan mid his hearpan, ond biddan þaet hi him *ageafen* eft his wif. Þa he ða ðider com, ða sceolde cuman ðaere helle hund ongean hine, þaes nama waes *Ceruerus*, se sceolde habban þrio heafdu, ond onfaegnian mid his steorte, ond plegian wið hine for his hearpunga. Ða waes ðaer eac swiðe egeslic geatweard, ðaes nama sceolde bion Caron, se haefde eac þrio heafdu, ond waes swiðe oreald. Ða ongon se hearpere hine biddan þaet he hine gemundbyrde ða hwile þe he ðaer waere, ond hine gesundne eft ðonan brohte. Ða gehet he him ðaet, for ðaem he waes oflyst ðaes seldcuðan sones. Ða eode he furður od he gemette ða graman gydena ðe folcisce men hatað Parcas, ða hi secgað ðaet on nanum men nyten nane are, ac aelcum men wrecen be his gewyrhtum; þa hi secgað ðaet *wealden* aelces mannes wyrde. Ða ongon he biddan heora miltse; ða ongunnon hi wepan mid him. Ða eode he furður, ond him urnon ealle hellwaran ongean, ond laeddon hine to hiora cyninge, ond ongunnon ealle sprecan mid him, ond biddan þaes ðe he baed. Ond þaet unstille hweol ðe Ixion waes to gebunden, Leuita cyning, for his scylde, ðaet oðstod for his heapunga; ond Tantulus se cyning, ðe on ðisse worulde ungemetlice gifre waes, ond him ðaer ðaet ilce yfel filgde ðaere gifernesse, he gestilde. Ond se *vultor* sceolde forlaetan ðaet he ne slat ða lifre Tyties ðaes cyninges, ðe hine aer mid ðy witnode; ond eall hellwara witu gestildon, ða hwile þe he beforan ðam cyninge hearpode. Ða he ða longe ond longe hearpode, ða cleopode se hellwara cyning, ond cwaeð: "Wutun agifan ðaem esne his wif, for ðeam he hi haefð geearnad mid his hearpunga." Bebead him ða ðaet he geare wisse, ðaet [he] hine naefre under baec ne besawe, siððan he ðonanweard waere; ond saede, gif he hine under baec besawe, ðaet he sceolde forlaetan ðaet wif. Ac ða lufe mon maeg swiðe nueaðe oððe na forbeodan: wei la wei! hwaet, Orpheus ða laedde his wif mid him, oð ðe he com on þaet gemaere leohtes ond ðiostro; ða eode þaet wif aefter him. Ða he forð on ðaet leoht com, ða beseah he hine under baec wið ðaes wifes: ða losade hio him sona.

(From J. W. Bright, *An Anglo-Saxon Reader* [N. Y., 1917], pp. 5-7, omitting editorial macrons, but retaining editorial italics and square brackets indicating departures from the base MS.)

[4] I follow Bliss's edition in this study.

[5] Nor can I feel that there is any influence upon *Sir Orfeo* of Ovid's account of Orpheus's sustenance while on the shore of the Styx ("Cura dolorque animi lacrimaeque alimenta fuere"—*Metam.* X:75), as Smithers suggests (pp. 85-86). The conceit—tears and sorrow as food—does not occur anywhere in *Sir Orfeo* (241-62), where Orfeo has real sustenance—roots, fruit, and berries—and his poor food is only one element in an elaborate series of contrasts between his former luxurious estate and his present destitute one. The whole passage in *Sir Orfeo* is a natural development from the situation of a *king* in the *wilderness*.

[6] Ða saedon hi þaet ðaes hearperes wif sceolde acwelan, on hire saule mon sceolde laedan to helle. Ða sceolde se hearpere weorðan swa sarig, þaet he ne meahte ongemong oðrum monnum bion, ac teah to wuda, ond saet on ðaem muntum, aegðer ge daeges ge nihtes. (Bright, p. 5.)

[7] There is one, but perhaps it is only a very interesting coincidence. The Otherworld in *Sir Orfeo* is a curious blending of the land of the living (Celtic) and the land of the dead (classic). When Orfeo enters the fairy castle court-yard, he sees

> Of folk þat were þider y-brouȝt,
> & þouȝt dede, & nare nouȝt. (389-90.)

These folk all are in the posture in which they had been when the fairies took them out of this world; and all these postures, as I interpret them, are those in which mortals may be at the moment of their death: without heads, without arms, with wounds through the body, in a madman's bonds, armed on horseback, strangled, drowned, burnt with fire, in childbed, or sleeping (my understanding of this passage follows K. Sisam's pointing [*Fourteenth Century Verse and Prose* (Oxford, 1928), p. 26, l. 402], rather than Bliss's). Orfeo sees Heurodis there sleeping under a grafted tree—just as she had been when taken by the fairy king. Now in Ovid's account, when Orpheus in the Otherworld sees Eurydice coming to him, she comes limping from the snake-bite on her heel. In both the *Metamorphoses* and *Sir Orfeo*, then, the lady has the mark upon her of the manner in which she entered the Otherworld.

⁸ Smithers, p. 87. The Latin runs thus (M. R. James [ed.], *Walter Map De Nugis Curialium* [Oxford, 1914]):

Miles quidam Britannie minoris uxorem suam amissam diuque ploratam a morte sua in magno feminarum cetu de nocte reperit in conualle solitudinis amplissime. Miratur et metuit, et cum rediuiuam uideat quam sepelierat, non credit oculis, dubius quid a fatis agatur. Certo proponit animo rapere, ut de rapta uere gaudeat, si uere uidet, uel a fantasmate fallatur, ne possit a desistendo timiditatis argui. Rapit eam igitur, et gauisus est eius per multos annos coniugio, tam ioconde, tam celebriter, ut prioribus, et ex ipsa suscepit liberos, quorum hodie progenies magna est, et *filii mortue* dicuntur. Incredibilis quidem et prodigialis iniuria nature, si non extarent certa uestgia ueritatis.

The same story is told by Map in a shorter form in Distinctio II, cap. 8, the only new contribution of the shortened form being that the ladies are dancing (a chorea).

⁹ Bliss, p. xxxiii. See also Smithers, p. 87.

¹⁰ R. S. Loomis and C. Davies believe that Map's *Filii Mortue* was one of the sources of the Breton *Lai d'Orphey;* G. V. Smithers and A. J. Bliss believe that the *Filii Mortue* is derived from the Breton lay. (See note 2 above.) Loomis argues that the absence in the *Filii Mortue* of any feature from the *Wooing of Etain,* which deeply influenced *Sir Orfeo,* indicates that Map's story was not derived from the Breton lay. Smithers argues that the large company of women in *Filii Mortue* is derived from the *Wooing of Etain,* and both he and Bliss believe that the fact that Map's lady had really died indicated that his story had *already* been contaminated with the classical legend. As the reader will see above, the evidence convinces me that Map's story was indeed influenced by the classical version and that it in turn influenced the Breton lay. It is difficult to see how some of the more striking features of the Breton lay—the hero as king, the hero as harper, the abduction, the rash promise—were not reflected in the *Filii Mortue* if that account were really derived from the Breton lay. If the *Filii Mortue* were derived from the Breton lay, one could, to be sure, understand how the classical element of the husband's long period of grief passed into the *Filii Mortue* at second hand through the Breton lay; but how could the fact that the wife had actually died (instead of having been abducted) get into the *Filii Mortue?* One would have to believe that death rather than abduction was a feature of the Breton lay, or that the classical story influenced the *Filii*

Mortue after the latter was derived from the lay. It is much simpler and more likely that the *Filii Mortue,* mingling, as it does, both classical and Celtic elements, is intermediate between a classical version and the Breton lay.

[11] Map: "He resolved to carry her off by force, in order to have the happiness that her capture would bring him if she were real, or to avoid the imputation of cowardice in holding back (if he were being deceived by an illusion)." ("Certo proponit animo rapere, ut de rapta uere gaudeat, si uere uidet, uel a fantasmate fallatur, ne possit a desistendo timiditatis argui.") Cf. *Sir Orfeo,* 331-42.

[12] For this tale see E. O'Curry, *On the Manners and Customs of the Ancient Irish* (Dublin, 1873), II:192-97; H. Arbois de Joubainville, *Cours de littéra-ture celtique* (Paris, 1884), II:311-22; A. H. Leahy, *Heroic Romances of Ireland* (London, 1905), I:23-32; T. P. Cross and C. H. Slover, *Ancient Irish Tales* (N. Y., 1936), pp. 82-92. In my summary I follow Cross and Slover, but O'Curry is authority for the song of Midir. See also Kittredge, pp. 191-92.

[13] C. Davis (see note 2 above) suggests that Marie de France was the author of the lost French *Lai d'Orphée,* that Marie is to be identified with Mary, Abbess of Shaftesbury, and that the account of Heurodis's abduction was influenced by the actual historical abduction of Ela, wealthy young heiress of William Fitzpatrick, Earl of Salisbury—an abduction which the Abbess certainly knew of. Aside from the fact that many of the details of Heurodis's abduction are paralleled by the abduction of Etain and not at all by the historical events, it is hard to believe that such a mundane ab-duction as that of Ela could have suggested the magical fairy disappearance of Heurodis.

[14] M. B. Ogle, in "The Orchard Scene in *Tydorel* and *Sir Gowther,*" *Romanic Review,* XIII (1922):37-43, doubts whether this feature is peculiarly Celtic; but see Bliss, pp. xxxv-xxxvii.

[15] Some of the Celtic tales which may have suggested isolated elements similar to these are discussed by Kittredge, pp. 186-97, and by Bliss, pp. xxxv-xxxix. Most interesting of these are *The Adventures of Connla the Fair* (Cross and Slover, pp. 488-90), which could have suggested the fairy mound, the Otherworld as the land of the living, and the situation of a mortal who is taken by fairy power to the Otherworld against the wishes of another mortal (a father here) who loves him; and the story of Herla (Map, *De Nugis Curialium,* Dist. I, cap. 11), which could have suggested the fairy army, the fairy hunt, and passage into a rock as entrance to the Otherworld.

[16] Kittredge, p. 185.

[17] Bliss, pp. xl-xli.

[18] L. H. Loomis, *JEGP,* LV:291.

[19] Smyser, p. 135.

[20] See Smyser, pp. 135-37, and Bliss, p. xliii. Smyser is right, it seems to me, in rejecting the peculiar defense of the final episode that it "gives the whole story its proper balance by making the scenes of enchantment, already psy-chologically central, physically central as well." The concept of psychological centrality is fuzzy and its specific application here to *Sir Orfeo* is debatable; also the critical assumption that the psychological and physical center should

coincide is questionable. My defense of the final episode is on quite other grounds.

[21] To be sure, the charming of the beasts with his harping (267-80) is present in the classical versions; but in *Sir Orfeo* the beasts are made to subserve the dominant mood of the king's sufferings, for when he left off harping the very beasts abandoned him to solitude again.

[22] It is interesting that the author does not suggest to us immediately the question, Will Orfeo find Heurodis? Indeed, there is no hint in Part II that Orfeo is abandoning his kingdom for the purpose of seeking Heurodis. On the contrary, the abandonment of all society and therefore of the kingdom is entirely an unreasoning expression of unbounded grief and overwhelming anguish of spirit. Orfeo does nothing to try to seek Heurodis out. He has no plan. He is not going anywhere. He is finally spurred into action only by the accidental sight of Heurodis among the crowd of ladies: then, and not till then, does he have incentive to win her back. Incidental remarks of some previous commentators suggest that this point has not always been clear to readers.

[23] I cannot feel that Orfeo's assumption of beggar's weeds in the final episode is a flaw, though it is quite true, as Smyser observes, that it may be a vestige of the return-and-recognition motif. (See Smyser, pp. 136-37; Bliss, p. 54.) When he returned Orfeo was still wearing the pilgrim's mantle which he had donned when he left, and, however long his beard, he would naturally have felt more secure from recognition in other clothing.

The Buried Lover Escapes

The second incident in a tripartite Icelandic tale that was written down several times at the end of the fourteenth or the beginning of the fifteenth century and was copied again at the end of the seventeenth century has a very curious history.[1] We can see only a part of this history and must hope for more texts to be discovered in order to see the whole. The tale is in brief as follows:

After hunting all day the sons of a king, duke, and earl spend the night in the woods. In order to pass the time the king's son proposes that each of them should tell the greatest danger he has experienced. The earl's son begins by telling how he once slipped over a cliff at night when he was going to visit his sweetheart. He landed on a ledge from which he was able to throw up a rope made by cutting up his cloak. In this way his servant rescued him. The duke's son tells of visiting his sweetheart, the daughter of a rich man. She was mortally sick and asked him to look at her treasures lying in a chest beside her bed. When he bent down to see the bottom of the chest, someone pushed him in and closed and locked it. The girl sent for her father and made him promise to bury the chest under her coffin. The lover remained silent while all this was going on because he thought disgrace was worse than being buried alive. She died that same night and the chest was buried as she wished. Since it was generally known that a chest lay beneath her coffin, thieves came and broke open its ends. The man within shrieked and having frightened away the thieves, buried coffin and chest again and escaped. The king's son then told his adventure that happened on a visit to his sweetheart. He was passing a gallows where three thieves were hanging. One of them cried out, claiming to be innocent, and asked to be cut down. The king's son approached but started back in fear. When he gathered courage, he returned and cut down the thief. The ungrateful thief, who said that he had been injured, tore the gallows from the earth and pursued the prince. The latter took refuge in a church, but a corpse that he had passed on his way through the church-yard rose and opened the church door for the thief. The prince defended himself as best he could against a double attack but finally fell in front of the altar. By a miracle the demonic dead men retired and he was saved.

As Reinhold Köhler, who helped Gering by adding parallels to the tales, points out in a note (*Æventýri*, II:174), this tale belongs to a cycle of tales in which one or more narrators tell of escaping from several dangers (usually three). As an example of the cycle, he cites a tripartite story in the *Dolopathos* in which a robber warns his three sons by telling of three dangers from which he escaped.[2] Although none of these dangers resembles those in the Icelandic tale, they are in part similar to those in a Scottish Gaelic tale collected in several versions by J. F. Campbell.[3] An incident in this latter tale concerns a man imprisoned in a grave and set free by grave-robbers. It also contains an incident similar to Polyphemus's adventure with the Cyclops, and both this adventure and that of the grave-robbers are found in the third and fourth voyages respectively of Sinbad the Sailor.[4] There is, furthermore, a story of *Andreuccio* of Perugia in the *Decameron,* II:5, with escapes from three dangers, one of them being imprisonment in a grave and the rescue by grave-robbers.[5] Whatever connections may exist among these tales, they do not involve the incident in our Icelandic tale except in the most general way.

Someone who may have been familiar with an oral version of the incident of the grave-robbers and the rescue chose to set it in a very simple frame of the three adventures of the noblemen on their several ways to visit their sweethearts. The first adventure was a simple story of a mishap and a fortunate rescue, the third was an appalling ghost story, and the second is the tale with which we are concerned. When, where, and in what form the Icelandic narrator or the man from whom he learned it found the tale we cannot guess. As Gering says (*Æventýri*, I, p. xxv), he took few stories from written sources. Those which have parallels in such sources show variations that suggest oral transmission. The original narrator of the Icelandic tale—I shall for convenience call him an Icelander—has arranged the incidents in a climactic order, proceeding from a traveller's accident to a sadistic love affair and ending with a ghost story.

With some minor but significant differences the incident of the lover and the grave-robbers was current in Italy in the first half of the sixteenth century as a historical anecdote. Matteo Bandello (1486-1561) tells it as an event that was commonly known. When he was visiting Messer Antonio Cappo, doctor of laws and gentleman of Mantua, who was then governor for the Holy See at Rimini, he heard this "story said to have befallen a little while before." [6] He goes on to say, "Albeit I know the true names, I think well, for apt reasons, to suppress them and avail myself of feigned names." According to Bandello:

A young and rich nobleman named Pandolfo del Nero loved Francesca, the wife of a rich gentleman, so passionately that he could not abide an hour without her sight. She finally gave ear to his pleas and "On this wise, then, they abode some two years' space, enjoying each other whenassoever they might." When Francesca fell grievously sick, her poor old husband, sparing no expense, sent to Bologna for a doctor. She realized that the end was near. "She had in her chamber a coffer, big enough to hold a man, the which had been provided of set purpose for the concealment of her lover in case of surprise, and it had sundry times befallen that Pandolfo had hid himself therein for four or five hours' space." She invited Pandolfo to come to her and told him of her wish that they might be buried in the same sepulchre. Pandolfo encouraged her as best he could but did not comment on this wish. While they were talking, Francesca's husband came to her room and Pandolfo took refuge in the coffer, while the maid locked up the house. As Pandolfo listened, Francesca made her husband promise to bury the coffer with her. Pandolfo did not dare to attempt to escape because he belonged to a contrary faction and would, if found in the house, be torn "limbmeal." Francesca died during the night and her coffin and the coffer were buried the following evening in the Dominican church of San Cataldo. After the funeral a nephew of the dead lady's husband enlisted the help of two comrades to break open the tomb. This they did without great difficulty. Pandolfo rose when the lock of the coffer was broken and bellowing fearfully, frightened away the intruders. He then collected the lady's jewels, closed the tomb, and made his way home. Bandello concludes with the remark that "all should beware of loving women who tender their own disorderly appetites dearer than their lover's lives."

According to Bandello, this was a historical event, although he has concealed the true names of the actors. He does not say when it occurred. We can fix the date when he wrote down his novella roughly in the first third of the sixteenth century. He was born at Tortona in northwestern Italy and removed to France in 1534. The manuscript of the *Novelle* was saved when his house at Milan burned and was brought to him across the Alps. After some revision and enlargement, a portion containing our tale was printed at Lucca in 1554. The story of Pandolfo de Nero differs in significant details from the incident in the Icelandic tale. In particular, the relationship of the lovers is adulterous. It is conceivable that the anecdote had been current in Italy for a century or longer and had made its way to Iceland during this time, but whether the Icelandic or the Italian version represents the original tale is a matter for conjecture.

The name Pandolfo identifies Bandello's historical or pseudo-historical anecdote. We can therefore derive all later versions of the story that contain this name directly or indirectly from Bandello's novella. For example, Simon Goulart (1543-1628) tells a French story about a Pandolfo—the family name is lacking—with its scene in Rimini about 1528 in his *Thrésor de histoires admirables et memorables de nostre temps.*[7] He cites his source as "Hist. d'Italie," by which he probably means an oral version of Bandello's novella. In other citations of sources he ordinarily gives an author's name and the title of the book with an adequate reference to chapter or page. In telling the story he differs in no way from Bandello beyond underscoring the moral implications. He says, for example, about the lady:

> Auint au bout de ce temps, que la iustice diuine commence à appeller à compte ceste adulteresse par vne griefue & incurable maladie . . .

and later, about Pandolfo in the chest:

> . . . mais sans penser à or ni argent il se disposoit à autres pensées, quand Dieu volut lui donner noueau respit pour penser à l'auenir à sa conscience, mieux qu'il n'auoit fait par le passé.

Such moralizing is easily added or omitted according to circumstances. The Thrésor is probably the source of the anecdote containing the name Pandolofo as found in a German miscellany (1663) put together by the indefatigable excerpter and compiler Erasmus Francisci (1629-1694), and the anecdote with the same name continued to appear, according to Bolte, in subsequent German miscellanies down to 1720. All of these, which I have not seen and have not troubled to run down, are presumably derived directly or indirectly from Bandello or Goulart. So, too, is a story in Carlo Casalicchio, *L'Utile col dolce,* where the name is Pandulfo.[8] There are minor differences, probably of Casalicchio's making. A rich man has an only daughter, whom he wishes to keep at home, even when she marries. Consequently, she is refused to Pandulfo and given to old Sempronio with a poor fortune. This mariage of May and December proves unhappy. Pandulfo pays court to his sweetheart and the rest follows much as in the novella. He realizes, however, the wrong that he has done and once freed from the sepulchre, "prima d'ogn'altra cosa si butta avanti dell'Altar Maggiore ringraziando il Signore, e confermando il voto, che avea fatto di Religione, e di castità, dipoi con una candela accesa in mano ritorna al sepolcro a pigliarsi quanto vi era di prezioso, per darlo a' povera, come poi subito fece" (p. 123). After going home, where he stayed many days, he went to the Dominicans, "col quale visse molti anni con molto fervore, e mori santamente." Casalicchio's description of Pandulfo rising from the sepulchre will be a sufficient sample of his style:

. . . ecco, che Pandulfo all'improviso da un' orribil mugito, come se fosse stato non solo un formidable, e terribile uomo del mundo, ma un vero demonio dell' inferno. Dal quale inaspettato evento atteriti, e mezzi, morti di paura, lasciate già e le chiavi, e l'armi quei due miseri giovani, scappan presto fuori, affermando tuttavia aver veduto con gl'occhi propri stare in quella cassa un diavolo d'inferno, che aveva le corna in fronte, e che butta fuoco dalla bocca, e dalle narici. . . .

More interesting than these reworkings of Bandello's novella is a curious version of uncertain origin. It is no doubt originally an Italian story, but I know a German form of it in the *Kurtzweilige und lächerliche Geschicht* (Frankfurt a.M.,

1583). This book announces itself to be a compilation of the best contemporary collections of jests and anecdotes, and contains our story on the very first page. I have used Bolte's reprint in his edition of the *Schimpf und Ernst* (II:110-12). It is told of an anonymous lover and a nobleman's wife of Bologna. She insists that her husband confirm, in the presence of her Franciscan confessor, his promise to bury the chest with her. After the burial the friars—not, as in the novella, the husband's nephew and companions—break open the chest, release the lover, and are frightened away. The story continues with new incidents: The lover squanders the treasure won with such difficulty. He sells jewelry to a goldsmith, who recognizes it and informs the dead lady's husband. When the lover comes a second time to the goldsmith, he is arrested and forced to confess. The husband realizes that further disclosure will bring disgrace and proceeds no further in the matter.

It is hard to say whether the setting of the scene in Bologna in this German tale can be connected with Bandello's allusion to bringing a doctor from Bologna to Rimini. The allusions to religious orders are similar in both tales, but concern different orders. The absence of the name Pandolfo makes it uncertain whether the tale is a derivative of Bandello's novella.

There remains one more version of our tale. At the end of the seventeenth century it was brought once more to Iceland and on this occasion was turned into verse. We may, for convenience, call it a ballad, since, as H. L. D. Ward says,[9] it seems to have been written in imitation of English or Danish ballads. The source of this ballad is somewhat uncertain. It does not seem to have been derived from the earlier Icelandic tale, although this was copied about 1690 by Jón Vigfússon, chamberlain of the Danish ambassador to Sweden and subsequently amanuensis in a library. This copy and the modern paper manuscript *Íslenzk bókmentafélag 139* of uncertain date (*Æventýri*, II:174, n. 1) are evidence that the medieval tale was known in modern times. This Icelandic "Kistu dans" has been printed in a review of the *Æventýri* and will soon appear again in an edition of the Icelandic ballads by a competent hand.[10] I content myself with translating Felix Liebrecht's summary:

A king's daughter who is mortally ill asks her lover who is secretly visiting her to choose a jewel in memory of her from the bottom of her chest. While he is bending over the chest, she pushes him in and closes the lid. Her father has been summoned and she asks him to bury the chest with her. This is done, but thieves dig it up and are frightened away so that the lover escapes.

A few inferences about the origin and connections of this Icelandic ballad are obvious. It is not one of those "ballads of a general character, which may have been invented by the writers."[11] As the reference to a "king's daughter" shows, it does not appear to be derived from the medieval Icelandic tale. Nor is it likely to have been based on the printed historical anecdote current in the Renaissance, unless we believe the Icelandic versifier removed the characteristic proper names and introduced the figure of the anonymous "king's daughter." The source was probably an oral tale derived ultimately from Bandello's novella or the historical anecdote but showing alterations caused by oral transmission. As Vigfússon and Powell say in the *Corpus poeticum boreale,* "One doubts whether they [the Icelandic ballads] were anything more than an attempt on the part of Gizur and his friends to imitate the ballads of the Continent or the British Islands" (quoted from Ward). We can, I think, look to Anders Sørenson Vedel (1542-1616), the tutor of Tycho Brahe, who with his brother pushed Vedel into publishing the first collection of Danish ballads, or possibly to Peder Syv (1631-1702), who was interested in folk tradition in the latter half of the seventeenth century and reprinted Vedel's collection with an additional hundred ballads (1695), as the men who inspired the Icelandic versifier.

This brief history has shown how tradition or learned men have adapted a simple tale to narrative fashions prevailing at various times. In the late Middle Ages the tale was fitted into a familiar tripartite pattern of the folktale. The original inventor of this version may possibly have been an Icelander. In any case, his invention appears to have had no success in oral tradition, although it was copied several times over a period of several centuries. A century and more after the Icelander retold the tale Matteo Bandello told it as a historical anecdote and gave it currency in Italy and north of the Alps for a couple of centuries. This characteristically literary tradition, or the story that lay behind it, seems to have enjoyed a small success as an oral tale. Finally, a seventeenth-century Icelander inspired by an interest in balladry that was characteristic of contemporary Denmark turned the tale into the "Kistu dans." In all these uses the little tale—which was no doubt originally a historical anecdote but one apparently earlier than the story employed by Bandello—changes its appearance like a chameleon.

ARCHER TAYLOR,
University of California, Berkeley

Notes

[1] See Hugo Gering, *Íslenzk æventýri* (2 v., Halle, 1882), I:232-39 (text), II:169-74 (translation). The text was first published in Konrad Gislason, *Fire og fyrretyve . . . prøver* (Copenhagen, 1860), pp. 410-15. Gering is using manuscripts which he designates as C¹ (*Æventýri*, I, p. xii) or AM 657B of the end of the fourteenth or the beginning of the fifteenth century; F (*Æventýri*, I, p. xxvii) or AM 586 of the same period; G (*Æventýri*, I, p. xxviii) or AM 335, which may be a little earlier; a (*Æventýri*, I, p. xxix) or Cod. holm. 66, which was written about 1690; and a more recent undated manuscript (*Æventýri*, II:174, n. 1) that he regards as worthless. I do not know why Johannes Bolte cites the tale as current in Iceland in the thirteenth century; see his edition of Johannes Pauli, *Schimpf und Ernst* (2 v., Berlin, 1824), II:444-45, no. 876.

[2] See Vistor Chauvin, *Bibliographie arabe* (12 v., Liége, 1892-1922), VIII: 204-05, no. 247, citing still another tale of tripartite pattern with some general resemblances as discussed in VI:22-23, no. 194.

[3] *Popular Tales of the Western Highlands* (4 v., Edinburgh, 1860), I:103-56, nos. 5-7.

[4] See Chauvin, *op. cit.*, VII:15-20.

[5] See M. Landau, *Die Quellen des Dekamerone* (2nd ed., Stuttgart, 1884), pp. 122-34; J. Bolte, ed., Martin Montanus, *Schwankbücher* (Stuttgart, 1899), pp. 582-83; A. C. Lee, *The Decameron* (London, 1909), pp. 30-34.

[6] *The Novels of Matteo Bandello, First Bishop of Agen, done into English prose and verse by John Payne* (6 v., London, 1890), Day III, Nov. 1.

[7] 2 v., Geneva, 1620. See I:254-56.

[8] I have used an edition published at Venice in 1741. See Decade Settima, Arguizia prima (pp. 119-23). Bolte cites ed. Venice, 1723, "nr. 61," which is probably a printer's error.

[9] See *Catalogue of the Romances in the British Museum* (3 v., London, 1883-1910), II:98, no. 30.

[10] Felix Liebrecht, *Zur Volkskunde* (Heilbronn, 1879), p. 508. For the text of the ballad see Liebrecht's review of the *Æventýri* in *Germania*, XXIX (1884):357-58. The ballad was first mentioned in a library report in *Antiquarisk tidsskrift*, 1852 (for 1849-1851), p. 225, no. 30.

[11] Ward, *Catalogue*, II:90-91.

Middle English Metrical Romances and Their Audience

In my article "Die Überlieferung der mittelenglischen Versromanzen," [1] I have tried to draw some conclusions on the various interests of the producers or initiators of the MSS. in which the texts of those romances are preserved. The contents of the MSS. also seem to suggest conclusions as to the interests and the social status of people for whom they had been destined. Fragments of MSS. are left out of consideration, since they do not reveal anything for our purpose.

In the thirteenth century, reading and writing were probably confined to persons of a clerical education. MSS. were therefore of use only to such persons, either to read privately, or to be read aloud to an audience interested in their contents. In the latter half of the fourteenth century the art of reading gradually became widespread. At the same time the knowledge of French in England gradually decreased. In the fifteenth century general education was spreading even among citizens in the towns. It is, therefore, no wonder that MSS. became more numerous, although undoubtedly the use of paper instead of costly parchment partly accounts for this. It is no wonder that MSS. containing romances are scarce in the thirteenth and early fourteenth centuries and only become numerous from the middle of the fourteenth century onwards. Middle English metrical romances have come down to us chiefly in MSS. of the later fourteenth and fifteenth centuries; a few are of the sixteenth century and some in the early prints. Quite a number also are contained in the Percy Folio MS. of the middle of the seventeenth century (British Museum Additional MS 27 879), some of which may have been copied from printed texts no longer extant. None of those MSS., with the single exception of the Auchinleck MS. (National Library of Scotland, Adv. 19.2.1) of the first quarter of the fourteenth century, shows costly execution, like that of some religious MSS. of the time, or some of the later Chaucer MSS. (e.g. the Ellesmere MS.), or the numerous fine MSS. of French prose romances of the fifteenth century, especially those of the Burgundian School. Even the Achinleck MS. contains only a certain number of quite good, if hardly artistic illuminations, but the text is, though well written, not too reliable. Its five or six scribes were decent penmen, but certainly not over-careful copyists. One of them even had difficulty in spelling English. He very likely was an Anglo-Norman, or one skilled only in copying French (or Latin) texts, for he constantly confuses such English letters as ʒ and þ, *sch* and *ch*.[2] This MS. may very well be the product of an early London bookshop[3] which employed various scribes without looking at their proficiency except as penmen. Rich people in England possibly did not care much for metrical romances; early printings of the romances do not go back to Caxton, who looked to aristocratic and rich book-collectors as likely buyers, but to Wynkyn de Worde, or Copland. These later printers printed the romances in comparatively cheap, small books that would find buyers among the middle class.

The only MS. containing romances which was written in the second half of the thirteenth century is Part II of MS. Cambridge University Library Gg. 4.27 (Part I of the volume is of later date and was bound up later with Part II). Since the MS. is not quite intact, several leaves being missing at the beginning and at the end, conclusions as to its original contents are not entirely sure. In its present state it contains a copy of *Floris and Blauncheflour,* followed by *King Horn* and the religious poem *The Assumption of Our Lady. Floris and Blauncheflour* is a pretty close English adaptation of the so-called "aristocratic" version of the French romance *Floire et Blancheflor* (as it is called by its editor, Édélstand de Méril, Paris, 1856, who names the second, more popular French version *"la version populaire"*). The translation is in fairly regular octosyllabic couplets. It is clearly the work of a learned poet, who knew French and English well. The English version of this story of the two devoted lovers, who after most strange adventures are happily united, was undoubtedly destined for persons of refined taste, educated upon French models, who did not understand French well and preferred an English translation. They might have been ladies. Another copy was the source of the other texts of this romance: MS. British Museum Egerton 2826 (*olim* Duke of Sutherland) from the end of the fourteenth century, which contains various other romances; the badly mutilated MS. Cotten Vitellius D III, which contained, as far as we can tell from the extant fragments, an Anglo-Norman poem on the history of Mary and Jesus and must therefore have been intended for bilingual readers; and the Auchinleck MS. (National Library of Scotland Adv. 19.2.1). *King Horn* is different in origin, even though the story deals also with two lovers who after many vicissitudes are united. It is based upon the Viking invasions of the British Isles and uses various motifs found in popular stories of Northern Europe, while *Floris and Blauncheflour* is connected with Oriental stories that became known in France as a result of the Crusades and the trade connections with the Orient. Perhaps *King Horn* was first told in alliterative verse by itinerant minstrels, for the existing version uses short couplets, commonly associated with minstrels, somewhat similar to the verse form of Layamon's *Brut*. In spite of French forms of many personal names, *King Horn* hardly goes back to a French romance, even though the story has been dealt with in an Anglo-Norman *Geste* by Maistre Thomas in the late twelfth century (preserved in three MSS. of the thirteenth century). *The Assumption of Our Lady* is very likely based upon a French poem on this apocryphal biblical subject. It is also in regular octosyllabic couplets and was copied very often. This poem is found in five fifteenth-century MSS. containing only religious pieces. Therefore it seems likely that the Cambridge MS. was compiled by a clerk connected with a gentleman's house, perhaps for its ladies, who wanted the two love stories, which they had heard somewhere, to be preserved, but in English because they did not know enough French. The clerk may have added the biblical story, because of his patron's interest in religious legend.

King Horn is found in two more MSS., both of the early fourteenth century, in a not very different text. But these MSS. are different in their other contents and probably also in their origin. One is the well-known Harley MS. 2253 of the British Museum, compiled by a monk of Leominster Priory near Hereford about 1310 or a little later.[4] Why this man chose to copy *King Horn* into the midst of his very varied collection of all sorts of French legends, religious and didactic poetry, Latin legends and religious poems, and English religious and secular shorter poems, even political ones, must remain a mystery. Most likely this man of very wide literary interests and curiosity had heard *King Horn* recited somewhere, obtained a text, and copied it into his MS. The third MS. of *King Horn* is Laud Misc. 108/II (Summary Catalogue No. 1486) of the Bodleian Library, Oxford, of about the same date. Here *King Horn* follows *Havelok*. The MS. does not seem to have contained anything else; Part I of the present volume is a copy of the *Southern Legendary* of an earlier date; Part III is a good deal later and contains also legends; the parts were bound together at a later date. From various misplacings and omissions of lines it has been urged that both poems were copied from a small portable volume of some twenty lines to the page, such as might have been the property of an itinerant minstrel.[5] It may be that the existing copy was meant to serve the same purpose.

Havelok deals with a story that must have developed on British soil. It is, like *King Horn*, connected with the Viking invasions, and tells of various incidents that could not have failed to attract popular audiences. But it is far less courtly and knightly than *King Horn*. The existing text is probably one recited by a minstrel on market days in town squares (cf. ll. 13-16 and the end). We have no other full text of it, but three short fragments exist in another fourteenth-century MS., now Cambridge University Library 4407 (19). Thus it is not unlikely that it was mainly used for reciting. The Havelok story was, however, also dealt with in an Anglo-Norman *lai* (preserved with other Anglo-Norman poems in a thirteenth-century MS.), of which a shortened version was incorporated into the *Estoire des Engleis* by the Yorkshireman Geoffrey Gaimer. The story was thought to contain historical facts, as is attested to by an allusion to it in the Anglo-Norman chronicle of another Yorkshireman, Pierre de Langtoft, of the first half of the fourteenth century. A short extract is also in the older MS., the translation by Robert Manning of Brunne (finished, as he says himself, on May 25, 1338) Lambeth Palace MS. No. 131 (middle of the fourteenth century), while the later MS. Inner Temple Petyt 511 (end of the fourteenth century) suggests doubt of its historical truth since the story is not told in the Latin Chronicles. Also the name Havelok was remembered. In the Auchinleck MS. of the *Short Metrical Chronicle* (ed. E. Zettl, EETS, OS, 196, l. 430) the Danish King who fights against Æthelred I is given the name of

Havelock. In the MS. British Museum Royal 12 C XII (first quarter of the fourteenth century), and in MS. Cambridge University Library Ff.V.48 (fifteenth century) the Danish King who fights against Æthelred II (*ibid.*, l. 729), is also given this name, although here the name is spelt *Avelot*. From the MS. *stemma* it seems likely that the latter was in the original text (see Zettl's ed., p. xlv) and that the Auchinleck MS. changed it. The other MSS. of the *Chronicle* omit the name.

The story of *King Horn* likewise seems to have continued to be known in one tradition. The more popular version of it, in tail-rime stanzas, *Horn Childe and Maiden Rimnild* (Auchinleck MS.) may go back to somebody who had heard it and wanted to refashion it. The name *Horn* is preserved in the Scottish ballad *Hind Horn* (Child, *English and Scottish Popular Ballads*, No. 17), which retells only the banquet scene.

Most of the other MSS. of metrical romances seem to have been destined for readers. This is certainly the case with the long works in short couplets by the London "skinner" Henry Lovelich (or Lonelich): his *History of the Holy Grail* (23,784 lines, beginning lost) after the French prose *Grand Saint Graal;* and his *Merlin* (27,822 lines, end lost) after the French prose *Merlin,* both contained in the late fifteenth-century MS. Corpus Christi College Cambridge 80, and his *Geste Historiale of the Destruction of Troy* in 14,044 alliterative long lines (MS. Hunterian Museum, Glasgow). Variants in texts preserved in several MSS. are not to be accounted for by oral transmission, but by the carelessness of scribes who simply exchanged one stock-in-trade phrase for another, or invented new lines when they had difficulties in reading their originals, or transposed a text from one dialect into their own, etc.[6] Some poems which we usually classify as "romances" were in their day considered to be legends or pious tales, similar to sermon exempla, and thus were copied into purely religious MSS., as, for instance, *Joseph of Arimathea* (preserved only in the purely religious Vernon MS.), or *Roberd of Cicyle*, or *The King of Tars* (also in the Vernon MS., in the similar "Simeon" MS., and in others). Other romances were copied into MSS. containing historical reading matter. Owing to their historical or pseudo-historical background they must have been believed to contain real history. Such are *Merlin*, in irregular short couplets[7] inserted into a Latin Chronicle of the kings of Britain in the *Liber Rubeus Bathoniae* and only preserved there; *Arthur and Merlin*, of which fragments were inserted as late as 1560 into the MS. Harley 6223 of the British Museum in a prose chronicle, although usually it is contained in MSS. of romances, or in MSS. containing romances and religious material; and *Richard Coeur de Lion* (in a version without the purely romantic matter, but with four short historical additions) in two historical MSS., i.e., Harley 4690 (containing a prose chronicle) and College of Arms H D N 58 (containing a copy of the verse chronicle ascribed to Robert of Gloucester and a prose chronicle).

Most of the Middle English metrical romances are in short octosyllabic couplets or in the peculiar English tail-rime stanzas. Only later ones are in the so-called ballad stanzas, e.g., the *Geste of Robin Hood*, but this seems to be just a conglomeration of single ballads. Alliterative long lines with or without end-rime and in tail-rime stanzas seem to have been in fashion in the west of England from Herefordshire (cf. *William of Palerne*, translated from the French for Sir Humphrey de Bohun, Earl of Hereford, who died in 1361) in the south to Cumberland in the north and later in Scotland. Except for the *Destruction of Jerusalem* (*Titus and Vespasian*) that is preserved in seven MSS., owing to its religious bias (based as it is upon the French *La Venjance Nostre Seigneur*) and also in MSS. that contain otherwise only religious poems, and the *Awntyrs of Arthur at Tarne Wathelyne* (four MSS.) none of them is preserved in more than one MS. The reason is hardly the fact that alliterative poetry was not liked in other parts of the country. The *Vision of Piers Plowman* is preserved in fifty MSS. from various parts of the country and was printed in 1550 and 1561. It is more likely their contents did not appeal to readers in other areas and that perhaps also the widespread use of dialect words made it difficult to understand them elsewhere. Still the Yorkshireman Robert Thornton copied some of these alliterative poems into his two MSS. (Lincoln Cathedral Library A.5.2, formerly A.1.17, and British Museum Additional 31, 042) and we owe their preservation to him. Some others are in the Ireland MS., empty pages of which were later (late fifteenth century) used for entries of the Court of Hale (Warrington, Lancashire), so that it may safely be inferred that the MS. had remained at this place unfinished. It probably was in the possession of a local gentleman's family. The interest in alliterative romances and alliterative poetry seems to have been predominant among the upper class in the remoter parts of the British Isles, not among town people. Thus it seems likely that the most striking and original of all Middle English romances, *Sir Gawayn and the Greene Knight,* together with the other poems in MS. Cotton Nero AX, was associated with a noble family of northwest England, and the poet may have had such a person as his patron. This idea is strengthened by the fact that the MS. was in the possession of Henry Saville (1568-1617) of Banke in Yorkshire.

KARL BRUNNER,
Innsbruck, Austria

Notes

[1] *Anglia* LXXVI (1958):64-73.

[2] See my edition of the *Seven Sages of Rome,* Southern version, EETS, OS, 191, p. ix ff.

[3] Cf. Laura Hibbard Loomis, "The Auchinleck MS. and a possible London Bookshop," *PMLA,* LVII (1942):595-627.

[4] Carleton Brown, *English Lyrics of the Thirteenth century* (Oxford, 1922), pp. xxxv-xxxvii.

[5] Skeat's edition of *Havelok* (Oxford, 1923), p. vii, after Zupitza.

[6] Cf. Albert C. Baugh, "Improvisation in the Middle English Romance," *Proceedings of the American Philosophical Society,* CIII(1959):418-54.

[7] Ed. Furnivall, EETS, OS, 2.

The Comic Element in the Wakefield Noah

Not surprisingly, critical evaluation and scholarly interest in the English Cycle play have concentrated heavily on the works of the Wakefield Master and, most particularly, on the celebrated *Secunda Pastorum*. Past criticism of the group as a whole is best exemplified by Millicent Carey's admirable comparison of the Wakefield plays with other treatments of the same biblical topics;[1] past scholarship on the *Secunda Pastorum* has centered on the question of the folkloric background of the Mak story.[2] Perhaps the most significant change in the past twenty-five years is one which reflects (if I may use a much maligned phrase) a shift in sensibility: that is, from the treatment of the plays as primarily dramatic history in stanzaic form to an evaluation of them as thematic poetry in the dramatic mode. Too frequently, it has been assumed that these two approaches involved an *entweder/oder*, despite the fact that the immense amount of mutual confirmation strongly indicates a case of both/and.

The first suggestion that the folkloric might be dramatically functional came as an almost casual aside by Empson in *Some Versions of Pastoral* in 1935,[3] and, while this relationship has been periodically rediscovered,[4] it probably received its widest support when Professor E. K. Chambers referred to the sheep-stealing episode as "an astounding parody of the Nativity itself."[5] The various articles written in the past two decades concerning the structure of the *Secunda Pastorum*, emphasizing as they do the unity achieved through the Mak episode, have tended increasingly to regard the play as an artistic whole, capable of a minute analysis of both its thema-

tic and imagistic structure. Such a line of criticism leads ultimately to Professor Speirs's conclusion: "The best of the
Cycle plays yield their fuller meaning when they are recognized as poetic drama. They have to be responded to fully
as *poems*." [6] While it is true that such interpretations have
often been excessive in their author's view of irony,[7] myth
and ritual,[8] they have opened a profitable approach to the
play,[9] and indeed to the Wakefield group as a whole. It does
not, in sum, seem outrageous to regard the Wakefield Master
as a master not only of metrics, but of poetic structure as
well. If such a concession is justifiable, then we must assume
that he was fully aware of dramatic structure; we must assume,
unless there is strong evidence to the contrary, that he intentionally merged folkloric comedy and biblical narrative, and
that he produced a unified effect thereby. Such assumptions,
as I have mentioned, underlie the interpretations that have
been made of the *Secunda Pastorum;* but no other play has
been fully analyzed along these lines. If, then, we could
demonstrate that a similar technique exists in another of the
Wakefield Master's plays, it would greatly strengthen the
argument that he wrote with a very strong sense of poetic
and dramatic unity.

The prevalence and importance of the Noah legend can
hardly be gauged.[10] It merged with the classical legends of
Prometheus, Ogyges, Saturn, Deucalion, and Janus;[11] it very
early became a prefiguration of Christ's resurrection;[12] it en-
dured as the central theme in one of the most heated and
significant controversies of the seventeenth and eighteenth
centuries.[13] But, above all, the story of Noah was the story
of the second creation, the recommencement of history
following the flood's purgation of a sinful and chaotic earth.
Ludus Coventriae IV states the theme explicitly:

In me Noe þe secunde age
in dede be-gynnyth as I ʒow say
afftyr Adam with-outyn langage
þe secunde fadyr am I in fay   (L.C. IV:14-17)[14]

It is quite fitting, then, that the Noah of the Wakefield play review the history of the first era in the opening nine stanzas: the formation of the universe; the creation of the angelic hierarchy, followed by the fall of Lucifer; the creation of man to fill the place of the fallen angels, and then man's fall; the saving oil of mercy[15] to overcome the rampant sins that Noah sees around him; the patriarch's fear of the Lord's vengeance; and, finally, his plea for mercy.

Noah's account stresses the two basic contrasts of the *Processus*. First, there is the traditional contrast between Justice and Mercy,[16] between God's vengeance and His love, represented dramatically by the Flood at the opening of the play and the prayer for eternal salvation at the conclusion. Secondly, the chaotic world of sin is contrasted to pre-lapsarian harmony. The anarchic society is described by Deus:

In erth I se bot syn reynand to and fro
Emang both more and myn, ichon other fo
With all thare entent.   (111-13)

It is a world that has rejected "degree, priority and place":[17]

I repente full sore that euer maide I man;
Bi me he settys no store, and I am his soferan.   (91-92)

God's chastisement of man must be carried out because all other methods have proven ineffectual. God's proffered, ennobling love has been blatantly rejected:

Euery man to my bydyng shuld be bowand
Full feruent,

That maide man sich a creatoure,
Farest of favoure;
Man must luf me paramoure
By reson, and repent.

Me thoght I shewed man luf when I made hym to be
All angels abuf, like to the Trynyté;
And now in grete reprufe full low ligys he,
In erth hymself to stuf with syn that displeasse me
Most of all.　　　　　　　　　　　　　　(76-86)

and even the last appeal to order has been disintegrated by
sin:

for me no man is ferd.
As I say shal I do—of veniance draw my swerd,
And make end
Of all that beris life　　　　　　　　(102-105)

The disordered, anarchic state of man in the last moments
of his first era is in direct contrast to the harmony which
reigned at the first creation:

Of the Trinité bi accord, Adam, and Eue that woman,
To multiplie without discord, in Paradise put he thaym (30-31)

The strong biblical parallel [18] of the first and second creations
is stressed by the Wakefield Master in Deus's benediction:

Noe, to the and to thi fry
My blyssyng graunt I;
Ye shall wax and multiply
And fill the erth agane[19]　　(177-80)

With the recognition of these two complementary themes—
God's just chastisement and His merciful salvation, and man's
disordered world and God's harmonious creation—we can
turn to the question of the comic element in the play.

There were actually two diametrically opposite traditions of the character of Noah's wife during the Middle Ages. Professor Mill's excellent article points up the difference:

To the orthodox theologian Uxor was the meek and virtuous woman of the French *Mistère,* the Old Testament prototype of Mary. "Noe significat Christum, uxor eius beatam Mariam." [20] As early as the fourth century, however, a development of the character had taken shape among the heretical sects. Thus, according to Epiphanius, Heresy XXVI, the Gnostic *Book of Noria* seems to have registered a certain truculence on the part of Uxor, an alliance with the powers of evil, and a desire to thwart her husband in his heaven-sent mission through setting fire to the Ark repeatedly, so that the building dragged on for many years. . . .[21]

As Professor Mill so ably demonstrates, the tradition of the shrewish Uxor "is widespread in art and folklore, as well as literary sources";[22] it frequently parallels, and on occasion is identified with, the story of Eve.[23]

As in the specific case of the Mak story, the comic element that is found in the Noah plays derives from folklore; but the Wakefield *Noah,* it is here suggested, integrated the comedy into the theme and dramatic action in an extraordinary manner. The Wakefield Master, by a series of slight but brilliant changes, made the Uxor episode parallel the theme of disorder, chastisement, and re-established harmony that is the very substance of the biblical level of the play. This is not a matter of irony—that much abused term has led to much excess; rather there is a comic descant on the main theme, a bringing together of the biblical *vox principalis* (to follow the musical metaphor) with the popular, folkoric, perhaps even ritualistic, *discantus supra librum.* A comparison of the Wakefield Noah with that of Chester and of York will, I believe, help to demonstrate the suggestion that has just been made.[24] Let us look first at the two scenes of contention between Noah and his wife, and then at the dramatic function of Uxor in the non-comic portion of the play.

The Towneley play alone has two comic episodes, the one preceding the building of the Ark, the other involving the attempt to make Uxor come aboard. The first is, as we shall see, far more the comedy of slapstick and name-calling than is the second.[25] Interestingly enough, this preliminary scene is in neither York nor Chester, both of which have the abuse limited to Uxor's refusal to leave. Here, one extremely important difference stands out starkly: in the York and Chester plays,[26] Uxor strikes Noah, but he does not return the blow; indeed, in the York play, his only reply is "I pray þe, dame, be stille" (121), and in Chester, it is scarcely more: "A! ha! mary, this is hote,/ it is good to be still" (243-44). In Wakefield, on the other hand, we are more fully prepared for a termagant even before the first scene of contention begins by Noah's trepidation:

> For she is full tethee,
> For litill oft angré;
> If any thyng wrang be,
> Soyne is she wroth   (186-89)

Noah, however, stands up to both her tongue and her hand:

> *Noe.*   Wel hold thi tong, ram-skyt, or I shall the still.
> *Uxor.* By my thryft, if thou smyte, I shal turne the vntill.
> *Noe.*   We shall assay as tyte. Haue at the, Gill!
>   Apon the bone shal it byte.   (217-20)

and, despite the claims of superiority from the two combatants (224-32), the battle is even and ends only because of Noah's sudden, almost comic, recollection of his mission: "Bot I will kepe charyté, for I haue at do" (235). The Towneley play, then, differs from the other cycles not only in having this preliminary scene but also in Noah's meeting force with force. Were these the only unique elements of the Wakefield *Noah*, we would have scarcely more than an interesting variation of the conventional disobedient, shrewish Uxor and henpecked, passive Noah; but the reasons for this variation and for relegating the *bataille rangée* to the preliminary scene become evident in Noah's explicit statements when he attempts to get Uxor to enter the Ark.

The first reason is that of comic motivation. In both the Chester and Wakefield plays, Uxor helps to load the Ark, but in the former, this comes *after* her refusal to obey Noah's request that she come aboard (Chester, 97-104). In the Wakefield play, the disobedience is held back until the question of her boarding the ship comes up. Where the Chester play gives no motivation whatever for her helping to load the Ark, the Wakefield play employs a device of characterization, namely Uxor's sense of ever more proximate danger. Noah's revelation to her of the coming Flood, paralleling that of Deus to Noah, momentarily frightens her into assistance. "I dase and I dedir," says she, "For ferd of that tayll" (314-15). Both in the York play (where Uxor comes up to the Ark out of curiosity) and in the Chester play, we are presented directly with the broad comedy of Uxor's stubbornness. In Wakefield, however, general fear gives way to more specific fear; the terror she had felt on hearing of the promised Flood disappears before her immediate dread of the Ark:

> I was neuer bard ere, as euer myght I the,
> In sich an oostré as this!
> In fath, I can not fynd
> Which is before, which is behynd.
> Bot shall we here be pynd,
> Noe, as haue thou blis?   (328-33)

It is only when there is no choice left that she rushes into the ship:

> Yei, water nyghys so nere that I sit not dry;
> Into ship with a byr, therfor, will I hy
> For drede that I drone here.   (370-72)

While the York play does stress her fear of the ship (77-78), it gives none of the careful, comic motivation of the Wakefield play. Indeed, in both York and Chester, Uxor is kept aboard the Ark by physical force (York, 101), or brought aboard by at least the threat of coercion (Chester, 239-40). The broad comedy of physical action by the sons is replaced in the Wakefield play by a series of plausible arguments from the sons' wives who are already on the ship; the first wife points out that the sun and moon are overcast; the second exclaims that the winds are blasting and "thise floodys so thay ryn"; and when Uxor replies "yit will I spyn," the third wife tellingly argues, "If ye like ye may spyn, moder, in the ship."

It is at this point that we come to the second reason for the rearrangement of the material, and to the most startling change that the Wakefield Master has made. It will be recalled that the York and Chester Noahs, once Uxor is aboard, passively receive from her a blow that they do not return. In the Wakefield scene of Uxor's refusal to enter the Ark, the disobedience is firmly chastised:

Noe.   Dame, securly
> It bees boght full dere ye abode so long by
> Out of ship.   (372-74)

and to Uxor's insolent reply ("I will not, for thi bydyng,/ Go from doore to mydyng"), Noah asserts his authority:

> In fayth, and for youre long taryying
> Ye shal lik on the whyp.   (377-78)

When fear, the last appeal to order, has no effect ("Thise grete wordys shall not flay me"), the chastisement begins.

Noe.   Abide, dame, and drynk,
     For betyn shall thou be with this staf to thou stynk.
     Ar strokys good? say me.
Uxor.   What say ye, Wat Wynk?
Noe. Speke!
     Cry me mercy, I say!
Uxor. Thereto say I nay
Noe. Bot thou do, bi this day,
     Thi hede shall I breke!   (381-87)

With comic suddenness, the author arrests the action. Uxor addresses the wives of the audience on the hard lot of married women and explains that many of them—like herself—would be "at ese and hertely full hoylle" if they were widows. It is then that Noah, speaking to the husbands, stresses not only the moral of this episode but the dramatic function of the comic element in the play as a whole:

> Yee men that has wifys, whyls thay ar yong,
> If ye luf youre lifys, chastice thare tong.
> Me thynk my hert ryfys, both levyr and long,
> To se sich stryfys, wedmen emong.
> Bot I,
> As haue I blys,
> Shall chastyse this.[27]   (397-403)

And these last three lines, as we shall see again from the specific changes of the Wakefield *Noah*, will prove quite literally true. Like God's chastisement of disobedient man with its subsequent harmony of the new creation, Noah's human,

realistic chastisement of his wife will reassert order and bring
them into a completely harmonious relationship. Undoubtedly,
when the comic action resumes with the same suddenness
with which it had stopped, Uxor does not stand still—the
Wakefield Master has far too fine a sense of dramatic realism
for that. But it is equally undoubted that it is Noah who
continues to administer the real drubbing:

Noe.   I shall make þe still as stone, begynnar of blunder!
  I shall bete the bak and bone, and breke all in sonder.
Uxor. Out, alas, I am gone! Oute apon the, mans wonder!
Noe.   Se how she can grone, and I lig vnder!
  Bot, wife,
  In this hast let vs ho,
  For my bak is nere in two.
Uxor. And I am bet so blo
  That I may not thryfe.[28]   (406-14)

The final portion of the Wakefield play shows a radical
divergence from the other two versions which we have been
considering. In the York play, Uxor has but three impersonal
speeches (197-98, 267-70, 303-5) once the Ark is under way;
it is the sons who converse with Noah and sail the ship. In
the Chester play, Uxor is heard from no more; the remaining
action of the play is described by Noah and Deus. In the
Wakefield play, it has been suggested, the chastisement of
Noah's wife, like the divine chastisement of mankind, has
purged out all disobedience, discord, and disorder. Without
some such analogy to the biblical theme of the play, the
remainder of the *Noah*—the total change in Uxor's character,
her dramatic position which is second only to Noah's, the
harmony that reigns between husband and wife—in almost
every aspect would be dramatically meaningless.

The harmonious tone is set almost at once. As Uxor looks
out to see "the seven starnes," Noah is concerned for her

safety ("This is a grete flood, wife, take hede"—l. 424).
His prayer for God's help is echoed, in the plural, by Uxor:
"Help, God, when we call!" (432); and, quite significantly,
she dutifully takes the helm as he makes his three soundings:

> *Noe.* Wife, tent the stere-tre, and I shall asay
> The depnes of the see that we bere, if I may.
> *Uxor.* That shall I do ful wysely.   (433-35)

Of the 138 lines devoted to the voyage of the Ark, 92 are
given to Noah, 43 to Uxor, and one each to the sons. But even
this does not sufficiently stress her importance; for, not only
are a number of Noah's lines devoted to her (as opposed to
description of the voyage), but, even more important, almost
every major dramatic event is described by her. It is Uxor
who, after the long storm, first sights the new dawn:

> The son shynes in the eest. Lo, is not yond it?   (453)

it is she who gives voice to their renewed joy and asks where
they are (463-65); it is she who recognizes the emergent hill-
tops as "mercy tokyns full right" (471); it is she who selects
—albeit incorrectly—the raven as the bird to bring "of mercy
som tokynyng";[29] it is she who excitedly spots the long-
awaited dove:

> Hence bot a litill she commys, lew, lew!   (507)

it is she who interprets the meaning of the olive branch ("A
trew tokyn ist we shall be sauyd all"—l. 517); and it is she
who, with a note of humanity that is startling in a play that
sets forth the divine plan, inquires almost plaintively about
the fate of all those who have perished. The second creation
is to begin in harmony, like the first:

Of the Trinité bi accord, Adam, and Eue that woman,
To multiplie without discord, in Paradise put he thaym.   (30-31)

Here there is no discord, no disorder, no disobedience. When Uxor inquires of Noah, "What grownd may this be?" (465), he answers with what could well be a brilliant example of paranomasia, "The hyllys of Armonye." And Uxor replies, "Now blissid be he/ That thus for vs ordand!"

"The hyllys of Armonye" are to be the site of earth's second creation, but Noah, with Uxor certainly in mind, prays for the final mercy of ultimate salvation:

> As he in bayll is blis, I pray hym in this space,
> In heven hye with his to purvaye vs a place,
> That we,
> With his santys in sight,
> And his angels bright,
> May com to his light.
> Amen, for charité.   (552-58)

If what I have suggested here has any validity, the *Processus Noe* and the *Secunda Pastorum* are constructed on surprisingly similar patterns.[30] In both, biblical material, beautifully transposed, furnishes the main plot and the main themes; in both, folkloric material, artfully integrated, provides the comic element and a descant upon the main themes. Such an interpretation assumes that the Wakefield Master fully knew what he was about and was master not only of the metres of poetry but of the themes of poetry as well. Why he merged these two seemingly disparate levels is probably a question to which he himself could not have given any single answer—if he could have given any answer at all. Perhaps it was to engage his audience, perhaps it was to show them how their version and the biblical version were really the same, or perhaps he felt that between the universal plan and the pitiful humanity that carried it out, between the macrocosm and the microcosm, comedy almost inevitably becomes the vehicle for such a *reductio ad absurdum*. We cannot know; we can only wonder.

HOWARD H. SCHLESS,
Columbia University

[1] Millicent Carey, *The Wakefield Group in the Towneley Cycle, Hesperia*, Ergänzungsreihe XI, (Göttingen: Vandenhoeck & Ruprecht and Baltimore: Johns Hopkins Press, 1930).

[2] See, for example, A. C. Baugh, "The Mak Story," *Modern Philology* XV (1918):729-34. A recent attempt at summarization and interpretation is made by R. C. Cosbey, "The Mak Story and Its Folklore Analogues," *Speculum* XX (1945):310-17.

[3] William Empson, *Some Versions of Pastoral* (London: Chatto & Windus, 1935, 1950), p. 28.

[4] For an excellent, selective bibliography, see the recent edition *The Wakefield Pageants in the Towneley Cycle*, edited by A. C. Cawley (Manchester University Press, 1958), pp. xxxiv-xxxviii. Unless otherwise noted, quotations from the plays will come from this edition. For the full cycle, see England and Pollard. *The Towneley Plays*, EETS, ES, 71 (London: Kegan Paul, 1897; repr. 1907, 1925, 1952).

[5] E. K. Chambers, *English Literature at the Close of the Middle Ages*, (Oxford: Clarendon Press, 1954 [first published 1945]), p. 38.

[6] See the two articles by John Speirs, "The Mystery Cycle: Some Towneley Plays," *Scrutiny* XVIII:2 (Autumn 1951):86-117, and XVIII:4 (June, 1952):246-65. The present quotation will be found on p. 265; the italics are Speirs's.

[7] See, for example, Eugene E. Zumwalt, "Irony in the Towneley Shepherds' Plays," *Research Studies of the State College of Washington* XXVI (1958):37-53.

[8] Spiers, on occasion, goes beyond his evidence in support of ritual drama. *Vide supra;* also *Scrutiny* XVIII:3 (Winter 1951-52):193-96.

[9] For an admirably balanced interpretation, see Homer A. Watt, "The Dramatic Unity of the 'Secunda Pastorum,'" *Essays and Studies in Honor of Carleton Brown* (New York: New York University Press, 1940), pp. 158-66.

[10] See the remarkably fine study by Don Cameron Allen, *The Legend of Noah* (Illinois Studies in Language and Literature, Vol. XXXIII, Nos. 3-4; Urbana: University of Illinois Press, 1949).

[11] *Ibid.*, pp. 74-75, 83-84.

[12] *Ibid.*, pp. 138-39. Also, Josef Fink, *Noe der Gerechte in der Frühchristlichen Kunst* (Beihefte zum Archiv für Kulturgeschichte, Heft 4; Münster: Böhlau-Verlag, 1955).

[13] Allen, *op. cit.*, pp. 92-112. For the most thorough treatment of the controversy and its implications, see Marjorie H. Nicholson, *Mountain Gloom and Mountain Glory* (Ithaca: Cornell University Press, 1959).

[14] *Ludus Coventriae*, ed. K. S. Block. EETS, ES, 120 (London: Oxford University Press, 1922).

[15] The implications of this highly important theme are fully discussed in Esther Quinn, *The Legend of Seth and the Holy Cross* (unpubl. Ph.D. dissertation, Columbia University, 1960; available on microfilm).

[16] These, of course, are the personifications that plead before Deus in *Le Mistère du Viel Testament,* ed. James de Rothschild, SATF, No. 36, Vol. I, ll. 5606-49.

[17] *Troilus and Cressida,* I, iii. The conventionality of Ulysses's speech on order is underlined by the many parallels to Deus's view given here.

[18] Genesis I:28 and IX:1, 7.

[19] As Miss Carey points out (p. 52), this is quite close to *Le Mistère du Viel Testament,* ll. 6165-66: "Croissez, multipliez sur terre/ Car ma grace vous est donée." Speirs summarizes one aspect of this particular contrast (p. 96): "The play of Noah has for *its* theme a pattern of destruction and renewal, destruction of what was created, because it has fallen or declined, and its subsequent renewal or recreation. The play moves with a sure rhythm throughout to the completion of its ordered and unified structure; it is a dramatic poem, complete in itself, yet a significant part of a larger whole."

[20] A. de Laborde, *La Bible Moralizée, illustrée,* t. I (Paris, 1911), P 1. 9 (Mill's note).

[21] Anna Jean Mill, "Noah's Wife Again," *PMLA* LVI (1941):615.

[22] *Ibid.*

[23] *Ibid.,* p. 624, n. 50.

[24] I shall be following generally the very useful comparative outline that Miss Carey has given us (*op. cit.,* pp. 71-75). For her evaluation of other plots, see Section II, *passim.*

[25] I am intentionally avoiding the term "flyting" which has, I feel, been too loosely applied to the Uxor episode.

[26] *York Plays,* ed. Lucy Toulmin Smith (Oxford: Clarendon Press, 1885); and *The Chester Plays,* ed. Hermann Deimling, EETS, ES, 62, Part I (London: Oxford University Press, 1892; repr. 1926).

[27] Cf. the remarks on wives and the admonishment to the audience by Secundus Pastor in the *Secunda Pastorum,* 64-108.

[28] It is quite possible, of course, that Noah's sore back comes from Uxor's blows; but it is equally possible, considering his speeches and Uxor's groans, that it is the result of the drubbing that the patriarch has administered. Certainly, Uxor gives voice to none of the triumphant description that she had used in her first combat; likewise, it should be recalled that physical exertion had similarly affected Noah in the building of the Ark: "A! my bak, I traw, will brast! This is a sory note!/ Hit is wonder that I last, sich an old dote,/ All dold,/ To begin sich a wark." (264-67.)

[29] Miss Carey has pointed out the change in the relationship of Noah and Uxor (p. 95: "He tactfully asks his chastened wife's advice as to which bird would best bring them tidings of good"; and p. 97: "She subsides because she is chastened by her beating. . . ."), but her view of Noah as merely "the henpecked husband" prevents her from seeing the relationship of the episode to the play as a whole.

[30] Speirs has suggested (*op. cit.,* p. 258) that in the Towneley *Iudicium* "The demons with their rolls have now assumed the aspect of lawyers— or of clowns burlesquing lawyers—and the episode thus evolves into a parody of the Judgment."

The Conclusion of the Perceval
Continuation in Bern MS. 113

The Old French *Perceval* romance, or *Conte du Graal,* which was begun by Chrétien de Troyes about 1180 or 1181, had an unusual fate in that the completion of it was several times deferred. Chrétien himself probably died while still at work on it, for Gerbert de Montreuil,[1] one of his continuators, says

> Ce nous dist Crestiens de Troie   6984
> Qui de Percheval comencha,
> Mais la mors qui l'adevancha
> Ne li laissa pas traire affin.

A first continuator, whose name is unknown, took up the story at the point where Chrétien was interrupted (vs. 9234), and carried on the narrative of the adventures of Gauvain for many thousands of lines.[2] However, in spite of the length of the First Continuation, the hero, Perceval, does not reappear, and quite naturally no acceptable ending of the original story was possible without him. A second continuator,[3] also anonymous, brought Perceval back into the story, making it clear that he was picking up the thread at the point where Chrétien had last spoken of him; that is, at Perceval's departure from the house of his Hermit Uncle, where he had arrived on Good Friday and had remained until after Easter.[4] In that scene Chrétien had said that he was going to tell about Gauvain and that Perceval would not soon reappear:

> De Percheval plus longuement   6514
> Ne parole li contes chi,
> Ainz avrez molt ançois oï

De monseignor Gavain parler
Que rien m'oiez de lui conter.

The second continuator spins out his story for more than 12,000 lines, and although he manages to keep Perceval in the center of the stage most of the time, with only an occasional episode devoted to that much more fascinating character, Gauvain, he loses sight of the Grail, the Bleeding Lance, and the Fisher King for long stretches of the narrative. He relates instead a series of miscellaneous adventures, which are interesting enough and some of which are quite well told, but which are in no way different from the episodes which fill dozens of other romances of adventure, and which have no connection at all with the central theme of the *Conte du Graal*. At the same time the second continuator waits until almost the very end of his story to take into account a new element which had been introduced into the Grail story by his predecessor, the first continuator. This new element is the question of vengeance for the knight from the Grail Castle who had been mysteriously killed while Gauvain was escorting him to the presence of Queen Guenevere.[5] The predestined avenger of the slain knight is to be recognized by his success in joining the pieces of a broken sword which the Fisher King presents to each knight who comes to the Grail Castle. Gauvain, in the long version of the First Continuation, had twice tried unsuccessfully to join the pieces of the sword;[6] and when Perceval finally arrives, in the last episode of the Second Continuation, at the Grail Castle, he too undergoes the test.[7] Almost incidentally as it were, Perceval also asks the famous question ("Cui on en sert")[8] concerning the Grail which he had failed to ask (in Chrétien's poem) during his first visit to the Castle; but the question has by now apparently lost its significance, for nothing happens and the attention of

Perceval and the Fisher King is centered upon the sword test. Unlike Gauvain, Perceval succeeds in joining the pieces of the sword; the Fisher King embraces him and welcomes him as his successor:

> Li rois lo voit, grant joie an a,   34921
> Ses deus bras au col li gita
> Conme cortois et bien apris.
> Puis li a dist: "Biaux doz amis,
> Sire soiez de ma meson;
> Je vos met tout an abandon
> Quanque je ai, sanz nul dongier."

At this point the second continuator might very well have brought the story to a suitable conclusion, if he had been working only with the elements which had been introduced by Chrétien. But by accepting from his predecessor the motif of the vengeance which must be performed by the knight who successfully joins the pieces of the broken sword, the second continuator made it impossible to end the story immediately after Perceval's successful visit to the Grail Castle. It was necessary to write a series of episodes which would lead up to the incident of the vengeance.[9]

This task was finally performed, after a lapse of some twenty-five or thirty years, by two continuators, Manessier and Gerbert de Montreuil, who seem to have worked at about the same time, but quite independently of each other. They both wrote long, rambling accounts, into which they introduced numerous secondary characters and episodes extraneous to the Grail theme, but they eventually brought the long tale to a satisfactory conclusion: Manessier in a little more than 12,000 lines and Gerbert in more than 17,000.

In the interval after the second continuator ceased to work on the story and before Manessier's and Gerbert's conclusions appeared, it seems certain that a number of manuscripts of the incomplete story were copied. Even among those now extant, almost all of which were written after the middle of the thirteenth century—i.e., well after the time when Manessier and Gerbert wrote their continuations—there are several which do not reach a conclusion. With one notable exception they all begin with Chrétien's part of the cycle, but several of them (*B C F H*) stop even before the beginning of the First Continuation; one (*R*) goes on for only about fourteen hundred lines after the end of Chrétien's section; another (*A*) stops after the first eight hundred lines of the Second Continuation; and still another (*L*) breaks off exactly at the end of the Second Continuation. All the others (*E M P Q S T U V*) give one or the other of the conclusions by Manessier and Gerbert.[10] It seems probable, therefore, that the text of MSS. *A* and *L*, at least, goes back ultimately to exemplars copied before these conclusions were written.

The exception mentioned above is MS. *K* (Bern 113), which contains neither Chrétien's work nor the First Continuation.[11] In MS. *K* the Second Continuation appears as an independent, self-contained romance, which opens with a very brief introductory passage:

> Do roi Artu lairai atant   fol. 87a
> Et si orés d'or en avant
> Le bon conte de Percheval
> Et le haut livre do Greal

and which replaces the long and tedious conclusion of Manessier by a short passage of fifty-eight lines. This independent ending, which is found in no other manuscript, finishes the story in conformity with the ideas and conceptions of Robert de Boron, as set forth in his *Joseph d'Arimathie* and in the Didot *Perceval*, and not at all in accordance with the basic assumptions of the stories told by Chrétien and the first two continuators.[12] It cannot be regarded as the original ending of the Second Continuation, as some scholars[13] have considered it to be, but it does give testimony at a relatively early date of the effort to combine the pseudo-historical and religious traditions of Robert's cycle of romances with the courtly and adventurous spirit embodied in the several parts of the *Conte du Graal,* which is the most striking trait of the Didot *Perceval* in the rewritten and interpolated form in which it has survived.

The special conclusion of the Bern manuscript was first printed by Alfred Rochat in a dissertation which he presented at the University of Zurich in 1855, under the title *Ueber einen bisher unbekannten Percheval li Galois.* On pages 90-92 of this little book, Rochat gives a fairly accurate transcript of the passage, but he omits lines 9 and 10 for no discernible reason, perhaps through inattention. Eight years later Charles Potvin also printed the concluding lines of Bern 113 on pages 40-42 of his *Bibliographie de Chrestien de Troyes* (Bruxelles, Leipzig, Gand, 1863). Potvin does not mention Rochat, whose dissertation he may not have known; but it is strange that he also omits lines 9 and 10, and that, like Rochat, he adds the word "Explicit" after the last line of the text, although it does not appear in the manuscript.[14]

The loss of a couplet from such a passage as the Bern conclusion might have been of no particular importance, but the omission of lines 9 and 10 from the only two printings ever made was unfortunate, because it is precisely in those two lines that the author refers to the legend of Longinus,[15] the blind soldier who pierced the side of the crucified Christ with a lance and whose sight was miraculously restored when he rubbed his eyes with his hand upon which the Holy Blood had fallen:

C'est la lance tot vraiement   5
Dont li fix Deu soffri torment
Quant en la crois fu estendus.
Ens el costé en fu ferus,
Li sans contreval en glaça,   9
Longis s'en terst et raluma.   10

Neither Chrétien nor Robert de Boron mentions the name of Longinus, and the Bleeding Lance which appears in the Grail procession in Chrétien's poem (vss. 3192-3201, 6373-77) is certainly not the lance of the Crucifixion (cf. vss. 6166-71). Robert mentions no lance at all in his *Joseph*. The Didot *Perceval* (*E* 1850; *D* 1516-17) refers to "li lance dont Longis feri Jhesucrist en le crois," but does not speak of his blindness nor its cure. Most of the MSS. of the First Continuation associate the lance at the Grail Castle with the lance of the Crucifixion, but only two of them mention Longinus (*T V* 13471), without alluding to his blindness or to its miraculous cure. The author of the Second Continuation refers to the Bleeding Lance on several occasions (vss. 22258, 26244, 28104, 34580, 34748), but he never identifies it with the lance of the Crucifixion and he does not mention Longinus at all. It is apparent, therefore, that the author of the Bern conclusion either used versions of the Didot *Perceval* and the First Continuation which have not survived, or drew upon his own acquaintance with a popular medieval legend in order to elaborate the final scene of the Second Continuation.

Since this text has not been printed for nearly a hundred years and since both Rochat's and Potvin's books have long been extremely rare, it seems appropriate to make the passage available in an accurate copy, with no corrections or changes in the readings of the MS., but with enough punctuation and capitalization for ready comprehension. The last five lines

of the Second Continuation which immediately precede this
passage in the Bern MS. are printed in italics at the beginning.

[34930]   *Atant revint cil a esploit*
             Qui l'espee avoit aportee,
             Si l'a prise et envolepee
             En un cendal qu'il en reporte;
[34934]   *Et Perchevaus se reconforte.*
             Forment li plaist et li agree,
             Et de la lance a demandee.
             Li rois li dist: "Jel vos dirai,
             Ne ja de mot n'en mentirai.   4
             C'est la lance tot vraiement
             Dont li fix Deu soffri torment
             Quant en la crois fu estendus.
             Ens el costé en fu ferus,   8
             Li sans contreval en glaça,
             Longis s'en terst et raluma."
             Aprés li a dit Perchevaus,
             Qui tant estoit preus et loiaus,   12
             Que del Graal wet il fis estre,
             Cui on en sert et que puet estre.
             Li rois saut sus isnelement,
             Tos est garis, nul mal ne sent.   16
             Puis dist: "Amis, or m'entendés
             Et vostre non ne me celés;
             Dites le moi, jel wel oïr."
             Et cil respont: "A vo plaisir: 20
             Perchevaus, voir, sui apelés;
             A Sinadon, la fui jo nes;
             Et mes peres par verité
             Alains li Gros fu apelé."   24
115b   —"Ha, Perchevaus! t'iés mes amis.
             Alains li Gros, il fu mes fix.
             Enigeüs ot non sa mere
             Et Josepf si refu ses frere,   28

A cui Jhesucris fu bailliés
Quant de la crois fu destaciés.
Et Pilate qui li bailla
Por ses soldees li dona.   32
Nichodemus le despendi
Et a Joseph si le rendi.
Ses plaies prisent a saignier;
Cest vaissial fist aparellier,   36
Ens degouterent sans mentir,
Vos le porés ja bien veïr.
Et sacrement fist ens Jhesu
Le jor del jusdi absolu.   40
  Ore, biaus niés, si est bien drois,
Ains que vos avant en saçois,
Que vos corone d'or portés
Sor vostre cief et rois serés;   44
Car ne vivrai mais que tier jor.
Ensi plaist il al Creator."
Adont en vait a son erale
U la corone ert delitable,   48
Et les ados a aportés
En sa chapele de biautés.
Percheval sacra et beni
Et sa corone li rendi.   52
Rois fu Perchevaus apelés,
De trois roiames coronés,
Ains que li rois fust trespassés;
Mais al quart jor fu enterrés.   56
De chevaliers trois mil i ot
A l'enterer, car a Deu plot.

WILLIAM ROACH,
University of Pennsylvania

Notes

[1] *La Continuation de Perceval*, ed. Mary Williams, 2 v. (Classiques français du moyen âge, 28, 50; Paris, 1922-25), I, 214.

[2] The First Continuation is extant in several redactions, which vary in length from about 9,400 to more than 19,600 lines. For a description of the redactions, see *The Continuations of the Old French Perceval of Chrétien de Troyes*, ed. William Roach, Vol. I (Philadelphia, 1949), pp. xxxiv-xxxix; Hilmar Wrede, *Die Fortsetzer des Gralromans Chrestiens von Troyes* (Göttingen diss., 1952), pp. 52-62; and *Les Romans du Graal dans la littérature des XII ͤ et XIII ͤ siècles* (Paris, 1956), pp. 107-18.

[3] The names Pseudo-Wauchier and Wauchier de Denain for the first and second continuators have now been quite generally abandoned in favor of the simple numerical designations; cf. A. W. Thompson, in *Arthurian Literature in the Middle Ages*, edited by R. S. Loomis (Oxford, 1959), p. 206.

[4] The standard critical edition of Chrétien's *Perceval* is by Alfons Hilka, *Der Percevalroman (Li Contes del Graal) von Christian von Troyes* (Halle, 1932). Quotations from the *Perceval* in this article are from my own more recent edition, *Le Roman de Perceval ou le Conte du Graal*, 2d ed. (Textes Littéraires Français, 71; Geneva and Paris, 1959), which is based on MS. 12576 of the Bibliothèque Nationale (MS. *T*), but which preserves the line-numbering of Hilka's edition.

[5] This episode occurs in all the redactions of the First Continuation, with only minor variations in the details of the story; cf. *Continuations*, I, vss. 12878-13002; II, vss. 16997-17114; III, MS. *L*, vss. 6923-7038; MS. *A*, vss. 6906-7018.

[6] *Ibid.*, II, vss. 3891-3923, 17439-48.

[7] Charles Potvin, *Perceval le Gallois*, V (Mons, 1870), vss. 34884-34908.

[8] *Ibid.*, V, vs. 34775; cf. Chrétien's *Perceval*, vss. 3245, 6414.

[9] The best discussion of the numerous complications and contradictions which were occasioned by the introduction of the vengeance motif and the sword-test is still that given by Richard Heinzel, *Ueber die französischen Gralromane* (Vienna, 1891), pp. 29-31.

[10] The MS. sigla here used were established by Hilka in his edition of the *Perceval* (see above, n. 4). They have been accepted by all subsequent editors and critics.

[11] A very full description of MS. *K* is given by Edmund Stengel in his edition of *Durmart le Galois* (Bibliothek des literarischen Vereins in Stuttgart, CXVI; Tübingen, 1873), pp. 448-67. Cf. also *Continuations*, I, p. xix.

[12] Cf. E. Brugger, *ZFSL*, LIII (1930), 435-36; and Wrede, *op. cit.*, pp. 129-30.

[13] Notably Gustav Gröber, in *Grundriss der romanischen Philologie*, Vol. II (Strassburg, 1902), Abt. I, pp. 506 and 509.

[14] Potvin's text is somewhat less accurate than Rochat's in details of spelling. He says in a note on p. 37 of his Bibliography: "Je dois mes renseignements sur les deux MS. de Berne à M. H. Michelant, qui a bien voulu mettre à ma

disposition, à Paris, la copie qu'il en a faite." Because of the rather surprising similarities between Potvin's and Rochat's texts, one is tempted to believe that Michelant might have copied some of his information from Rochat. Potvin makes no mention of the Bern conclusion in the notes to his edition of the Second Continuation in Vol V (Mons, 1870) of his *Perceval le Gallois,* but at the end of a rather sketchy chapter entitled "Les Manuscrits" in Vol. VI (Mons, 1871), he says: "Nous avons collationné à Berne les deux manuscrits qui s'y trouvent et que nous connaissions déjà, grâce à l'obligeance de M. Henri Michelant" (p. lxxxiii).

[15] Because of the omission of these two lines by Rochat and Potvin, the reference to Longinus in the Bern MS. is not noted by Carl Kröner, *Die Longinuslegende, ihre Entstehung und Ausbreitung in der französischen Litteratur* (Münster diss., 1899), nor by Rose J. Peebles, *The Legend of Longinus in Ecclesiastical Tradition and in English Literature, and Its Connection with the Grail* (Bryn Mawr, 1911).

Readings from Folios 94 to 131
MS. Cotton Vitellius A XV

The three Old English prose texts recorded in the *Beowulf* codex, folios 94-131,[1] were edited by Stanley Rypins for the Early English Text Society in the hope of "producing an edition which, from a textual standpoint, might be considered authoritative."[2] In this EETS edition each printed page represents a page, each printed line a line of the MS. text. The sequence of texts, however, is the reverse of that in the MS.: Alexander's letter comes first, the Christopher fragment last. Moreover, the editor printed the misplaced folios 110-17 in their proper place between folios 125 and 126. Again, the editor did not reproduce the spacing of the MS. text; his spacing serves only to keep words apart. Thus, line 1 of fol. 98v reads S *eoland buend onfruman* in the MS. but *Seo land-buend on fruman* in the printed text.[3]

Rypins represents by & the MS. abbreviation for *ond* or *and*. He uses the circumflex to represent the accent mark more commonly represented by the acute. He uses italics to mark not only his expansions of the MS. abbreviations but also letters more or less illegible. His square brackets set off conjectural restorations of the text. An italic letter so set off represents a letter present but wholly illegible in the MS.

In the following paragraphs, each devoted to one page of the MS. text, the readings are set off by slanting lines, *R* marking Rypins's, *M* my own readings. Three dots indicate that the reading gives less than a full line of the text. *R*'s notes, when quoted, are set off by quotation marks. My comments, if any, follow the readings or quotations. My readings and comments grew out of a study of (1) the MS. itself and

(2) photographs of the MS. pages, taken by British Museum photographers. In general, I take up only points in which I disagree with *R*, but now and then I depart from this principle.

Fol. 94r. 1. *R* . . . ac þ[u / *M* . . . ac þu *ea*[rt / The *u* of *þu* is somewhat distorted by a crease but certain; I read *ea* at the edge but not with certainty. 7. *R* . . . swungon g[e / *M* . . . swungon . . . / The letter after *swungon* is not *g*. 10. *R* . . . cemp[an / *M* . . . cempa[n / 12. *R* . . . acwellan / *R* did not note the point that follows *acwellan* in the MS. 13. *R* . . . cynig[e / *M* . . . cyninge / Of the last two letters only traces remain, covered with transparent paper. 14. *R* . . . geþ[oh]t / *M* . . . geþo[h]t / The last letter looks like *o* but must have been meant for *t*. 15. *R* . . . tintre[go / *M* . . . tintreg[o / 16. *R* . . . beobrea[d / *M* . . . beo bread / A bit of the *d* can be seen. 17. *R*'s footnote: "After *scamol* a letter (*l?*) seems to have been erased. After *se* there seems to have been either *o* or *t*." The erased letter, if any, is certainly not *l;* after *se* comes what looks like a point, probably accidental. 18. *R* . . . wæs / *M* . . . wæs / 19. *R* . . . aset[tan / *M* . . . asettan / The second *t* is a bit distorted but certain; the last two letters are not readily legible but seem to be *an*. 20. *R* . . . crist[o / *M* . . . cristo /.

Fol. 94v. 3. *R* fyre[s . . . / *M* fyres . . . / The *e* is partly, the *s* wholly covered but the top of the *s* can be made out through the paper covering. 4. *R* . . . fulle . eles . . . / What looks like a point here is part of the *e* of *fulle*, the end of the final bottom flourish. 9. *R* s]te[fn]e . . . / Most of this word is covered but parts of *t* and of the two *e*'s and the top of *f* can be seen. 16. *R* f]orus . . . / The *f* is faint and partly covered but can be seen.

Fol. 95a. 2. *R* . . . nigoþa[*n* / The *a* is shrunken and the *n* covered. 3. *R* . . . hyn*e* / This word is progressively shrunken and its *e* nearly all covered. 11. *R* . . . &swarode . . . / The *s* was put in later but seemingly by the same hand with the same ink. 12. *R* . . . mæg*e* / A hole in the leaf, over *g*, has damaged the part of *æ* that overhangs *g;* third leg of *m* faded; *g* somewhat faded; *e* shrunken. 14. *R* . . . *t*[i]*d*[e / The *e* and part of the *d* covered but visible through paper; whole word can be made out. 15. *R* . . . byst / Only part of the *s* legible and this letter should be italicized. 16. *R* . . . of *þyssum* / Here *of* and *y* are barely legible; *þ* is clear, and *ss* can be read, though very faint except at the top; of *um* only the very top can be made out. 17. *R* . . . bysen þar*a* / Top of *s* faint, final *a* somewhat shrunken and partly covered.

Fol. 95v. 1. *R* word & *o*nsaga . . . / *M* word & onsaga / All the letters are clear. 2. *R* . . . ðe gegear / These words are separated by a point in the MS. 4. *R* symle . . . / This word is not clear in the MS. but comes out clearly in photograph. 7. *R* Se] . . . / *M* Se . . . / Most of this word covered and upper part gone but there can be little if any doubt about the reading. 8. *R* m[*i*]celnesse . . . / In the photograph the *i* is a bit faint but clear. 9. *R* m*a*nnes . . . / M mannes . . . / All letters clear in photograph. 13. *R* þa *s*cotedon . . . / First word shrunken and top of *þ* and s covered. 21. This line, the last on the page, is blank except at the extreme right, where some recent interpolator, in a modern imitation of the insular hand, wrote the word *forðon,* followed by a point and the figure 96, but the 6 of this figure has been crossed out and the figure 1 set over it. The next folio in the MS. as it now stands is 91, original foliation, but 96, present foliation. This folio begins with the word *forðon*. *R*'s note on the interpolation is inaccurate. The deed was obviously done after the adoption, in 1884, of the present foliation of the MS.

Fol. 96r. 1. *R* . . . wolde / The *de* is covered but can be read through the paper covering. 2. *R* . . . dæge / There is a point after this word in the MS. 3. *R* . . . halga[n / The last letter is shrunken and covered but can be read through the paper covering. 7. *R* . . . twa / Leaf torn between *t* and *w*; last two letters shrunken and mostly covered but can be read through paper. 11. *R* . . . þ[u / *M* . . . *þu* / Bottom part of this word covered but top part readily legible. 13. *R* . . . dryht[en / *M* . . . dryht*e*[n / Here the *e* is partly, the *n* wholly covered. 17. *R* . . . ny[m / Part of *y* and whole of *m* covered; *m* shrunken and its third leg gone; rest can be seen through covering but not well. 18. *R* . . . gemartyro[d / *M* . . . gemartyrod / Whole word clear in photograph. 19. *R* . . . þine / H[erzfeld] þine [twa] / There is room for *twa* at the end of the line and what looks like traces of *wa* can be seen in the MS., but the photograph shows nothing after *þine* and *R*'s reading must be accepted.

Fol. 96v. 2. *R* *f*ram þinra . . . / The first two letters are shrunken and the bottom of *f* is a bit displaced to the left, but *r*, at least, is plain and needs no italics; the *a* might have been italicized, since it is badly faded and hard to make out; in *þinra* the bottoms of *þ* and *r* are faded. 3. *R* *t*]id . . . / This word is badly shrunken and partly covered by opaque paper but the right-hand part of the *ti* ligature can be made out and the *d* is partly visible. 4. *R* on]fêhð . . . / *M* o]*n*fehð . . . / Part of the *n* is covered but part can be seen; the mark over *e* may be the dot of an accent but is more likely not. 5. *R* to drihtne . . . / *R* failed to note the point after *drihtne*. 15. *R* þær . . . / First letter ð, partly covered and most of cross-mark gone or covered but the right end of this stroke remains.

Fol. 97r. 3. *R* . . . hyr[a / A hole in the leaf has damaged *r*, which besides is faded at bottom; *a* covered but can be seen dimly through paper. 11. *R* . . . lar*e* / Last letter nearly all gone and shrunken remnants covered; *re* in spite of *R* is not a ligature. 13. *R* . . . hundteontig . & fiftyne / Where *R* has a point the MS. has a slanting row of three dots. There *is* a point (not noted by *R*) at the end of the line. 15. *R* . . . hyn[e / Leaf torn between *y* and *n*, damaging *y* somewhat; *ne* shrunken and part of *e* gone, rest covered but visible through paper.

Fol. 97v. 2. *R* on þrowigende . . . / The þr is unmistakable, though the very bottom of þ is covered and the long leg of *r* is faded at the foot. 4. *R* cr*i*stoforus . . . / The *i* is plain in the photograph. 19. *R* . . . noht . . . / MS. has *naht*.

Fol. 98r. 2. *R* . . . will[an / The last two letters are covered but traces of them can be seen, though not identified, through the paper. 3. *R* full . . . / The first letter was first written as a long *s* and then changed to *f*. 8. *R* . . . & *ge* / The *ge* is perfectly clear in the photograph. 12. *R* . . . *of* / The last letter is almost certainly *f* rather than *n*. It was badly damaged by a tear in the leaf and only a part of its left side remains. 16. *R* . . . tear[*um* / *M* . . . tear*u*[m / The *u* is partly covered but its first leg is plain.

WONDERS OF THE EAST

Fol. 98v. *R* f]rom . . . / *M* *f*rom . . . / Most of *f* is gone or covered but part of its top is still visible. 3. *R* l]ande . . . / *M* *l*ande . . . / Most of *l* is gone or covered but its bottom can still be seen. 4. *R* rime þæs . . . / There is a point in the MS. between these words. 5. *R* tæles þe . . . / First letter looks like *g* and the scribe may have written *g* by mistake (dittography) instead of the *t* that the context requires; the MS. has a point after *tæles*. 11. R overlooked the point at the end of this line.

Fol. 99r. 4. R . . . leo[nes / M . . . leon / Second leg of *n* gone, and first leg covered, along with most of *o* and part of *e*, but the covered parts can be seen through the paper. 12. R . . . eal his / Some of *l*, much of *h*, most of *i*, and all that is left of *s* are covered but the covered parts can be seen through the paper; *s* is damaged but fragments remain.

Fol. 99v. 1. R . . . deor / R's footnote, "MS: ðeor," is in error. There is something that might be taken for a cross-mark but it lacks the usual head at the right end and is probably not a cross-mark. Above it and parallel to it is another mark, even fainter but of the same kind. 4. R *þe*]os . . . / First two letters covered but traces of capital "thorn" can be made out through the paper. 6. R *leo*hte . . . / The first four letters are shrunken and the top line of the *e* can hardly be made out. 12. R *from* . . . / The bottom of *fr* is gone and the *m* torn. What looks like a point after *babiloniā* is only the end of the flourish of final *a*.

Fol. 100r. 3. R . . . bið / The last letter is shrunken, and a bit damaged by a hole in the leaf. 9. R . . . mænego / R does not note the point after this word. The point, the *o*, and part of the *g* are covered but visible through the paper.

Fol. 100v. 9. R & . . . ûp / The abbreviation is torn but both top corners and part of the down stroke can be made out. The mark over *up* is unlike the usual accent and is probably accidental. 13. R . . . stedan þa . . . / The MS. has a point after *stedan*.

Fol. 101r. 16. R Betwih . . . / M Betwih / Part of the capital is covered but the covered part can be seen through the paper.

17. *R* . . . bryxontes / *R* in a footnote says "*tes* very faint" but the tip of the *s* is plain enough.

Fol. 101v. 1. *R* On . . . mænego / Capital *o* is partly covered. The first part of the digraph *æ* is blurred by what seems to have been an imperfect erasure. The scribe may have tried to turn *æ* into *e* by erasing the *a* part of the ligature. 5. *R* fota lange & hy hab / The first letter is partly covered but the covered part can be seen, indistinctly, through the opaque paper. *R* did not note the point after *lange* in the MS. 8. *R* s]et . . . / *M* f]et . . . / 21-22. *R*'s footnote: "At bottom of page in a later hand: oððe him hw[ilc man] folgian[de]." These catchwords make lines 21 and 22, in the right-hand corner of the lower margin. They anticipate the first words of fol. 102r and were presumably added after the foliation of the MS. became disturbed (viz., when fol. 101 came to be followed by fol. 104). Cf above, under fol. 95v.

Fol. 102r. 2. *R* . . . gewende / There is a point after *gewende* in MS. 17. *R* footnote: "Lacuna after *ran*" / There is an abrasion here and the right-hand upper corner of *n* is gone but there is no hole in the leaf.

Fol. 102v. On this page there are a number of interlinear words in a Middle English hand. The interlineations are not true glosses. In part they give a modernized handwriting only and in part they also give a modernized phonetic form; in only one case is the interlineation a word different from the one it annotates. *R* gives an inadequate account of the interlineations. In the following I proceed without regard to his note on the subject. 2. Over *heafdū* and *habbað* are written *hefdū* and *habbyt*. 3. Over *on hyra breostum* is written *on hyre brestū*. 5. Over *eahta* is written *at afote;* the space between *at* and *afote* is filled by the long upright stroke of the *h* of *eahta*.

It seems possible that *at a* serves to annotate *eahta;* certainly *fote* annotates the *fota* of the next line (see below). One would have expected not *at a* but *ahta* or *atha* (the *h* properly comes before *t* but was often set after *t* instead), but perhaps the annotator thought it needless to write *h*, since the upper part of the long stroke of the *h* of *eahta* (the word he was annotating) stood right after the *t* of his interlineation. 6. Over *fota* there are traces of an interlineation, presumably *fote*. It seems not unlikely that the annotator by anticipation wrote *fote* as well as *at a* over the *eahta* of line 5 (which ends its line) and then repeated the *fote* in its proper place, over the *fota* at the head of the sixth line. Later, when the MS. leaf was torn, only traces of the interlineation over *fota* were left. Over *lange* the annotator wrote what looks like *ling* plus some illegible letter. But what I read as *i* may be merely a bad *a*. Over the *eahta* of this line (more precisely, over its latter part) is written what looks like *cte* but here only the *t* is certain. 7. Over *fota brade* is written *fote brode*. 11-12. The interlineations here seem to be in a different hand. 11. Over the *ar* of *Ðar* is written *þar;* over *þa, þa;* over *beoð, beth;* over *on, on;* over *lenge, lenþe,* with *g* (or possibly *c*) superscript between *n* and *þ*. 12. Over *fot* is written *fot;* over *mæla, mele;* over *lange, lange;* over *⁊, x̄;* over *fiftiges, fifty*. After *fiftiges* there is a point (not noted by *R*) but this is obscured by an ink smear. 16. *R* F]rom . . . / Traces of an erased small *f* can be seen; a capital was set in the margin to replace the small letter but this capital is nearly all gone.

Fol. 103r. 1. *R* . . . miclan / The *i* is torn through and the top of the *l* is gone; some of the *m*, nearly all of what is left of *i*, and the upper parts of the other letters are covered but can be seen through the paper; there is a point (not noted by *R*) at the end of the line. 10. *R* footnote: "MS: el reord . ge m̄" / There is no point in the MS. between *reord* and *ge*. 18. *R* . . .

læssan / The last two letters are shrunken but clear. 20. *R* does not note the dim point after the numeral.

Fol. 103v. 1. *R* On þisse . . . / *M* On þisse / The first s (long) torn in two and the top of þ covered. 2. *R* footnote: "MS.: lawernbeabe" / *R* ignores the point in the MS. under the first *b*. The scribe wrote *beabe* (by dittography) instead of *beame* and by mistake pointed the first *b* (instead of the second) for correction but the correction was never made. 8. *R* .c.li & þæs . . . / *M* .c.li & þæs / The point after *i* is very dim in MS. but clear in photograph. 9. *R* Ðon[ne is s]um ealond / *M* Ðonne is sum ealond / The su is not perfect but there can be no doubt of the reading.

Fol. 104r. 1. *R* . . . beswicað . . . æfte[r / The ð is plain and part of the *r* is visible, though covered. 17. *R* . . . hræd-lece swa is / *M* . . . hrædlice swa is / 20. *R* . . . man / There is a point after *man* in the MS.

Fol. 105r. 20. *R* . . . leon / There is a point after *leon* in the MS.

Fol. 105v. 1. *R* & loxas . . . / *R* did not note the point after *loxas* in the MS. 7. There is a point (not noted by *R*) at the end of the line. 15. *R* &]hi . . . / MS. has *hy*, though the *h* is shrunken and covered and not legible with certainty. The long stroke of *y* is badly faded except for its tip.

Fol. 106r. 11. *R* . . . beo / *M* . . . beoð / 20. R don fela cyninga ./ MS. has a point before as well as after *cyninga*.

Fol. 106v. 8. *R* al]exander . . . / The *d* is plain in the photograph, though it looks like *n* in the MS.! 10. *R* driende . . . / *M* drende . . . / 14. *R* s]tanas . . . / *M* stanas . . . / The first *s* is legible enough; *R* in his footnote wrongly says that there is "only a trace" of it. 17. *R* sweartes hyiwes on onsyne / The *e* of *hyiwes* was freshened by a later hand, who turned it into an epsilon-like character. The *s* of *onsyne* was written too close to the preceding *n* and a later hand gave this *n* a new second leg, closer to the first.

ALEXANDER'S LETTER TO ARISTOTLE

Fol. 107r. 10. *R* footnote, "MS.: freon nis se" / The MS. actually has *frecni nis se* or possibly *frecin nis se* and *R*'s emendation *frecennissee* is needless. 20. *R* . . . þeoh / MS. has *þeah,* with a squarish *a* unlike the scribe's usual triangular *a* but practically identical with his *a* in *gleawnis* 107v1 and *fram* 108r13, both read *a* by *R*. See also below, under 109r.

Fol. 107v. 1. *R* . . . naniges / *M* . . . næniges / 4. *R* . . . ic . in / The dot between *ic* and *in* is very small and probably accidental. 14. *R* . . . æteowed / MS. has two small dots after this word. 18. *R* . . . hiowa / MS. has a small dot after this word.

Fol. 108r. 1. *R* . . . hwæt (footnote, "Part of *t* gone") / The *t* is practically whole. 3. *R* . . . rihtes / There is a point after this word, covered but visible through the paper. 4. *R* . . . m[id / This word is shrunken, scorched, and displaced upward; the first leg of the *m* is torn off; of *i* only the upper part is left; a trace of *d* remains. 12. *R* urum weorode . for / After *weorode* there is a colon in the MS., not a single dot.

Fol. 108v. 3. *R* t]um þê ic þe sende . . . / The first þe (rel. pron.) may have an accent mark by mistake for þe "thee" (next word but one).

Fol. 109r. 1. *R* . . . læton . . . / *M* . . . lætan . . . / MS. has the squarish *a* mentioned above (under 107r). 2. *R* . . . þæ[m (footnote: "No trace of *m* visible.") / The first leg of *m* can still be seen. 20. *R* . . . metdon. Ond'his healle / *R*'s *metdon* is a traditional reading, taken from earlier editors, but

the MS. has *in eodon* here, translating Latin *inuasimus*. The
final *e* of *healle* is torn in two and its middle part is gone; a
later hand wrote another *e* over the tear in the leaf.

Fol. 109v. 2 *R* ro]n . . . / The second letter is *a*, not *o*. It is
covered but visible through the opaque paper. 5. *R* be þ]æm
. . . / A bit of the rounded part of þ can be seen at the edge of
the paper framing. 7. *R* gr]es . . . / The *e* is practically whole,
though shrunken. 9. *R* g]yldenne . . . / A bit of the bottom
of *g* can be seen; a bit of *y* covered but covered part can be
made out through the opaque paper. 20. The reading *hwite*
at the head of this line is clear in the photograph, though not
in the MS.

Fol. 110r. 1. *R* . . . bryne / A letter that looks like a shrunken
g follows *bryne*. 6. *R* . . . & . lii / There is a point after as
well as before *lii;* it is covered but visible through the paper.
14. *R* . . . eac missenlices wæs . . . / There is a point between *missenlices* and *wæs* in the MS. 16. *R* . . . swulton mid
. . . / There is a point between *swulton* and *mid* in the MS.
17. *R* beorendan lyfte þe . . . / There is a point before þe
in the MS.

Fol. 110v. 3. *R* ne ælc . . . / The *æ* of *ælc* has over it a
macron-like mark that *R* does not note. 7. *R* ces . . . / Before
c the *æ* of *þæt* (110r7) shows through the leaf. 8. *R* b]runes
. . . / M *brunes* . . . / Only part of bottom of *b* is visible
verso but the whole of the rounded part of the letter can be
seen recto through the leaf; the stem of the *b* is gone. 9. *R*
*c*lea . . . / M c]lea . . . / What looks like the top of *c* is only
the *æ* of *stræ* recto (110r9) showing through the leaf. 13. *R*
wæron mid . . . / There is a faded point after *wæron* in the
MS.

Fol. 111r. 8. *R* . . . fæst (footnote: "After *t* something un-
decipherable.") / M . . . fæste[n / After *t* there is a frag-

ment of a letter that I take for *e;* cf *þæs londes fæstenum* 111v.
9. *R* lond & . . . / *M* lond . & . . . /

Fol. 111v. 2. *R* cen ða . . . gemæro / MS. has point after *cen*
and colon after *gemæro.* 4. *R* hæfdon micle . . . / *M* hæfdon
micel . . . / 5. *R* . . . wicode / MS. has point after *wicode.*
10 *R* . . . truwode þonne / MS. has point after *truwode.*

Fol. 112r. 1. *R* . . . sæde . / At the end of the line is a mark
that looks like the abbreviation for *ond.*

Fol. 112v. 2. *R* . . . gehyrde / MS. has a point after *gehyrde.*
6. *R* . . . wolde & . . . / MS. has point after *wolde.* 8. *R* s]wa
. . . / *M* swa . . . / Most of *s* gone but tip remains; it can also
be seen recto through parchment. All but bottom of *w* covered
but can be seen through paper. 20. *R* . . . kyning . / There
are two points at the end of the line, though one is faded;
over the heavy point stands an ink mark.

Fol. 113v. 2. *R* s]ecgan . . . / *M* secgan . . . / The *s* is covered but can be seen through the opaque paper when the leaf
is held up to light. 6. *R* . . . duna be . . . / MS. has point
between *duna* and *be.* 9. *R* be þæm sæ . . . / M be þæm sæ̂
. . . / 19-20. These lines are clear in the photograph, though
not in the MS.:

> 19 don adrogad . & fen & cannon & hreod
> 20 weoxan ða cwom þær semninga sū

Fol. 114r. MS has point after *breostum* 6, *dæges* 19, and *noman*
20.

Fol. 114v. 13. *R* . . . swin gesawon / MS. has accent over *i*
of *swin.*

Fol. 115r. 10. MS. has point (perhaps accidental) at end of
line. 11. *R* sona . . . stan / Mark over o may be accent,
though too far to left; there is a perfectly normal accent over

the *a* of *stan* (overlooked by *R*). 18. MS. has point at end of line.

Fol. 115v. 19. *R* . . . geweox on / MS. has macron-like mark over *g;* presumably the scribe started to write *ge* by abbreviation and then absentmindedly wrote it in full. 20. *R* þone æfen ða cwom . . . / *M* þone æfen . ða cpom . . . / The *p* is an obvious scribal error for wynn.

Fol. 116r. 1. *R* . . . feolle / *M* . . . feolle / Final *e* is shrunken and scorched but readily legible. 8. *R* . . . us . . . / MS. has accent over *u* of *us; R* notes it but takes it only for a meaningless dot. 20. *R* . . . gode siðþan / MS. has point after *gode.*

Fol. 117r. 16. MS. has point at end of line.

Fol. 117v. R . . . to / MS. has point after *to.* 3. *R* mær]lices . . . / Traces of *r* can be made out through the opaque paper. 4. *R* tað] / *M* ta]ð / Traces of *ð* can be seen through the opaque paper and also recto through the leaf. 8. *R s*[p]recende . . . / *M* sprecende . . . / The first two letters are covered but can be read with ease when the leaf is held up to light.

Folio 118r. 2. *R* . . . ðar inge / *M* . . . ðær inge / 7. *R* fatu & . . . / MS. has point after *fatu.* 12. *R* . . . lond mid . . . / MS. has point after *lond.*

Fol. 118v. R . . . fleondon porru*m* of / MS. . . . fleondon . porrū . of / The proper name is set off by points. 10. *R* ladþeowa & . . . / MS. has point after *ladþeowa.*

Fol. 119r. 9. *R* . . . nytlicra / *M* . . . nytlicra / *R*'s footnote "Lower half of *l* rubbed away" is inaccurate; the lower part is faint but the whole can be made out.

Fol. 120v. 4. *R* ða . . . / MS. has point before *ða.* 6. *R* & wintreow . . . / *M* & pintreow . . . / 7. *R* . . . wridode / MS. has point after *wridode.*

Fol. 121r. 3. R . . . ungemet / After *t* there is another letter, seemingly a shrunken and otherwise damaged *e*. 20. R . . . þa in . . . / The *n* seems to be a scribal misreading of *u*, and *þa iu* is a variant form of *þa geo* "already."

Fol. 121v. 1. R .o . . . / M t]o . . . / If the MS. actually once had *to*, this was presumably the adverb, in the sense "besides." If so, modern punctuation would require a colon after *to*. 14. R . . . þus ic . . . / The original reading was *ꝥ us ic* but this was changed to *þus ic* by rubbing out the cross-mark. 20. R . . . treowcynne þe on þære / MS. has point after *treow-cynne*.

Fol. 122r. 2. R & geworht . . . / R fails to note the point set below the final flourish of the *t*. 13. R fæstor hyddan . . . / MS. has point after *hyddan*. 20. R mera . . . / MS. has *nicra* (see Norman Davis, *RES*, NS, IV (1953):141 ff.). R's reading goes back to Cockayne.

Fol. 122v. 14. R . . . byman . . . / R mentions a "heavy dot" over the *y* but does not take it for an accent. Actually there are two marks over the *y*, the usual dot and the accent.

Fol. 124r. 17. R . . . reode su / MS. has point after *reode*.

Fol. 124v. 7. R . . . wunnan huru . . . / MS. has point after *wunnan*. 9. R . . . ehton / MS. has point after *ehton*.

Fol. 125r. 8. R . . . swulton / MS. has point after *swulton*. 12. R does not note that the numeral xx is enclosed in points. 18. R micle & . . . / After *micle* there is a point on an erasure.

Fol. 125v. 6. R þ]ar . . . / MS. has *æ*, not *a*. 12. R . . . becwom / MS. has *be cwoṁ*, which sohuld be expanded to *becwomen*, late OE for *becwomon*. 17. MS. has point before as well as after *dentes tyrannum*. 19. There is a point, perhaps accidental, at the end of this line.

Fol. 126r. 1. Photograph shows *mec þa* at end of line, though the *þa* cannot be read with certainty. 2. R . . . me[r / M mær / Only part of the r is visible. 7. *R* . . . pore / There is an erasure after *o*, presumably of some letter to be replaced by *r*, but this *r* was not written in. 14. *R* . . . ðæm . . . / MS. has accent over æ.

Fol. 126v. 1. *R* hie] wæron / MS. has *wæran*. 12. *R* . . . earan him þurh þy / MS. has point after *earan* .15. R . . . gegerwed / MS. has double point (..) after *gegerwed*. 19. *R* . . . wolde . þa . . . / MS. has triangle of points (not single point) after *wolde*.

Fol. 127r. 2. *R* . . . wif (*R* footnote, "MS.: wig after which a fragment of a letter") / *M* . . . wig*f* / Most of *f* gone but much of the long vertical stroke remains. The *g* here seems to be the familiar spelling device for marking the preceding vowel long. The context requires the gen. pl. *wifa*. 5. *R* na mid me þrio . . . / MS. has point before *þrio*. 9. R . . . so / Cf. *sole* (fol. 138v5), where likewise we find *o* for *ā* (late OE rounding). 15. *R* treowu gongan þa . . . / MS. has point after *gongan*. 20. *R* . . . monan / MS. has point after *monan*.

Fol. 127v. 4. *R* hea]nisse . . . . / *M* h]*eah*nisse . . . . / There is a great tear in MS. before *n*, leaving only the top of the second *h*; the shrunken remains of *ea* are displaced a bit downward. 6. *R* . . . wende þ / MS. has point after *wende*. 8. *R* de] . . . / *R* says, "Of *d* a little of the upper stroke remains" but I find no trace of this stroke.

Fol. 128r. 1. *R* footnote: "After *ænig* is an unintelligible stroke." Here the *c* of [*be*]*cuman* verso shows through the leaf. 2. *R* ten cwealde . . . worhte / MS. has points after *ten* and *worhte*. 5. *R* re ondswarege ondwyrdum þara / MS. has *re ondsware ge ondwyrdum þara* 14. MS. has slanting stroke, not dot (as *R* would have it) over *u* of *ut*.

Fol. 128v. 4. The *cwæd* of the MS. (which *R* rightly keeps) is of interest; compare ME *quod*.

Fol. 129r. 8. *R* . . . acwellanne / *M* . . . acwellanne / Most of *ll* gone (by abrasion) but tops and bottoms left (*R* has no note).

Fol. 129v. 17. *R* . . . getreowestan / MS. has point after this word. 19. *R* . . . gân . . . / The mark over the *a* does not look like the usual accent mark. 20. R se bisceop þa . . . / MS. has points before and after *bisceop*.

Fol. 130r. 2. *R* . . . wæd / MS. has *pæd* (by mistake, of course) but *R* fails to say that his *w* is an emendation. 3. *R* . . . genihtsumiað & be ðæm / MS. has point after *genihtsu-miað*. 7. *R* . . . bylifigeað & þon*ne* / MS. has point after *lifigeað*. 8. *R* . . . hie / MS. has point at end of line (after blank space). 19. *R* dan scoldon . þa . . . / MS. has semicolon after *scoldon*.

Fol. 130v. 11. This line ends with the symbol for *ond* (not noted by *R*). 14. *R* . . . ne ne . . . / MS. has a smeared *c* set between these words and a bit below them.

Fol. 131r. 1. The last word in the line is clearly *wop*, though part of *o* and most of *p* are gone. The first letter is wynn (not *p*, as *R* says in his footnote). 19. *R* . . . lifes & eac / MS. has point after *lifes*.

Fol. 131v. 7. *R* fin;t . . , / MS. finit . . , /

KEMP MALONE,
Johns Hopkins University

Notes

[1] Fragment of Life of St. Christopher, fol. 94-98r; Wonders of the East, fol. 98v-106; Letter of Alexander the Great to Aristotle, fol. 107-31.

[2] Original Series, 161 (London, 1924), p. v.

[3] If, however, a word is divided between two lines in the MS., it is so divided in the printed text as well.

Some Notes on Anglo-Saxon Poetry

In an earlier paper on "The Theme of the Beasts of Battle in Anglo-Saxon Poetry," [1] I briefly discussed the function of the theme[2] in helping an oral singer to carry on and or to embellish his narrative. From the earlier paper it is clear that once fighting was to be discussed the singers were disposed to introduce as props the three beasts of battle, the wolf (*wulf*), the raven (*hræfn*) and the ern or sea eagle (*earn*). It is a priori most likely that Anglo-Saxon singers possessed many themes suitable for giving added point or appropriate embellishment to various recurrent situations, and like all the rest of the diction these would have been developed over centuries to facilitate the composition of traditional songs, that is, versified compositions with a non-Christian background, mostly stories going back to pre-conversion times,[3] as opposed to songs in similar meter and mainly similar diction with such new or non-traditional topics as saints' lives, biblical paraphrases, moral injunctions, and the like. Whereas it is obvious to me that the singers were able in a rather remarkable way to adapt much of the traditional diction to these "new" matters, it is likewise obvious that the traditional themes would only rarely be appropriate to such new topics. It is a happy chance that the beasts of battle turn up in the non-traditional songs *Elene*, *Exodus*, and *Judith*, where severe fighting takes place, thus providing us with more examples of this theme than one might reasonably have expected to find.

Like a formula, a theme must occur at least twice to be recognizable as such; and though the surviving traditional songs, particularly the so-called "heroic poems" among which the *Béowulf* song[4] are pre-eminent, may contain many a theme which we might recognize as such had we appreciably more

273

preserved traditional verse for it to turn up in, there are only two besides the beasts of battle which thus far I feel sure are themes. These are "the grateful recipient" and "the gesture of the raised shield and/or brandished spear," the latter used to introduce certain speeches.

I. THE GRATEFUL RECIPIENT

This theme lets the singer highlight the value and splendor of a gift by dwelling briefly on the pride which the recipient takes in it.

1. The first instance occurs in *Béowulf* 1024b-26 on the occasion of the giving of a splendid cup to the hero at the great banquet at Heorot (ll.1008b-1237a):

> Bío-wulf ȝeþaeg
> full on flette; ná hé þǽre feoh-ȝifte
> for scéotendum scamian þorfte

(Béowulf received the cup; he had no reason at all to be ashamed of that valuable gift in the presence of bowmen.)

2. Almost immediately after this (ll.1046-49) the same point is made in a general, somewhat impersonal way:

> Swá mannlíce mǽre þéoden,
> hord-weard hæleða heaðu-rǽsas ȝeald
> méarum and máðmum swá híe nǽfre man líehþ

(Thus in noble fashion did the illustrious prince [Hróthgár], treasure-guardian of warriors, repay onslaughts of battle with horses and treasures in a way that one will never find fault with them.)

3. Near the end of the visit to Gamle Lejre (ll.1880b-85a) the singer remarks on the hero's pride in the gifts received:

> Him Bío-wulf þanan,
> gúþ-rinc gold-wlanc, græs-moldan træd
> since hrœmiȝ . . .
> Þá wæs on gange ȝiefu Hróþ-gáres
> oft ȝe-eahtod

(Then [from Heorot] Béowulf, battle-warrior proud in his gold, walked along the turf. . . . Then as they went along, Hróthgár's gift [i.e., general munificence] was often praised.)

4. The last passage (1900-03a) is in some ways the most attractive with its account of the boatman's almost childlike pleasure in Béowulf's parting gift:

> Hé þǽm bát-wearde bunden golde
> sweord ȝesealde þæ hé siþþan wæs
> on medu-benće máðme þý weorðra,
> ierfe-láfe.

(He [Béowulf] gave the boatman a sword strapped with gold so that the latter was afterward the more distinguished on the mead-bench by virtue of the treasure, of the heirloom [sword].)

Though these passages are united in the theme in question, it is noticeable that, contrary to the case of the beasts of battle, there are no recurring formulas. The matter is put this way or that depending on the somewhat varied character of the particular situations involved. The point is, I assume, that the identity and number of gifts and persons and circumstances of the giving would in the nature of things be too varying to make any one or even a small group of special formulas useful to a singer.

II. THE GESTURE OF THE RAISED SHIELD
AND/OR BRANDISHED SPEAR

On Béowulf's arrival on the coast by Gamle Lejre in Denmark he is confronted by a Scielding coast-guard, who somewhat extensively interrogates the Gautish party on their intentions. The atmosphere is one of caution, not of hostility. The coast-guard introduces his speech with a gesture (ll.235-36):

> þeʒn Hróþ-gáres, þrymmum cweahte
> mæʒen-wude mundum, mæðel-wordum fræʒn

(Hróthgár's representative, he vigorously brandished a big wooden spear with his hands, asked with solemn words . . .).

If this were the only passage in the preserved corpus to introduce a speech with such a gesture, there would be little or no reason to suspect that one had to do anything like a theme. But this very gesture, occasionally elaborated by the simultaneous brandishing of a sword, to give solemnity to words that follow occurs five times in the *Maldon*, leaving no doubt as to what sort of literary device this is.

1. The first instance is in *Maldon* 42-44 where Beorhtnóth is speaking forcefully and angrily in reply to a Danish emissary; his gesture is made to reinforce his answer, not as any immediate physical threat:

> Beorht-nóþ *maðelode, bord hafenode*,
> wand wacne æsc, wordum mælde

(Beorhtnóth spoke, raised his shield, flourished his slender ash-wood spear, uttered words.)

The remaining instances occur in the last third of the surviving text which is essentially devoted to solemn reaffirmations of earlier vows (*bíotas*) of undying loyalty to the now deceased leader.

2.   Offa ȝemǽlde, æsc-holt ascóc
                              (*Maldon* 230)

(Offa spoke, shook his ash-wood spear.)

3.   Léof-sunu ȝemǽlde and his linde ahóf,
           bord to ȝebeorge   (*Maldon* 244-45a).

(Léofsunu spoke and raised his linden-wood shield, his protective shield.) It may be noted that *to ȝebeorge*, with the translative *to*, is adjectival in function; there is no question here of the shield serving as an immediate protection, hence not "as a protection."

4.   Dunnere þá cwæþ,   daroþ *acweahte*
                              (*Maldon* 255)

(Dunnere then spoke, brandished his spear.)

5.   Beorht-weald *maðelode, bord hafenode*—
           se wæs eald ȝenéat—æsc *acweahte*
                              (*Maldon* 309-10)

(Beorhtweald spoke, raised his shield—the latter was a tried retainer—he brandished his ash-wood spear.)

The wording of the *Béowulf* passage is, one might say, individual while the *Maldon* passages show certain similarities among one another and certain formulas and formulaic systems recur. All begin with an on-verse saying that so-and-so spoke, two (1, 5) with the familiar system *x maðelode*, two (2, 3) with the *x ȝemǽlde*. *Bord hafenode* occurs in 1 and 5, in both instances following an instance of the *x maðelode* system with which it rimes and almost forms a two-verse formula; the system *x* [for some word meaning spear] *acweahte* occurs in 4 and 5. The gestures in question are specific and limited, whence the emergence of formulas and formulaic systems is not surprising.

III. THE TEMPORARY MISINTERPRETATION

OF A SIGHT OR SOUND

I have already suggested that, had we more of the poetry, we might well see that various passages were in fact thematic. Generally speaking, however, it would be rather futile to start guessing around and grasping at this and that group of verses as possible, if unidentifiable themes. Yet this is precisely what I now propose to do on the basis of material far removed from Anglo-Saxon poetry. In the huge Karelo-Finnish corpus of traditional or oral poetry, for present purposes adequately represented in that interesting conflated and concatenated anthology, the *Kalevala*, there occurs a number of passages where a certain sight or sound is temporarily misinterpreted, this misinterpretation then being immediately corrected. The result of this device is to create suspense, then surprise, and the over-all effect can be rather nice. I will first quote two examples chosen at random from material published more fully elsewhere[5] and for a somewhat different purpose.

In the *Kalevala*, Poem 6, ll. 85-89, a brash young man Joukahainen, out to revenge himself on the eternal seer and singer Väinämöinen, is lurking about to shoot the latter on sight. One morning he sees a speck on the sea and asks himself:

> "Onko se iässä pilvi,
> päivän koite koillesessa?"

Ei ollut iässä pilvi
päivän koite koillesessa:
oli vanha Väinämöinen . . . .

("Is that a cloud in the east, daybreak in the northeast?" It was not a cloud in the east, daybreak in the northeast: it was old Väinämöinen. . . .) Later in the *Kalevala*, in Poem 21, ll. 12 . . . 17, Louhi, an almost Bergthóra-like grande dame and mistress of a great farm "North Farm" (*Pohjola*), hears a noise in the courtyard or home-field (ON *tún*); she asks herself:

"Suurtako sotaväkeä? . . .
ei ollut sotaväkeä,
oli suuri sulhaiskansa,
vävy keskellä väkeä . . .

("Is it a big armed force? . . . it was not an armed force; it was the bridegroom with his retinue, the son-in-law in the midst of his people. . . .)[6] It may be further noted that the device calls for a certain repetition in the negative to correct the wording used in the original question.

I would now take a jump to the opening lines (ll. 1-7a) of the *Finnesburg Fragment*:

. . . hornas biernaþ næfre."
Hléoðrode þá heaðu-ʒeong cyning:
    "Né þis ne dagaþ éastan né hér draca ne fléogeþ
né hér þisse healle hornas ne biernaþ,
ac hér forþ beraþ, fugolas singaþ,
ʒielleþ græʒ-hama, gúþ-wudu hlyneþ,
scield scæfte oncwiþ . . ."

(. . . gables are not burning at all." Then the king, inexperienced in battle, spoke: "Neither is the dawn coming up from the east nor is a dragon flying about nor are the gables of the hall burning; on the contrary [x] are carrying forward, birds [of battles?] are singing, the gray-coated one [wolf?] is howling, a battle-spear is whirring, shield parries shaft [of arrow?]. . . .) This passage offers many uncertainties of interpretation in detail, but nothing obscures the basic point that something has been seen (the gleam of armor and weapons in the moonlight? cf. ll. 7b-8),[7] which has been wrongly interpreted; and that Hnæf immediately sets out to correct this misapprehension and explains that it is the approach of armed men. This device of creating suspense may well be completely unique in the Anglo-Saxon poetic tradition, but since it is so very common in the Karelo-Finnish tradition one may perhaps not unreasonably at least ask whether this Anglo-Saxon passage may not reflect a traditional theme that might recur had we more of the traditional poetry.

IV. A NOTE ON THE EXCELLENCE OF THE *Maldon*

It is generally conceded that the *Maldon* is one of the most successful of the surviving Anglo-Saxon poems. I have, in fact, never known anybody, even including reluctant students, who did not confess to enjoying it, often to an almost extravagant degree. I should like to consider very briefly at least one reason for the poem's success. This reason is, I feel, not so much, or not necessarily, that it is the work of a singer of spectacular talent, but that it is the work of a singer singing about just the kind of material for which most of the diction was in the main originally created. A proper opportunity to exploit this traditional language to the full will give any singer the most favorable, best possible chance to produce a fine, fluent song, a song swifter paced and smoother running

than the careless care and giddy cunning of most lettered
poets writing in isochronous verse can produce.

The basis of the *Maldon* is a battle with hand-to-hand
fighting. Talk about weapons and equipment is in order, there
is a certain amount of seafaring terminology, the battle array
is up for consideration, and there is a reaffirmation by various
of the English principals of loyalty vows (*bíotas*) made in
former days to their now fallen leader, Beorhtnóth. As in the
song of Béowulf's death there are faithless retainers to be
castigated, and on occasion the language used recalls some
of Wígláf's words. In dealing with matters of this kind, so
traditional in character, the Anglo-Saxon singers must have
felt at their greatest ease and would naturally have performed
with corresponding facility and felicity. A rich supply of
formulas was at hand, and certain thematic materials were
ready for use as embellishments. Without the slightest intention of downgrading the singer of the *Maldon*, still less the
singers of the *Béowulf* songs, who are in a very similar
situation, I would at the same time hesitate to assume that
these were basically more competent or of greater talent than
many singers of non-traditional Anglo-Saxon songs, though
without some kind of competition on more or less equal
grounds no demonstration could be made along these lines.
In the religious songs the singers have had as best they could
to adapt a diction created for one purpose to quite another.
Indeed in the *Exodus* the story there told permits a very full
exploitation of the traditional diction, with the result that if
one were to substitute Germanic for biblical names one might
often think one had a traditional Germanic song of a high
order of excellence. But if one feels that, say, the *Elene* or
Juliana is a less successful work than the songs already
mentioned, one might do well to consider the limitations,
almost handicaps, under which the singer worked. Except in

the proem of the *Elene* dealing with Constantine's Balkan war, the singer had little opportunity to use the almost countless formulas and various themes and embellishing devices almost literally made to order for the singer of traditional tales. Give the singers of the *Béowulf* songs or of the *Maldon* the *Elene* story and one may seriously wonder if they could turn out a better job.

The wealth of compounds used by the *Béowulf* singers, and of course numerically many fewer by the *Maldon* singer, has often been remarked on and on occasion adduced as a sign of the singer's high inventive genius and the like.[8] From quite another point of view these can be viewed as a sort of weakness in the Anglo-Saxon poetic diction as opposed to chaster ways of the Norse singers of old.[9] Be that as it may, any examination of these will show that they are largely connected with warfare and the life of the comitatus and would be quite unusable in making verses about matters of religion or Christian morality whether the singer knew them or not.

FRANCIS P. MAGOUN, JR.,
Cambridge, Mass.

Notes

[1] *Neuphilologische Mitteilungen*, LVI (1955):81-90.

[2] *Op. cit.*, p. 83. See further Albert B. Lord, *The Singer of Tales* (Cambridge, Mass.: Harvard University Press, 1960), pp. 68 ff. ("The Theme"), where Lord at times seems to use the term "theme" almost for what folklorists describe as a motif (*Märchenmotif*). I prefer to think of a "theme" as something more limited in scope.

[3] As for instance the *Battle of Maldon*, composed certainly after the events of 991 and probably in the southwest of England.

[4] That the *Béowulf* may well be a concatenation of three songs see *Arv: Tidskrift för nordisk Folkminnesforskning—Journal of Scandinavian Folklore*, XIV (1958):95-101, esp. p. 101 *ad fin.*

[5] *Britannica: Festschrift für Hermann M. Flasdieck* (Heidelberg: Winter, 1960), pp. 183-85.

[6] Persons who do not read Finnish but who might care to consider the quoted passages in context can readily locate these in the line-for-line verse translation by the English entomologist William Forsell Kirby (1844-1912), *Kalevala* (Everyman's Library, 1907, and later printings).

[7] Such telltale sights were probably not uncommon in the past. Cf. the *Nibelungenlied*, stz. 1602, 2: *si sâhen in der vinster der liehten schilde schîn* "in the darkness they saw the gleam of the bright shields," and further stz. 1841.

[8] E.g., Arthur G. Brodeur, *The Art of Béowulf* (Berkeley: University of California Press, 1959), p. 6.

[9] F. P. Magoun, Jr., "Nominal Compounds in *Béowulf*," *Studies in English Philology: A Miscellany in Honor of Frederick Klaeber* (Minneapolis, 1929), pp. 73-78, esp. pp. 75-77.

A Middle English Medical Manuscript
from Norwich

The manuscript which is the subject of the present investigation is not entirely unknown to the world of scholarship. The first apparent mention of the volume is the brief notice given in the catalogue of the Phillipps manuscripts:[1] "Kalendarium. ¶ An English Poem on Medicine. *Incip.* 'These Lechys for seke mannys sake. Divers medicynys sumtyme gun make.' 18*mo. V. S.* xv. *in a blue paper case.*" Subsequently it appeared in two Sotheby sales (July 17, 1950, lot 27, and February 28, 1955, lot 169), being acquired, on the latter occasion, by the present writer. Since the manuscript was not recorded by Brown–Robbins,[2] and since it contains Middle English verse of medical interest, differing in minor details from related texts previously published, a full description of the volume seems to be warranted.

MS. 21, collection: Curt F. Bühler. Manuscript on vellum (6 1/8 x 4 1/2 inches. *Collation:* 1[6] (wants 1), 2[6] (wants 2-3); 3[8], 4[8] (wants 7-8); 5[8] (wants 3), 6-8[8], 9[8] (wants 8) = 61 leaves (folios i-ix; 1-52). *Note:* though leaves are wanting (possibly blank and cut away), there are no lacunae in the texts. Written by various hands in East Anglia, fifteenth century. Bound in the original binding of leather over oak boards, in a brown morocco case.

Contents: ff. i[r]-ii[r], blank.

ii[v], colored emblematical drawing (crown with spiral branches beneath, containing grotesques and mottoes). Three names in the same hand: Thomas Cotfold, Johannes Rothe, Robertus Halle;[3] also signature of Johannes Landes.

iii-vi, verses, proverbs, and medical recipes, English and Latin. Signature of Johannes Wylton on iii[r].

vii-ix, blank.

1-14, Calendar, Use of Norwich Cathedral; table for finding Easter; tables for finding Lunar (1429-1479) and Solar (1429-1462) eclipses.

15[r], recipe "ffor the tothe ache"; remainder of leaf, blank.

16, treatise on urines, English prose.[4]

17-25, Computus manualis:[5] "Incipit compotus manualis. In primis sciendum est quod pro littere dominicalis invencione secundum ordinem compoti . . . ffilius esto dei celum bonus accipe grates . . ."

26[r], blank.

26[v]-45[v], English Metrical Herbal [for details, see below].

45[v]-49[v], English Metrical Medical Treatise [for details, see below].[6]

50-52, English Prose Treatise on the Rosemary.[7] Begins: "Of þe vertu of rose mary. þe god erbe Rose mary is boþe tre & erbe boþe hot & drye . . . [ends]: Schrede hym not ne make hym not to bare of heys branchys but as it is seyd and if þou norche hym þus thow schalt haue Rose mary in plente & gret help & comfort þerby."

The first entries in the manuscript to draw our attention are the short texts on folio iii, recto. The first of these reads:

> I loue and y dare nouȝt
> y þenke and y sey nouȝt
> y spende and I paye nouȝt
> y wolde and I maye nouȝt
> do wel and dred nouȝt
> pley sekyr and sey nouȝt
> and be meke & stylle
> and þou shalt haue alle þy wylle[8]

This stanza is not included in the *Index of Middle English Verse*, at least as a separate poem under the present incipit.

Below these lines (written as four in the MS.), we find the following:

> Sey þe best or be stylle⁹
> Wyth thy tonge noman thou qwelle
> Suffyr and haue thy wylle¹⁰

> Optimam dic ve tace
> nullum perimat tua lingua
> suffer pacifice
> sic vota carpe tua

The English lines, obviously a translation of the Latin text, may be considered as verse, though the rhyme "still/quell/will" is very poor. In the fourth Latin line, another hand has interlineated the imperative "carpe" after "vota."

The calendar, which occupies folios 1-14, is a typical one of the early fifteenth century.¹¹ Since it specifically notes the feasts of St. Cuthbert (March 20), St. Dunstan (May 19), St. Ethelbert, king and martyr (May 20), St. Etheldreda (June 23), etc.,¹² the *Calendarium* was clearly of English origin. Pointing directly to Norwich is the entry for September 24 "Dedicacio ecclesie Norwicensis." Providing further evidence for the Norfolk origin of the calendar is the notation for the feast of Little St. William of Norwich. This entry ("Passio sancti williami norwicensis") also confirms the fact that, in the fifteenth century anyway, the feast of St. William was celebrated on March 24; the *Acta Sanctorum* and other authorities now cite the following day.¹³

On folio 15ʳ, one finds the remedy for a toothache which may appeal to the reader's interest, though it is unlikely that this will prove to be very beneficial in the hour of need:¹⁴

ffor the tothe ache

Take smythis synder & make yt rede hote in the ffyre Than put
them in a vesselle with a lytylle water but leve iij partes of the
synder drye than cast henbane sede upon the brennyng synder
than hold thi mouthe opyn there-ovyr & lett the ffume go yn-to
thy mouthe as myche as ye can but ye must couer your hed clene
yn with a schete & vse this for it is as gode as ony ys probatum
est.

The two chief items in the manuscript are the Metrical
Herbal and the Metrical Medical Treatise, both in the vernacular. Under different incipits, these poems are both listed
by Brown–Robbins, under the respective numbers 2627 and
1408. The incipits of the poems as given in the present
manuscript are not, however, cited in the *Index of Middle
English Verse;* they will be found below at the appropriate
places.

The herbal describes the following herbs: Betany (f. 26[v]),
Centory (f. 28[v]), Goolde (f. 29),[15] Celydonye (f. 30), Pymper-
nol (f .31), Modyrwort (f. 31 [v]), Verveyn (f. 33), Mortulaga[16]
/Mortagon (f. 34), Perwenke (f. 34 [v]), Rose (f. 35),[17] Lyly
(f. 36[v]), Henbane (f. 37[v]), Affodylle (f. 38[v]), Dragaunce/
Serpentin/Nedderystong[18] (f. 39), Astrologia (f. 40), Balde-
monye (f. 40[v]),[19] Egrimonye (f. 41),[20] Mynte (f. 41[v]),[21]
Sauge (f. 41[v]),[22] Rue (f. 42), Fenkel (f. 43[v]), Violet (f. 44),
Scharpe Burre (f. 44[v]), Isope (f. 44[v]), Fymeter (f. 45), and
Columbyne (f. 45).[23]

Of the thirteen manuscripts listed by Brown–Robbins under
number 2627,[24] only the Stockholm manuscript is of comparable length (965 lines).[25] The next longest are BM Addit.
17866 (753 lines)[26] and Cambridge University Library MS.
Dd. 10. 44 (some 600 lines). The remaining manuscripts, all
but one of which (Society of Antiquaries MS.) I have ex-

amined, are much shorter, some extending to only a few lines.

The manuscript here under discussion contains 918 lines,[27] most of which are identical with (or closely comparable to) lines either in the Stockholm manuscript or in the London one, or to be found in both these texts. Nevertheless, 132 lines in the present manuscript find no counterpart, at the same places, in the other codices. At least a third of these provide no new information, consisting mostly of conventional couplets of hackneyed phrases which serve chiefly as padding.[28] If three examples may be cited, these are typical lines of this nature:

> Of his flour wyl I not seye
> But grene it waxith be wode a weye
> > (Egrimonye, 716-17)

> Thow ne haue y not prouyd i-wys
> þe book tellyth þat soth it is
> > (Scharpe Burre, 889-90)

> þis gres wel for to discrye
> To me it is a gret maystrye
> ffor I knowe no-thyng of his flour
> Ne of his smellyng ne of his sauour
> And þou wold I þat hey & lowe
> Myt þis gres kendely knowe
> þer-fore haue I gretly in mende
> To tellyn of him & of his kende
> > (Dragaunce, 622-29)

Despite this fact, there are a good many lines in this herbal which are of more than passing interest and which do not occur either in the Stockholm or in the London texts; of these, we may print the following as typical examples:

These lechys for seke mannys sake
Diuers medicynys sum-tyme gun make
Of alle þe gressys þat growyn on rote
þat mown man & woman helpyn to bote
If þey kondyn þese gressys knowe
And had hem prouyt on hey & lowe
þey dedyn hem wryte wysly in boke
þat leryt & leuyt þeron myth loke
þerfore a leuyt man thour grace at nede
May help a sek man to wysse & rede
So þat he knowe his gressys alle
And thynggis þat þerto wyln be-falle
Now at betany I wyl begwynne²⁹
þat many vertuys beryth hym with-inne   (ll. 1-14)

A gracious grees is betany
ffor oþer vertuys hath he many
Weche þat I haue not in mende
þerfore of hym here I make an ende
At anothyr gres I wel be-gynne
þat on hunderyt vertuys hath hym with-inne
Centory it is nemelyd be name
It may don helpe to blynd & lame
To seke & fayre it may don helpe
I may not þer-of to fele ȝelpe
But þer-on a lytyl wyln I dwelle
And sumdel of his vertuys wel to telle
If it be sothyn in good wyn clerleche³⁰
And drunkyn XV dayys contuneleche
So þat it be mad cler & thynne
Wath maner of venym be man with-inne
It schal dystroye it & breke þe flesche
And dryuyn out þe venym nesche
Ley no thyng elles be þat wonde
Tyl þat he be heyl & sownde   (ll. 99-118)

The English version here under consideration also has some general remarks to make on the subject of herbalists which seem to find no counterpart in the Stockholm or London texts:

> Ho-so xal warkyn with gressys to sen[31]
> fful wyse & ware he must been
> But if he knowe hym in gressis wel
> He xal for-lesyn his warkys eche deel
> But if he wete what he xal done
> He may for-lesyn his craft ryt sone
> But he kendys of gressys knowe
> And here vertuys of hey & lowe
> Ho-so kendys of gressys knowe can
> He may be told a mayster þan
> ffor fewe leue noow vndyr sunne
> þat alle gressys mown knowe kunne
> þerfore be hym þat hath me bowth
> In here craft ne spede he nowth
> ffor he cun neyþer hende ne fare
> Knowe thynggis þat longyn to þe mayster
> Sweche mown be lekenyt to a blynd man
> þat may not seen but felyn he can
> þow he be felyng alone may goon
> Sone he may stumbelyn on a ston
> So faryth a leche man or woman
> þat wenyth to cun good & noon he can[32]
> Of feythful fenkel & of his kende
> I wele telle as y wrete fynde   (ll. 801-24)

For the Hyssop, the present manuscript adds these lines which do not appear in the printed versions of the other two texts:[33]

> It may be etyn & drwnk also
> But if his betyrnes it for-do

> þan men may sethyn it in swet lycour
> þat xal it make of betyr sauour   (ll. 897-900)

The medical treatise in the manuscript from Norwich consists of 202 lines, as compared with the 496 in the Stockholm
manuscript and 370 in the London volume. The only other
recorded manuscript to preserve this text is Trinity College
Cambridge MS. 911, "a disarranged and defective text"
(Brown–Robbins 1408), containing some hundred verses.

Twenty-six lines in the manuscript under consideration are
not duplicated in either printed version.[34] Here again some
couplets are introduced for the evident purpose of padding
the text, such as:

> Anoþer medecyn y fynde redende
> þat mannys heryng may mekyl mende   (ll. 133-34)

> Also y fynde for þis peyne
> þat prouyd is a fayre medecyne   (ll. 157-58)

Nevertheless, other lines provide material not previously
recorded in print, of which the following appear to be the
most interesting:

> Now haue y told ȝou þow y it ȝelpe
> Of gressys þat most mown men do helpe
> How þei waxyn hey & lowe
> And wherby a man may hem knowe
> Of here vertuys & of here kende
> In diuers bokys as wretyn I fynde
> But for þe loue of a lewyt man
> More xal I telle ȝet as I can
> And as I fynde wretyn in book
> þat leryd & lewyd moun on loke
> In iiij parteys of eche a man
> Be-gynnyth þe sekenes þat þei han
> In heed in wombe or in þe splene
> Or in þe bledder þese iiij I mene[35]   (ll. 1-14)

Through some inexplicable circumstance, the present writer's manuscript preserves the lines on the Euphrasy in the very middle of the medical treatise (f. 47 ᵛ). In the Additional MS., they appear, in almost identical wording, at the end of the herbal, the appropriate place for these couplets; they are not, however, included in either poem in the Stockholm MS. This would seem to be the earliest description of the Euphrasy in English, since the *O.E.D.* cites only a mention of this herb in a vocabulary of "circa 1475." In the new manuscript, the lines read:

> [E]ufras is of byt*ter* sauo*ur*
> A lytyl smal g*re*s whit is h*is* flo*ur*
> In metys & drynkys if he be doon
> He is medecynabyl boþe morwe & noon
> He castyth wel to eye h*is* syth
> þis medecy*n* is prouyd wel I plyth
> For helpe of syth mekyl haue I sowt
> And mor*e* to telle let wyl I nowt[36]   (ll. 95-102)

The first six lines also occur in Trinity College Cambridge, MS. R.14.51, f. 46, as the closing lines of the herbal.

The particulars here given set forth the chief characteristics of the newly discovered texts and emphasize the importance of this manuscript vis-à-vis those whose contents have already been printed. A line-by-line comparison reveals that the new manuscript stands in close relationship to the Additional MS. 17866, though it is slightly longer and (here and there) seems to offer more satisfactory readings. When the exhaustive treatment and critical edition of these poems is eventually undertaken, the present manuscript will serve, together with the Stockholm manuscript and Additional 17866, as the basis for the definitive edition of these poems of great medical interest.

Curt F. Bühler,
The Pierpont Morgan Library

Notes

[1] Sir Thomas Phillipps, *Catalogus librorum manuscriptorum in bibliotheca D. Thomae Phillipps* (Middlehill, 1837), p. 106, no. 7008.

[2] Carleton Brown and Rossell Hope Robbins, *The Index of Middle English Verse* (New York, 1943).

[3] None of these Norfolk individuals can be identified. A Robert Hall is named in a letter written by Margaret Paston on February 7, 1465, but there is no reason to believe that this is the same person. Cf. James Gairdner, *The Paston Letters* (London, 1904), IV:127.

[4] An unprinted treatise on urinoscopy, which may be related to this tract, occurs in the Stockholm MS. (for which see note 25), ff. 123-26.

[5] Listed in col. 266 of Lynn Thorndike and Pearl Kibre, *A Catalogue of Incipits of Mediaeval Scientific Writings in Latin* (Cambridge, Mass., 1937).

[6] For a poem of similar nature but more specific in character, see R. H. Bowers, "A Middle English Mnemonic Plague Tract," *Southern Folklore*, XX (1956):118-25, with important references.

[7] A treatise on the Rosemary, unpublished except for an extract, is also to be found in the Stockholm MS. X. 90, ff. 80-86 (Brodin, p. 60; cf. note 25). The extract was printed by Ferdinand Holthausen, "Rezepte, Segen und Zaubersprüche aus zwei Stockholmer Handschriften," *Anglia*, XIX (1897): 75-88.

[8] For similar proverbial rhymes with "nought," see Brown–Robbins no. 1163 and George L. Apperson, *English Proverbs and Proverbial Phrases* (London, 1929), p. 595.

[9] Compare Alexander Dyce, *The Poetical Works of John Skelton* (London, 1843), I:17: "A prouerbe of old, say well or be styll" ("Agaynste a Comely Coystrowne," l. 64). For an earlier citation (c. 1480), see Apperson, p. 551.

[10] Apperson, p. 608, cites "Suffer and expect" (Herbert, 1640).

[11] Calendars from various dioceses are printed by Francis Wormald, *English Kalendars before A. D. 1100* and *English Benedictine Kalendars after A. D. 1100* (Henry Bradshaw Society nos. LXXII, LXXVII, and LXXXI; London, 1934-1946).

[12] The Dog Days (*dies caniculares*) are here given as July 14–September 6.

[13] Official sources are not in complete agreement on the date. The *Acta Sanctorum* (Paris, 1863-1931), IX:586-88, lists St. William for March 25, while Paul Guérin, *Les petits Bollandistes* (Paris, 1880), III:619, prefers March 24. March 25 is chosen by Sabine Baring-Gould, *The Lives of the Saints* (London, 1897-98), III:461-66, and Sir Nicholas H. Nicolas, *The Chronology of History* (London, 1833), p. 102—though on p. 165 he adds the note: "According to Butler, March 24." Franz von Sales Doyé, *Heilige und Selige der römisch-katholischen Kirche* (Leipzig, 1929), II:546, cites both March 24 and March 25, while Frederick G. Holweck, *A Biographical Dictionary of the Saints* (St. Louis, 1924), p. 1035, suggests that the feast was transferred from March 25 to March 26.

[14] This recipe does not appear in Gottfried Müller, *Aus mittelenglischen*

Medizintexten. Die Prosarezepte des Stockholmer Miszellankodex X. 90 (Köl-
ner Anglistische Arbeiten no. X; Leipzig, 1929); Herbert Schöffler, *Beiträge
zur mittelenglischen Medizinliteratur* (Halle, 1919); Ferdinand Holthausen,
"Rezepte, Segen und Zaubersprüche aus zwei Stockholmer Handschriften,"
Anglia, XIX (1897):75-88; Gösta Frisk, *A Middle English Translation of
Macer Floridus de Viribus Herbarum* (Upsala, 1949; Upsala Universitet,
Essays and Studies on English Language and Literature, III); *The 'Liber de
Diversis Medicinis' in the Thornton Manuscript* (ed. Margaret S. Ogden,
EETS, OS 207 [1938], pp. 16-19, esp. 17. 11-18); etc.

[15] Marigolα. Modern English equivalents for the herbs are mostly not given
here, since these can easily be ascertained through the OED.

> Goolde is goode in sauo*ur*
> Fayer & yelew is his floure
> The golde flowyr is goode to sene
> It makyth syght bryght & clene   (ULC MS. Dd. 10. 44)

[16] Not in OED, though Mortulaca is cited under Mortagon.
[17] Except for the last two lines, which appear in the Stockholm MS., the
lines here printed are unique in this manuscript:

> To make þis playste*r* ho-so wyl cu*n*ne
> He hangyt in a glas in þe hete of þe su*n*ne
> And tho*ur* þe eyr & su*n*nys hete
> þe gressys xul moysty*n* & waxin wete
> And casty*n* [h]er*e* wate*r* all*e* be-dene
> Into þe glas ful fayr & clene
> þis wate*r* is good for eyne sm*er*tyng
> And for þe syth claryfying   (ll. 453-460)

Besides rose leaves, the glass was to contain Celidony, Rue, Fennel, and
Vervain.
[18] Or Adder's-tongue; see OED under Serpentine.
[19] Baldmoney; more commonly known as the Gentian.
[20] In the short version (c. 300 lines) in Sloane MS. 2457, the poem ends
on f. 7[v] with the lines:

> Of egrymonye y schal telle al-so
> ffor it nedeth and is to do
> Egrymonye to dringes and plastres is goode
> Als telles the maiste*r* of mylde mode
> Hit remewes postemes dronke wit wite wyne
> And washeþ the splene and the venyme
> Lay it vndere a mannes hed
> He schal slepe als he were ded
> He schal neuer of slepe a-wake
> Til hit fro vnder is hed he take

Similarly, Trinity College Cambridge MS. 1117 (112 verses) concludes with
these lines:

It remeuyth postymes dronkyn with wyne
And wascyth the splene & oþer venyme
Lay it vnder a monnis hede
He shalle slepe as he were dede
There shalle no drede hym wake
Tylle fro vnder þe hede it be take.

[21] The Additional MS. (ll. 607-612) includes some verses on Mint which do not appear in the Stockholm text. The present manuscript also includes this text on Mint, together with six lines on Rue which are not in the other two MSS. (lines 732-43):

Menta iuuat stomacum cor salgia ruta cerebrum
Ambiger extirpat tussym pectus stomacum
Mynte is for þe stomak good
As seyth þe mayster with mylde mood
Sauge makyth þe herte clene
þus seyn þis vers both be-dene
Rue also is good for syth
And for þe kernele & makyn eyne bryt
It is no nede þese gres to discrye
þis vers wytnessyth here maystrye
Saue þat sauge wyl don more ӡet
þer-fore of hym xal I speke bet

For the "cerebrum" of the new MS, read "celebrum"? The first six English lines are also to be found in TCC, MS. R.14.51, f. 44.

[22] Cur moritur homo dum salgea crescit in orto
þis vers is ful of gret pryce
And is þus to seyn on englische
ffor defaute whi deyyth man
þat sauge myth to his helpe han   (ll. 758-762)

The Latin line occurs in both other MSS., though neither of the next two lines are found there. For the English translation they offer:

For defaute whi dies þe mane
þat sauge & mynte to helpe hane   (Addit. 624-625)

Why of seknesse deyith man
Whil sawge in gardeyn he may han   (Stock. 832-833)

[23] Columbine is present in the Addit. MS., though not in the Stockholm one. In TCC, MS. R.14.51, f. 46, the text reads:

Of columbyne I wil you telle
Hys floure blewe ys like a belle
Thys columbyne berith a blak seede
That ys gode dronken for squynnasy at nede.

[24] Thirteen is the number given by Brown–Robbins, but eleven would seem to be the more correct total. The herbal in Pepys MS. 878 is in prose, not in verse. Thus the description of Betony reads (p. 176): "Beteyne is a[n] herbe of many uertuys qwat manere of man þat beres beten up-on hym þer schal no manere venomys best doo hym an harme whil he beryt it and qhow drynkes þe water I-styllid it schal make hym a gode colowr & of all þing it is gode for þe stomake & he use to drynke it fastyng it is gode for þe dropsye." The text in BM Additional MS. 12056 is also a prose herbal, if I read my notes correctly. Sloane MS. 147 of the British Museum has a long text (some 600 verses), but it is both late and poor.

On the other hand, not noted in Brown-Robbins is Trinity College Cambridge, MS. 921 (R.14.51). This contains the metrical herbal in just under 600 lines, having 22 pages with (normally) 27 lines to the page, beginning with folio 35 verso. The MS. is cited by Brown-Robbins under acephalous poem °40 as "A Book of Receipts in English verse and prose."

[25] The text of Stockholm MS. X. 90 was printed by Ferdinand Holthausen, "Medicinische Gedichte aus einer Stockholmer Handschrift," *Anglia*, XVIII (1896):293-331. For further particulars as to this MS., see Gösta Brodin, *Agnus Castus: A Middle English Herbal* (Upsala, 1950; Upsala Universitet, Essays and Studies on English Language and Literature, VI).

[26] Printed by Robert M. Garrett, "Middle English Rimed Medical Treatise," *Anglia*, XXXIV (1911):163-93.

[27] A line is omitted at line 477, and the proper numbering is restored by the introduction of the single Latin line at 1. 758.

[28] Such lines are not, of course, peculiar to this text but are present in the other manuscripts. Thus, the Stockholm MS. has at lines 409-10 of the Medical Tract:

> þis medycyne full well prowyd is
> As tellyth maystyr Galyeen i-wys

All three MSS. have the lines found at 825-26 of the new text under Fenkel:

> As tellyth mayster Macrobius
> He is a gres ful precyous

[29] Line 13 corresponds to line 7 of the Stockholm text.

[30] At this point, the text in the University Library Cambridge MS. Dd. 10. 44 (and almost identically in Pepys MS. 1661, pp. 290-291) reads:

> At betony ende I
> And begynne at Centory
> In gode wyne sodyn centory
> And be dronke 15 dayes by and by
> So þat it be made clere & thynne
> What maner venym be man wyth-Inne
> It shalle verili brest the fleshe
> And drevyn owt the venym neshe

In Trinity College Cambridge Ms. 1117 (O.2.13), the next two lines read:

> Lay no thynges be þat wounde
> Tyll it be made hole & sounde

The other manuscripts have comparable lines for the last eight as printed here.

[31] In Addit. MS. 17866, lines 660-63, the first four verses read:

> Who so shal wyrke with gres to sene
> War & wyse he moste bene
> But he hym knawe in gres welle
> He schal for lese his werk ilke dele

This passage is preceded by two French lines (plus six of English translation) which do not seem to appear elsewhere. Following it are the lines:

> Fenkill says maister Macrobius
> Is a gres ful precious

These compare to lines 825-826 of the new manuscript and 874-875 of the Stockholm text.

[32] After "he," another hand has interlineated "or thee."

[33] In place of these, Sloane MS. 2457, f. 4, supplies the lines:

> And fro the fende hit schal the schelde
> In hous in toun in wod and felde

Pepys MS. 878, p. 177, here reads: "Isop is a gode herbe for þe stomake & for þe lyuere & for þe longis & for þe dropsye. stampid and temperyd it wiþ water & ʒif it a womman to drynke þat is trauelyng wyþ child she schal haue gode deleueraunce be þe grace of god."

[34] A great many lines are duplicated in either the Stockholm or the Additional texts but not by both. Forty-four lines of the new text are not in the Stockholm one (but in Addit.), while twenty-two are not found in the Additional MS. (but do occur in Stockholm). The last twenty-two lines of the new text compare with the others as follows: four lines (181-82 and 189-190) are found in neither of the other texts; lines 183-88 and 191-96 = Addit. 884-95 (not in Stock.) and lines 197-202 = Stock. 133-38 (not in Addit.).

[35] Lines 11-14 correspond to lines 1-4 of the Stockholm "Gereimte Heilkunde."

[36] Lines 101-102 do not occur in Addit. butare paralleled by Stock. lines 85-86:

> For helpe of syth mekyl I hawe sowth
> And more to telle let wil I no[w]t[h].

A Manuscript of the Chronicle of Mathieu d'Escouchy and Simon Greban's Epitaph for Charles VII of France

The editor of the last printed edition[1] of the Chronicle of Mathieu d'Escouchy gives a list of the MSS. which he had consulted. This list can be augmented by the addition of two other MSS. The first, now in my possession[2] and the subject of discussion here, has not, so far as I can discover, been previously reported; the second, very briefly seen by me when it was recently on sale in London, is now in the United States.[3]

The first MS. is on paper, 16.5 cm. by 24 cm., and is bound in an elegant nineteenth-century binding, presumably carried out for a former owner, Sylvain van de Weyer,[4] a noted bibliophile whose bookplate appears inside the front cover. The MS. contains in all 976 pages, arranged as follows: front end-pages, unnumbered but here designated for convenience as pp. i-xxii; pp. 1-891 (numbered in the MS.) give the complete text of the Chronicle, which is immediately followed (pp. 891-917) by two poems attributed to Simon Greban; the reverse side of p. 917 is blank; then follows an Index, the pages of which are unnumbered but which, since they are an integral part of the MS., we may call pp. 919-941; the reverse side of p. 941 is blank; then follow a further six sheets of endpapers which we designate as pp. xxiii-xxxiv. Of the endpapers, the first two leaves (pp. i-iv) and the last two leaves (pp. xxxi-xxxiv) are obviously inserted by the nineteenth-century binder and can be ignored.

The front end-pages contain a number of entries important

for the dating of the MS. P. v bears in the top right-hand corner the number 955, written in a hand identical with the hand which has numbered the pages of the text. On the top edge it bears the date *5 juin 1609* and a name J. de Cantin (?), as well as four lines of notes referring to a passage on p. 815 of the text. P. vi is blank. P. vii is filled with brief entries relating to members of the Le Picart family. Pp. viii-x are blank. P. xi is filled with references to Mathieu d'Escouchy derived from the text. Pp. xii-xxi are blank. At the head of P. xxii is a note *cronique de mathieu descouchy depuis 1444 jusques en 1461 non imprimees,* followed by a further note in a different (late seventeenth- or eighteenth-century hand) *imprimé* (sic) *depuis et donné par Godefroy dans son histoire de Charles VII page 532.* The text starts on p. 1, which has, in the top left-hand corner, the date *26 febvrier 1609.* The text itself is cross-referenced and annotated throughout in the left-hand margins. The text ends on p. 891 with a simple *Explicit;* then follow the two poems. At the head of the first poem in the left-hand margin is the entry *vers composés par feu simon grebant,* and, at the end of the second poem on p. 917 the scribe has written *Explicit,* against which a different hand has added *9 Apvril 1609,* while a little lower down, in a third hand, occurs the statement *epitaphes du roy Charles 7 composés par feu symon grebant.* On the next page but one the 23-page, double-column Index starts, and is then followed by the blank end-pages.

Four different hands are to be found in the MS. The first is that of the scribe who wrote the text of the Chronicle and the poems, and also the details of the Le Picart family on front end-page vii. The second hand is that of the indexer, who has also been responsible for: the date (and possibly the name) and notes on p. v; the numbering of the pages of the text and the figures 955 on p. v; the notes on Escouchy on p. xi; the marginal annotations, corrections, and cross-references; the two dates on p. 1 and p. 917; and, from time to time, short passages of the text. The third hand, possibly that of a later owner, occurs in the first note (*cronique de M.d'E. . . .*) on p. xxii, and in the attribution of the poems to Simon Greban on pp. 891 and 917. The fourth hand, possibly again the hand of a subsequent owner, is found only in the second note (*imprimé depuis . . .*) on p. xxii.

Apart from the irrelevant endpapers inserted by the nineteenth-century binder, all the pages of the MS. are of the same paper, except front endpaper p. v, which has a different watermark. On the other hand the page number 955, as well as the handwriting and date, would seem to indicate that this page (incidentally an isolated cut half-sheet and not, like the rest, half of a folded sheet) formed part of the original collection of sheets. Whether or not the number 955 takes into account the unnumbered index is impossible to say; the numbered pages, together with the Index and endpapers, would add up to 950. The page had certainly been detached and incorporated at the front of the volume in an earlier binding, as is evidenced by the corresponding worm-holes in the front end-pages and the first few pages of text; similar evidence shows that the blank rear end-pages immediately followed the Index in the earlier binding as they do now.

Front endpaper p. vii is significant, not only because it is on the same paper as the text and in the handwriting of the scribe, but also because of the brief details it gives of six members of the Le Picart family.[5] One entry is important for the dating of the MS., that against Jacques le Picart, ". . . conseiller et adcat du Roy au Chlet de Paris receu en ce d. office le 18 mars 1608 . . ." Although this sheet could conceivably have been written on a different occasion, the identity of paper and handwriting suggest March 18, 1608 as a reasonable *terminus ab quo* of the MS.

The other two dates in 1609 at the beginning and end of the text, in the handwriting of the indexer-annotator (who could also have been the first owner; his annotations show him to have been a well-read, learned man, with an interest in history) would seem to indicate, not perhaps the date of copying of the text itself, but more probably the date on which the indexer started and completed the annotation and Index. The several passages which the indexer himself has contributed to the text (because the copyist had difficulty with the reading of his original?) and which fit neatly into the text, as well as the corrections and comments which the indexer has made from time to time against the text, and which suggest both constant surveillance and reference to the original, suggest that the copyist and the indexer-annotator worked closely together. The obvious *terminus ad quem* for the date of the MS. is the indexer's date of April 9, 1609.

Corroboration of the date of the MS. is provided by the paper itself which, with the exception of front endpaper p. v, has throughout the same watermark (two crowns, surmounted by a third crown of laurel branches, with the device Edmond Devise at the base of the crest). This paper is found at various dates between 1590 and 1612, and, in particular, at Paris from 1594 to 1612.[6] It seems safe to conclude, therefore, that the MS. dates from the early seventeenth century, and was probably written between March 1608 and April 1609.

Apart from giving details of this hitherto unreported MS., we are not concerned here with the Chronicle of Mathieu d'Escouchy[7] but with one of the poems ascribed to Simon Greban at the end of the text, namely the Epitaph for Charles

VII. The second poem, a ballade, is, I think, of doubtful authenticity as far as Greban is concerned; considerations of space preclude its treatment here, and it will be the subject of a separate article.

The name Simon Greban is nowadays primarily associated with the *Mystère des Actes des Apôtres,* but he evidently enjoyed a reputation as a poet in his own time and in the sixteenth century. In the first printed edition of the *Mystère* (1536), he is mentioned in the Prologue as " . . . Symon Greban, bon poete estimé . . . ," while Guillaume Alabat's preface states that the *Actes* were " . . . Traslatez par tres-eloquent homme et poete excellent maistre Symon de Greban docteur en theologie . . . "[8] Other sixteenth-century writers who praised the Grebans include Jean Lemaire de Belges,[9] Marot, du Bellay, Jean Boucher and La Croix de Maine.[10] Simon's Epitaph for Charles VII has been indicated in recent years by, among others, MM. Gröber,[11] Champion,[21] and Lebègue,[13] and another epitaph by him, for Jacques Milet, which also contains an acrostic in the last verse, has been published by A. Piaget.[14]

As far as I can discover, Simon Greban's Epitaph for Charles VII has only been printed once, and that as long ago as 1500.[15] Vérard's text is an indifferent one, erroneous in many places and also incomplete. The version of the poem given in our MS. is an improvement on Vérard in some respects, but itself lacks sixty lines and contains numerous errors, many of which seem attributable to the fact that the scribe, or the writer of his original, had difficulty in deciphering an earlier manuscript. The inadequacy of Vérard, and the errors of our MS., have led me to look for other MSS. and to produce below what I believe to be the first critical edition of Simon Greban's Epitaph.

MANUSCRIPTS

The MSS. used,[16] and brief details about them which can be amplified in most cases from the relevant catalogues, are as follows:

A = The text of the poem as found in the MS. of Escouchy's Chronicle described above.

B = B.N.1642. Paper, fifteenth century. Item no. 9 (f.414r.-f.423v) of a miscellaneous collection.

C = B.N.1661. Paper, fifteenth century. Item no. 11 (f.112r-f.121v) of a miscellaneous collection.

D = B.N.1956. Vellum, fifteenth century. Item no. 3 (f.61r-77r) of a miscellaneous collection. The text is followed by a quatrain in the same hand: *Ung clerc aplat dargent deliure/ dont a peu quil nyst hors du sens/ Soixant huit mil quatre cens/ En juillet acomplit ce liure;* the figures 1468 have been added at the side.

E = B.N.5053. Paper, end of fifteenth century. Ff.15 plus two front end-pages. The text has been corrected in places by a similar but different hand. At the head of the text a later (eighteenth-century?) hand has written "Bibliothèque de la Croix du Maine, p. 456."

F = B.N.5735. Paper, fifteenth century. F.lv-f.20v.

G = B.N.23283. Paper, fifteenth century. The Epitaph follows (f.186r-f.201r) the *Chronique de Charles VII* of Gilles le Bouvier.

H = Arsenal 3523. Paper, fifteenth century. Item no. 22 (p. 439-p. 460) of a miscellaneous collection.

J = Glasgow University Library Hunterian 234. Sixteenth century. Fragment (ll.1-236). Follows (f.209r-212r) a MS. of Jean Chartier's Chronicle of Charles VII;

the text of the poem is followed by four blank leaves ruled as for the text itself.[17]

V = Text as printed in A. Vérard, *Codicille et testament de maistre Jehan de Meung ou Clopinel*, Paris, 1500. The text is preceded by the *Testament maistre iehan de meun*.

In none of the MSS. used is the text absolutely complete, but *C*, *D*, *F*, and *H* each lack only two lines, and *E* only four.

The precise interrelationship of the MSS. is difficult to determine in detail. It is only rarely that common omissions can be used as a guide, and then usually only to show the kinship of *C* and *V*. The close relationship of Vérard's printed text to *C* is clear, but, even allowing for the vagaries and errors of the early printers, and the possible misreading of a scribe's hand, there are too many significant differences to permit the assumption that Vérard was completely dependent on this MS. The defective MS. *J* appears to be closely linked with *CV* and, in particular, with *V*. There is a suggestion of two major lines of tradition *ABDEFGH* and *CJV* but it is not constant and the sub-groups vary. *B* on occasion inclines to the second group, as do *D* (occasionally), *E*, *F*, *G*, and *H* (more frequently). *A* itself, which is often very individualistic in its readings and its omissions, sometimes shows affinities with *CV* or with *C*. *G* also has many individual readings. Possible sub-groups indicated are *EF*, *EV*, *AE*, *AG*. The rubric of the last verse suggests a relationship between *CDHV* (and also perhaps the Rennes MS., see p. 344 note 16).

The relationships of the MSS. used are not sufficiently clear-cut to permit the construction of a reliable *stemma* or to indicate the predominant suitability of any MS. as a base. *D* and *E* seem to offer the best choice, not only because of their relative completeness and the clarity of their readings but also because the fastidious neatness of the scribes inspires confidence in their care and accuracy. The early date of *D*, coupled with the fact that *E* has occasionally been amended by a later hand, has led to its selection as base MS.

ATTRIBUTION

Apart from the indication of authorship implicitly contained in the acrostic in the last verse—an acrostic which is paralleled in the Epitaph for Jacques Milet,[18] several MSS. directly indicate the name of the author; thus *CDHV* draw attention to the acrostic in their last rubric, while the scribe of *E* names the author at the head of his text. The attributions inscribed by later hands in *A* and *B* can be discounted as first-hand evidence. In view of the evidence of the MSS., coupled with that of the acrostic and the observations of La Croix du Maine,[19] there seems no good reason to doubt Simon Greban's authorship.

Epitaphes de Charles VII de France

En temps de deull que le roy Helion
Se vint asseoir ou trosne du Lion

Incipit] Sensievent les epitaphes touchans le regne et trespas du roy Charles de France, 7e de ce nom *A;* lepytaphe du feu roy Charles VIIe *B;* les epitaphes du roy Charles *C; missing in D;* epitaphe du roy Charles VIIe composees (*sic*) par feu symon grebant *E;* complainte pour la mort de Charles VII a Meung en 1461 *F; missing in G;* epitaphe ou lamentation du roy der trespasse *H;* epithedium sive lamentatio Karoli vij regis victormi *J;* cy fine le testament maistre jehan de meun et comence lepytaphe du roy Charles septiesme *V.*

1. Ou *ACEFGHJV;* doeil *A,* dueil *BCEFHJV,* doel *G;* elyon *A,* dylion *B,* dilion *CJ,* dylhon *F,* dhelion *G,* dit lyon *V.* 2. sen

Pour veoir Phebé s'amye face a face
Ainsy qu'il fault qu'en soy revolvant face
5 Retrograder de son chemin Saturne
Apres la nuyt seraine et taciturne
Qu'Aurora vient Orient enflamer,
Je m'esveillay d'un songe tres amer
Où mon esprit travailloit sans repos
10 Pensant sans fin a la fiere Atropos,
Ennemye du noble genre humain,
Qui ja tenoit une darde en sa main
De bois mortel, ferrée de souffrance
Pour trespercer le grant pasteur de France,
15 Ainsi pensif me prins a cheminer
Cuydant mon deul et tristesse miner.
Le midy vint, dont peu me resjouÿ,
Car ung petit apres une heure ouÿ
Par bois, par prez, par chemins et par plains,
20 Les plus dolens et plus angoisseux plains

H; en *A,* au *EF.* 3. saine *V.* 4. que en *C,* qun *G;* soy] se *CJV
missing in H.* 5. retrograde *CFGJV;* de *missing in V.* 6. seraine]
se treuve *C;* a. s. la n. *J.* 7. Qu'A.] En A. *CV;* vint *CEHJV;*
enflamber *A,* anflamber *B.* 8. me levay *AEGHJV,* my levay
B, me leve *CF;* sompne *E.* 9. esperit *ABHJV;* trembla *A,*
travaille *B,* travailla *CFHJV,* tramlla *G,* travailla *corr.* to travailloit *in E;* repoux *C.* 10. Antroppos *A;* s.f.] tousdiz *B.* 11.
Adversaire *BCHJV;* genre] sanc *A.* 12. la *BCHV;* avoit *C;* un
grand dart *A,* ung dart *H;* en] a *F.* 13. ferrée] et ferre *A,* ferre
DFGHJV. 14. *Missing in V;* trespercher *A,* transpercer *BE,*
tresperchier *G,* tresparcer *J;* grand *A;* pastour *CGHJ.* 15.
chevaulchier *A.* 16. doeil *A,* dueil *BEFHV,* deult *C,* duel *J;*
en *GJV;* mucher *A,* mener *C,* muer *FHV, missing in J.* Stanzas
divided after l. 14 in *BEF.*

17. dont bien peu mesioy *AH;* peu] pour *J.* 18. Car prestement aprez *A.* 19. prez] champs *A;* chemins] emmys *E;* et p.p.
missing in E. 20. dolens] piteux *A.*

Souspirs et pleurs, et les plus piteux criz
Qu'onques jamais furent faiz ne escriz
En cronicques, tant anciennes soient,
Que les bergiers du plat païs faisoient,

25 Car par trouppeaux s'assembloient aux champs
Crians: "Ha Dieu! que ferons nous meschans?
Las! comment veult ta clemence permettre
Que ceste mort nous oste nostre maistre,
Qui tant en paix nous laissoit laborer?"

30 Là eussiez veu maintes lermes plorer,
En regretant leur seigneur tres amé;
Mais dessus tous ung Cueur Loyal nommé
Se complaignoit par desolation:
Oyez pour Dieu sa lamentation.

Cueur Loyal

35 Assemblez vous de toutes pars,
Bergiers, où que soiez espars;
Assemblez vous, peuple menu,
Abandonnez brebis et parcs,
Et ne craignez loups ne liepars.

40 Plourez tous, le temps est venu,

---

21. piteux] hideux *A*. Ll. 21 *and* 22 *reversed in F*. 23. *Missing in H;* es *A;* En c.]et si oncques *C;* anchiennes *A*, ancienne *D*. 24. bergers *B*. 25. Car par grans t.*H;* troppiaux *A*, troppeaulx *BCEFGH*, troupeaulx *J*, tropeaulx *V;* sassemblerent *V;* aux]es *JV*. 27. voeult *A*, veulx *C;* ta c.]la sentence *H;* permectre *BCEFJV*, parmectre *H*. 28. metre *D*. 29. Tant qui *C;* labourer *ABCEFGH*, labour *J*, gouverner *V*. 30. eussez *F;* mainte larme *G;* larmes *ABCEFJV;* plourer *ACFGHJV*, plour *E*. 31. regrectant *F;* leur]le *AH;* amé]amer *C*. 32. par sus *EFG;* coeur *A;* leal *A;* ung leal cueur *G*. 33. complaindroit *G*. 34. Pour Dieu ouez *H*.

Rubric]*missing in DV*. 35. assembles *V*. 36. ou que]que ne *A;* soies *G*. soyes *V*. 38. pars *C*. 39. Ne c.ni l.ni l. *B;* craignes *GV;* cragnez *J;* ni *B;* liepart *B*, liipars *G*. 40. Plourez *ACFGHJV;*

Car celuy qui nous a tenu
En seureté et maintenu
En bonne paix le temps passé
Est de ce siecle trespassé.

45   Plourez par desconfiture
Sa tresplaisant pourtraicture
    Que Nature
    Par figure,
Qui tout a son gré figure,
50   Avoit si bien figurée,
Quant Mort, qui tout deffigure,
L'a fait mettre en sepulture
    Par poincture
    Si tres dure
55   Qu'il n'est homme qui l'endure,
Tant soit de longue durée.

Traistresse deffigurée,
A tout mal faire asseurée,
    Maleurée,
60   Conjurée,
De tout plaisir separée,
Ta douloureuse morsure
Ne peut estre reparée,
Ne sa vie bienheurée,

---

p.t.] et plourez *H*. 41. cheluy *A*, celluy *BEV*, cellui *CGJ*. 42.
Missing in A; entretenu *H*. 43. En]soubz *BG*. 44. monde *CHJV*.
No division after 1.44 *in ADG*. 45. Plourons *BEFG*. 50-51.
Missing in A. 50. figure *CFHJV*, figurer *E*. 51. *Missing in H*.
52. mectre *BCEFHJV*. 53. *Missing in G;* peniture *V*. 56. fust *A*.
No division after 1.56 *in ABDEG*. 57. O beste *AF*, O tristesse
BHJV, o triste *C*, o triste mort *E*, o traistre *G*. 58. faire]faict
AFH, missing in V. 59. *Missing in C*. 60. comme juree *A*. 62-64.
Missing in B. 62. moisure *A;* malheureuse *CJV*. 63. peult *AEF*,
poet *G*, peust *J*. 64. vie]joye *AG*.

65   Esperée,
            Desirée,
            Ne sera assez plourée
            Tant que ce monde cy dure.

            Car comme l'espine flourie
70   Est en may courtine serie
            Soubz quoy pastoureaulx vont manger,
            Ou comme la rose cherie
            Est par royalle seigneurie
            L'honneur et le chois du vergier,
75   Ainsi le gracieux bergier
            Estoit, comme l'on peult jugier,
            En preudommye et loyaulté
            L'honneur du siecle et la beaulté.

            Ha! pastour sumptueux
80   Quant ton bras vertueux
            Par jours laborieux
            Du jardin gracieux
            De France bienheureuse
            A osté l'epineux
85   Ayglantier rapineux,
            Au peuple rigoureux

---

67. seras *B*. 68. cy dure]cya duree *H*.

No division after 1.68 *in A*. 69. florye *EGJ*, fleurie *V*. 70. cointe et serie *JV*. 71. qui *EG*; pastouriaulx *A*, pastoureaulx *BV*, pastoreaulx *EH*. 72. Ou]que *JV*. 73. royal *G*, realle *J*; seignourie *ABCFG*. 74. clos *A*; bergier *DGJ*. 75. grignour *C*, greignour *V*; vergier *J*. 76. on *AG*, len *HJ*, sen *V*; poeult bien bien jugier *G*; peut *ABCHV*, peust *J*. 78. sa *F*.

No division after 1.78 *in AD*. 79. pasteur *CEFJ*. 80. Qua *A*; precieux *E*. 81. labourieux *FHJV*. 82. *Missing in F*; Au *E*. 84. As *ABCEFGJV*. 85. englantier *A*, esglentier *BCHJV*, lesglantyer *E*, eglantier *F*, anglentier *G*. 86. *Missing in A*; Du *DF*; vigoureux *F*, dangereux *E*.

Car c'est bois dangereux
De plante venimeuse;

     Quant du lis precieux
90   Noble et delicieux
     Montoit jusques ès cieulx
     Pour resjouÿr les dieux
     L'odeur delicieuse,
     Par ung coup furieux,
95   Pas de mort doloreux,
     As passé, dont nos yeulx
     Lermoyent qui mieulx mieulx
     Et font chiere piteuse.

     Faulse Mort, pire qu'interdicte,
100 De ta condicion maudicte
     Fuys ceulx qui de vivre sont las,
     Mais par ta cruaulté despite,
     Qui jamais homme ne respite,
     Tens sur les vigoreux tes las;
105 Ainsi, sans autre cause, allas
     Tuer nostre bon maistre, helas!

---

87. lois *G*.
No division after l.88 *in ABDFGH*. 89. de *C*. 90. nobles *C*.
91-93. *Missing in G*. 91. aux *BCHV*, au *J*. 94. cop *AHJ*. 96. Ayt
E, A *G*, Est *V*; dont tous *JV*. 97. Larmoient *ABFGV*, larmoyait
E; qui m.m.] qui de mieux *A*, qui mieulx *H*.

No division after l.98 *in ADH. Ll*. 101-108 *missing in J, except for two lines* qui jamais homme ne respite prends ceulx
qui de vivre son las. 99. qu'i.] quentredicte *A*, que inter-
dicte *EFV*, quindecite *C*, quinterditte *G*, *missing in J*. 100.
maldicte *A*, malditte *G*. 101. Finis *A*, Fuy *H*, Sur *CFV*. 102.
Missing in V; ta *missing in A*. 103. *Missing in F*. 104. sur *missing in H*; tens le vigourex te las *C*, tens tes faulx et rigoreux latz
V. 105. *Missing in V*; autre]mettre *ABH*.

T'en est il venu grant prouffit?
Onques a homme ne meffit.

Helas! qui pourra vengier
110   Ce noble et puissant bergier,
Que Mort a fait abreger
    Et soubz terre mis?
Helas! qui pourra vengier
Celuy qui sens nul dangier
115   Aux champs se venoit loger
    Entre ses amis?
Qui le pourroit aleger
Ou sa vie prolonger
Par cueurs en lermes plonger
120   En douleur soubmis,
    De joye desmis?
Les yeulx endormis
Seroient a corriger,
    Car aux loups famis,
125   De France ennemis,
    Doulans et remis
A faict pasture changer
Et soubz terre mis.

---

107. grand *A*, nul *E*, une *F*.
   No division after l.108 *in ACDV.* 109-112. *Missing in A.* 109.
H. qui] helas et qui *H;* pourroit *H.* 110. Le *BC;* vergier *J.* 111.
Qui *V.* 112. muer *V.* 113. H. qui]helas et qui *H. Extra line*
helas qui pourra venger *between* l.116 *and* l.17 *in B.* 117.les *H;*
porroit *A*, pourra *CJV*, polroit *G.* 118. Ou]Ne *G.* 119. *Missing*
in AB; pleurs *J;* larmes *EFGV.* 120. *Missing in E;* doulours *A,*
doleur *B*, douleurs *C*, doulleur *F*, dolours *G.* 121. De]Et de *G;*
definis *DJV*, definie *F.* 123. Feroient *A*, fauldroit *B*, soient *JV;*
a *missing in B.* 125-6. *Order reversed in G.* 125. ennemie *D.*
126. Dolans *AB*, doulens *C*, dolens *EFGHJV.* 128. Est *V;* mis
missing in C. L.127. *struck out and reinserted after* l.128 *by*
different hand in E.

Fermez vos guez, dame Thetis,
130 Que les trouppeaux grans ne petiz
Ne boivent pour l'eure presente;
Pallas, deffendez les patiz
Qu'on ne coure vos appatiz;
L'ombre soit aux bestes absente
135 Affin qu'en chemin et en sente
Toute chose vive se sente
De la tristesse continue
Qu'aujourduy nous est survenue.

O vous, nymphes et seraines,
140 Et vous, nereïdes saines,
Les deesses souveraines
Sur les rivieres prouchaines
        Et loingtaines
Et sur la mer qui ondoye,
145 Soyez nous si treshumaines
Que de vos profons domaines
Convertissiez vos fontaines
Et vos fleuves en nos vaines,
        Qui sont vaines,
150 Affin que chacun lermoye.

No division after l.128 *in AD.* Ll.129-138 *occur after* l.172
in G. 130. troppeaux *AF,* troppeaulx *BH,* troupeaux *C,* troupeaulx *J,* tropeaulx *V,* bergiers *G;* grands *A,* grand *F.* 131. vien-
nent *A.* 132. Palez *D,* Pales *F,* Palas *J;* pastis *ABEGV,* pastilz
H. 133. coeurent *A,* courre *B,* treuve *C,* tourne *JV;* apatis *AEF,*
apastis *BGH.* 134. Lerbe *G.* 135. sante *C.* 136. Tout *F;* sen *G.*
137. continuee *J.* 138. Qu'a]qui a *BE;* venue *B.*
    No division after l.138 *in AC.* 139.et]si *AG.* 140. *Missing in*
E; bereides *C,* nieraydes *V;* nereïdes saines *missing in J;* fines
C. 142. prochaines *AH.* 144. la]le *A;* undoye *BCHV.* 146. par-
fons *ABCGH,* parfaitz *JV;* demaines *ACFGJV.* 147. Convertis-
sez *ABCEFGHV,* convertisses *J.* 150. larmoie *ABEFGJ.*

314   *Studies in Medieval Literature*

O dryades que j'amoye,
Oyez la requeste moye;
Toute herbe qu'on marche ou broye,
Tout bois qu'à present ombroye
155   Et verdoye,
Soit fait plus sec que la plaine
Sur quoy le souleil flamboye,
Si que tout plaisir se noye
Et que l'ombre jamais n'oye,
160   Pour or fin ne pour monnoye,
    Chant de joye
Ne quelque chose mondaine.

O vous, Pana, dieu des pastours,
Puis que la Mort ne fait pas tours
165   En qui desormais nous fion,
Muez en deul tous vos atours
Et que plus ne chante d'amours
La challemye d'Amphion;
Mais en desert nous en fuyon
170   Où la faulse Mort deffion,
Qui a le bon pastour surprins
Où tous biens estoient comprins.

---

151. *Missing in A;* duades *V.* 152. Oyez la res *J;* r.m.]r.de m.
H. 153. ou]et *ACGJV.* 153a. *Extra line* Et que lamenter on voye
in A. 154. qu'a] qui a *JV,* qui *D.* 156. Sont *C.* 157. qui
BCEFGJV. 158. Et *J.* 159. et que plus chanter on noye *H;*
que]que en *AB,* quen *EFG.* 160. or fin] onys *C.*

No division after l.162 *in D.* 163. Panas *A,* pan le *B,* panna *E.*
165. fuyons *A,* fions *BV.* 166. Mirez *A,* menez *C,* mues *V;* doeil
AG, dueil *B,* deueil *C;* noz *C.* 167. chantez *V.* 168. *Blank space
in E;* demphion *BF.* 169. fuyons *J,* fions *V.* 170. deffion]dam-
phyon *A.* 171. sousprins *A,* suprins *BEV,* seurprins *C,* soubpris
F, sourprins *G,* sourpris *H,* surpris *J.* 172. compris *FH.*

Helas! et que dira
Quant ceste mort sçaura
175 La bergiere de France?
Qui la confortera?
Las! comment portera
Cette grant doleance?
La Mort par arrogance
180 Cuyde leur alliance
Rompre, mais non fera;
Tant comme elle vivra
En aura souvenance
Et le regretera;
185 Car si grant habundance
Entre eulx deux d' amour a
Que quant par l'ordonnance
De Dieu deffinera
Es cieulx, c'est ma fiance,
190 Son esprit l'amenra.

Au moyns pour nos piteux recors
Faictes, grant Dieu, misericors
Que la tumbe où il sera mis
Luy soit aussi plaisant au corps
195 Comme d'ung fleuve les accors

No division after l.172 *in AD*. 173. quen *BFGH*, que en *E*;
diras *D*. 174. verra *A*, sara *G*. 175. bergire *E*. 176. le *A*. 180.
qui de *JV*. 181. ne *A*; porra *A*, sera *J*. 182. que elle *ABFH*;
vivera *AB*. 183. ara *A*. 184. la *C*; regrectera *FHV*. 185. grand
A. 186. En *G*; deux *missing in AEFH*; d'amour a]damour y
a *A*, demourra *C*, damours a *EH*, amour a *V*. 189. est *CHJV*.
190. ame *A*, esperit *GH*, espoir *JV*; laymera *ABDG*, lamenera
V.

No division after l.190. *in CD*. 191. nos *missing in A*; recorder
A. 192. granz *B*, grans *CE*; dieux *BE*. 193. tombe *ABEF*. 194.
plaisante *E*. 195. de un *A*, dun *CEGHJ*, au *F*; d'ung f.] din-

Aux gens sur la rive endormis,
Affin que plus ne soit submis
Aux labeurs de ce bas païs
Où nous n'avons heure ne terme,
200   Car au monde n'y a rien ferme.

Donc puis qu'en si briefve espace
Ce que Nature compasse
      Passe
Plus tost assez que le pas,
205   Et qu'à chacun pas qu'on passe
La Mort est, qui nous menasse
      Nasse
Pour nous happer au trepas,
Prions le Dieu qui repasse,
210   Le Juste qui ne trespasse
      Passe
Ne loy faicte par compas,
Que tellement le parface
Qu'en le voyant face a face
215   Face
De gloire son doulx repas.

---

struments *D;* ators *V*. 196. A *D;* la rive] les rives *C*, rivage
D, la rivex *G*, rivez *J*. rivieres *V*. 197. soient *B*. 198. bas]plat
G. 199. nous n'avons] il ny a *G*, nous navons ny *V*. 200. n'y
a] na *V; riens CEFGHJV*.

No division after l.200 *in ADF*. 201. que en *AG*, que *CF;*
si *missing in CJ*. 202. *Missing in D*. 204. P.t. a.] a.p.t. *G*. 205.
qu'on passe] compasse *CJV*. 206. est] a *BEFG, missing in*
CJV, a *struck out and* fort *added between* qui *and* nous *in H*.
209. *Missing in G;* que *J;* qui]qui tout *A*, quil *V;* compasse *D*.
210. Le]et le *B;* quil *CD*. 212. No *A*. 213. ie *V*. 214. *Missing in*
A; qu'en le v.] que le voient *B*, quen len voye *C*, quant ie
voy *V*. 216. De la gloire *A;* repas] trepas *DF*.

L'acteur

A ces motz la voix luy failly
Et cheut, comme ung homme assailly
De mort, sur ceulx qui gemissoient.
220 Là eussiez veu autour de luy
Maint visaige blanc et pally,
Car leurs cueurs de deull perissoient:
Des grans soupirs qui en yssoient
Tous les bois en retentissoient.
225 Jamais ne fut veu tel meschief;
C'est grant deul de perdre bon chief.

Quant sa vigueur ot recouvert
D'un manteau gris s'est descouvert,
Puis a escript de son cousteau
230 Sur l'escorce d'un laurier vert,
Par en hault de feuilles couvert,
Ung epitaphe tout nouveau;
En gros langaige pastoureau,
Non pas si orné ne si beau
235 Comme font les grans advocas,

Rubric]Missing in ADE. Ll. 217-226 *missing in V.* 217.
faillit *A.* 218. chut *AG,* chiet *B;* homme]font *G.* 220. Et *J;*
eussez *G;* autours *C,* entour *J;* ly *E.* 221. paly *BFJ.* 222. leur
H; cueurs]cueur *H. blank space in J;* doeil *A,* deul *B,* dueil
CEFHJ, doeul *G.* 223. Et si g.s.y jettoient *G;* De *ABDF;*
grands *A;* quen *C.* 224. Que *G;* li *C;* retondissoient *C.* 225.
Onques *G;* ne]nen *H.* 226. grand *A;* doeil *A,* dueil *BCEFGHJ,*
doeul *G;* son *BCH,* son *corr. to* ung *by different hand in E;*
chef *BCE,* cheff *F.*

No division after l.226 *in AD. Ll.*227-236 *missing in V.* 227.
sa v.] la voys il *B,* sa vie *J;* eut *BCE,* eult *G.* 228. D'un m.g.]
De son manteau *AG.* 230. *Missing in A;* lescorche *CG,* les
corte *J.* 231. *Missing in A;* en]le *D,* cy *F;* hante *F.* 232. tant *J;*
langage *G.* 234. orné]rime *AFG,* lime *BCEH,* luysant *J;* biau
G. 235. ces *D,* ses *C.*

Chacun parle selon son cas.

    Le premier epitaphe
Il y avoit en l'escripture
Jadis menay paistre en pasture
Ung tropeau, le plus beau des beaux,
240   Et plantay dedans ma clousture
Deux arbres de meisme nature,
Portans tous les ans fruiz nouveaux;
Et lors que les bons pastoureaux
Y amenoient leurs aigneaux
245   En l'ombre pour eulx refrechir
Mort m'a fait en terre flechir.

    L'acteur
Adonques Ysembart le roux,
Qui par tristesse avoit desroux
Ses cheveux et sa cotte grise,
250   Se leva en son grant courroux
Et dist franchement devant tous:
"Je feray plus haulte entreprise."
Alors a sa houlette prise
Et dessus une pierre bise
255   Grava comme savoir pourrez
L'epitaphe que vous orrez.

---

236. son]le A. *Text ends at* l.236 *in* J.

Rubric]Epitaphe AF, *missing in* E. Ll. 237-246 *missing in*
V. 237. en e. H. 238. mene BCGH; pestor C. 239. biau G;
biaulx G. 240. cousture C. 242. nouviaulx G. 243. *Missing in*
E; bons *missing in* G; pastouriaulx G. 245. rafrechir GH. 246.
en terre]en lheure A, cy lombre F.

Rubric]*Missing in* AE, le deuxieme epitaphe B. Ll. 247-256
missing in V. 247. Ysembars D; doulx C. 248. de roux A,
desfroux C. 249. robe A. 251. prestement B. 252. grant C.
253. A.a. sa h.p.]Et lors sa h. a p.A, et alors sa h. a p.CF,
adonques sa h.a p. BEG. 255. Grava]grans C; porres G. 256.
orez G

Le ii epitaphe

Charles suy, grant pastour de France
Qui de mes pastiz par puissance
Chassay jadiz maint loup sauvage,
260   Et bergiers par bonne ordonnance
Feis chanter en grant concordance
Chant de paix, soubz le bois umbrage;
Et ores, sans passer oultre aage,
La Mort, par son cruel oultrage,
265   A eu sur mes biensfaiz envie
Et m'a deserité de vie.

L'acteur

Alors le bon homme Thierry
Qui estoit doulent et marry
S'en vint à travers les herbiz
270   Et a dit du pasteur chery
"Feray dictié plus seignoury.
Laissez-moy oster mes habiz
Et, me deust couster ma brebis,
J'escripray sur ce marbre bis."
275   Mais mieulx eust anté une graffe,
Neantmoins fist cest epitaphe.

Rubric]*Missing in ABEF;* La *G.* 257. grant]le *H.* 259.
Chace *B;* saulvaige *A,* sauvaige *BEF,* sauvaiges *C.* 260.
bergiere *D;* bonne]grant *G.* 261. Fis *ABFH,* Faiz *C.* 262.
Champs *C,* Chanp *G,* Chantz *H;* bois *corr. to* bel *by different
hand in E.* 263. *Missing in E, where different hand has added*
La mort par son cruel oultrage *in margin;* eaige *A,* eage *B,*
age *G.* 265. biensfaiz]biens *C,* bienfaiz *F.*

Rubric]*Missing in E. Ll. 267-276 missing in A.* 267. Lors *F,*
Tantost *G;* tierry *BF,* thery *H,* therry *V.* 268. dolent *BEGH,*
dollent *F,* doulant *V.* 269. sen va *CV,* passa *G;* au *CGV;* ses
CFV, des *G;* brebiz *CFGV.* 270. a dist]dist *G;* du]pour le *G;*
egery *V.* 271. seray *FV;* ditie *BF,* dist il *E,* dit *V.* 272. ester *V.*
273. mes *C.* 274. escipre *B.* escriray *V;* barbre *V.* 275. ente

Le iii epitaphe

Je suis le pastour qui jadis
Le jardin françois deffendis
Contre l'ivernalle froidure,
280   Et en tel estat le rendis
Que c'estoit humain paradis,
Flourissant et plain de verdure;
Mais Mort, dont la rigueur trop dure,
A mis soubz une pierre dure
285   Mon corps par maniere de lame.
Priez à Dieu qu'il en ait l'ame!

L'acteur

Quant leurs dictiez furent assiz
A grans troupeaux de cincq a six
S'en vont vers le chasteau courant,
290   La face encline, tous pensiz,
Les coeurs doloreux et transiz,
Comme gens qui s'en vont mourant.
Là veïssiez maint homme plourant
Lors les bergiers du demourant
295   De leurs lermes firent devoir;
Ung piteux fait l'autre esmouvoir.

BG, ame C, hante E; grac C, graphe EF. 276. fist]il fist
CEFGH, feit il D; ceste C.

Rubric]Missing in E. Ll. 277-286 *missing in* A. 277. pasteur
BCEFHV. 278. vergier G; de france F, franchois G. 279.
infernale CV, invanalle E, inernale G. 281. estoit E. 282.
Florissant EGHV; et p.de v.]contre la brodure G. 283. tant
CV, est EG. 284. *Missing in* C; sur V; une ceste D.

Rubric]missing in V. 287. lours F; dictez B, dites F, dittiers
AG, dictes V. 288. de]a ABFGV, ou C, les E; chincq A; a]ou
C, les E. 289. la chartre A. 290. pensifz BCEFH. 291. *Missing
in* A; coeurs G, meurs V; pensifs CV. 292. C.g.] Comme font
gens C; s'en]se C. 293. vindrent AG; plorant E. 294. le G. 295.
debvoir A. 296. Lun GV.

Les ungs veïssiez pourmener
Destordans leurs mains et mener
Aspre deul excessivement,
300   Les soupirs des nobles sonner,
Clameurs par les airs resonner,
En lamentant piteusement.
Je croy a mon entendement
Que depuis le commancement
305   Qu'en France y ot roy couronné
Ne fust si tresgrant corroux né.

Si leur deul vouloye descripre
Il me faudroit forme d'escripre
Changer, qui est grosse et rustique;
310   Car qui de noblesse veult lire
Par raison il y doit eslire
Figure trop plus autentique,
Elegie ou chant eroïque.
Si fineray ma bucolique
315   Pour nouvelle matiere prendre
Qui m'est bien haulte a entreprendre.

---

297. veissies *AV;* les uns veissiez la p.*B,* les uns lors v.p.*D,* les uns veissiez vous p.*V.* 298. Detordans *A,* Destortans *BV,* destordant *G;* bras *CV.* 299. excessantement *V.* 300. de *AFG.* 301. *Missing in A;* leurs *H;* oirs *F,* hoirs *V;* raisonner *C.* 302. lamentans *E.* 303. a]en *ABEFG.* 304. commenchement *A.* 305. y *missing in B;* eut *CEV.* 306. si tresgrant] aussi grant *B,* ung si grant *CV.*

307. Si de *B;* leurs dis *G.* 308. fauldra *V;* fournir *F.* 309. grose *C.* 310. qui de]que *V;* noble *F;* voet *G,* vueil *V.* 311. y]*missing in CV,* luy *FG.* 313. Elegie]En son engien *A,* Lege *C,* Elegre *G,* Helegre *V;* au *A;* chant]autre *CV,* hault *G;* herricque *A.* 314. Cy *CHV;* princolique *C.* 315. prandre *E.* 316. bien missing in *CV;* hault *AH.*

Le proheme sur la complainte de Noblesse et parle
    L'acteur
Ou trop peu suis du feu d'amour espris,
Ou si grant pois de charge ay entrepris
En presumant reciter de Noblesse
320   Le deul piteux qui durement nous blesse;
Qu'en contemplant ses tresdoloreux faiz
Mon povre engin tremble dessoubz le fais
Et n'ose à peu ma matiere assaillir,
Tant doubte et crains que n'en puisse saillir
325   Fors par le pas de reprehension.
Mais vraye amour me donne impression
Du cas piteux, et me vient inciter
A ces dures complaintes reciter,
Disant: "Mieulx vault de venir à l'ataincte
330   Que la memoire en fust du tout extaincte."

Rubric]Lacteur *A;* sensuit le prologue sur la complainte de Noblesse *B;* sensuit le proesme sur la complainte de noblesse et dit lacteur de rechief; Prologue de lacteur voullant introduyre Noblesse *E;* Le prologue sur la complainte de noblesse et dit lacteur *F;* sensieult le proesme sur la complainte de noblesse et de rechief lacteur dist *G;* sensuit le proesme sur la complainte de leglise (*sic*) et dit rechief lacteur *H;* sensuit le proesme sur la complainte de noblesse et dit lacteur *V.* 317. Ou t.p.s.]Ou je s.t.*A,* ou t.je s.*BF;* amours *BCDHV.* 318. poix *BEFGHV,* pris *C.* 319, poursuivant *BCV;* reciter]le onour *C.* 320. doeul *AG,* dueil *BEFH,* doulx *C;* clerement *CV.* 321. si *E,* ces *V;* fayz *corr. to* faitz *by different hand in E,* ditz *V.* 322. tramble *FG,* tremblant *H,* trouble *V.* Ll. 323 *and* 324 *reversed in G.* 323. ma *missing in V.* 324. tant que souvent men commēt tresaillir *G;* ne *V.* 326. vroy *B,* vray *D;* oppression *ACV.* 327. et me veult *ABEFGH,* je me vueil *CV.* 328. ses *GH;* tresdures *H.* Ll. 329-330. *missing in G.* 329. de]te *CV,* den *EF;* latainte *BCV,* lattainte *FH.* 330. memore *A;* fut *F.* 331.

D'autre cousté crainte, qui mon coeur touche,
Ne veult souffrir que j'entreuvre la bouche,
Car trop seroit à l'oeuvre derogante
S'elle n'estoit plus haulte et elegante.
335 Ainsi ne sçay laquelle preferer;
L'une entreprend, l'autre veult differer,
Par quoy je suis en guerre continue.
Si ce ne fust que Raison est venue
Sur ce debat plus n'eusse dit mot d'ame;
340 Mais la treshaulte et excellente dame,
Qui à tous rent sa portion esgalle,
A decreté par sanction legalle
Qu'il vaut trop mieulx d'en dire aucune chose
Que la pitié fust reposte et enclose
345 En la prison d'Oubliance la sourde.
Pourtant, affin que la douleur en sourde
Par chant piteux et par voix lamentable
Es sept climatz de la terre habitable
Et qu'ès suppostz de l'ente paternelle
350 Soit reluisant en memoire eternelle,

---

coste *EFGV;* cremeur *A;* que *CV,* qui plus a *F.* 332. je en
oeuvre *AF,* je treuve *G,* ie oeuvre *V;* ma *ABGH.* 333. soit *B.*
334. Celle *E;* estoit *C;* eslargante *C.* 335. proferer *CV.* 336.
entreprens *B;* vieulx *B.* 337. Par ce *A,* Pourtant *G,* Ainsy *CV.*
338. et si ne f.R.qui est v.*E;* se me *F.* 339. neussiez *H;* de ame
F. 340. treshault *GH;* elegante *V.* Ll. 341 *and* 342 *reversed
in B.* 341. rend *ABE.* 342. decide *A;* sa s. *V.* 343. Qui *ADF;*
Disant mieulx vault *G;* en *ACEF.* 344. memoire *BF;* recluse
A, repouse *C,* rebouste *D,* repouste *F.* 346. Affin quaucune
chose en sourde *B;* doulceur *A,* dolceur *H;* enfrondre *G.*
347. Pour *B;* chans *A,* champ *G;* lamentables *A,* lamentelle
C. 348. Es elemens *A.* Ll. 349 *and* 350. *missing in B.* 349.
que es *ADEF,* que *CH,* le *G* quelz *V;* suppos *A,* supost
G, supportz *H;* lante *C,* langue *E,* leur *V;* paternalle *H.*
350. *Missing in V.*

Devers Clyo me convient recourir
En luy priant qu'en moy face courir
La fontaine de divine eloquence
Ou face en moy l'esperit de lactance
355   Ressusciter, si qu'en ma bouche afflue
Son beau parler et langue melliflue.
Donc moy voulant en elle confier
Commanceray à vous versifier
De Noblesse la complainte sensible
360   Pour le moyns mal qui me sera possible.
        Noblesse parle
Dieu immortel, qui soubstenez l'empire
Où jamais rien ne dechet ne empire,
Faictes mon cueur mollifier et fendre
A celle fin qu'à mon ayse souspire
365   Et qu'en tel deul que nul n'estoit soubz pire
Puissent mes yeulx fleuves de lermes rendre,
Puis que la Mort, qui chacun veult offendre

---

351. Vers elle cy *A*, Denant *C*, Devant *V;* recouvrir *V*.
352. A celle fin *B;* ouvrir *V*. 354. lespeoir *A*, lesprit *C;*
latance *C*, lactence *EFH*, lattente *GV*. 355. si et *AC;*
la *H*. 356. Son]De *A*. 357. Dont *ABCEFGH;* voeillant *A*,
vueillant *CEV*, vaillant *FG*, veillanz *H*. 358. veriffier *V*.
360. Par *AEFGH*, Dont *C*, Tout *V;* les *F;* mains *ACGH;*
quil *AGV*.

Rubric]La complainte de noblesse *B*, senssieult la complainte de noblesse *G*, Noblesse *ACEFHV*. 361. dieux *BCEFG;*
immortelz *BCEFGH;* soustenes *A*, soustenez *BCEFGH*. 362.
riens *ABGHV;* dechiet *ACHV;* ny *G*, ou *BCHV;* yeulx *F*,
yeux *corr. to* cueur *by different hand in E;* molestez en fondre
C. 365. *Missing in A;* en *B*, quant *V;* dueil *BEFHV*, deueil *C*,
doel *G;* que]ou *G;* ne soit *BCEH*, nosoit *FV*, ne poet *G;*
suspire *C*, souffire *G*, soubz mis *H*, soubzrire *V*. 366. mes
missing in V; larmes *AEFGV*. 367. que la]qua *H;* qui]que

Sans pardonner, preserver ou deffendre,
A convaincu par sa mortelle guerre
370 Roy le plus craint qui fust dessus la terre.

C'estoit de Mars le fort bras laudatoire
Lequel dompta par triumphant victoire
Le grant orgueil du Liepart redoubtable.
C'estoit le mur et seur repositoire
375 Qui le salut des Françoys et la gloire
Faisait flourir en haultesse admirable.
C'estoit un roy sur tous inexpugnable,
Dont le povoir et force inestimable
Faisoit trembler par faiz plains de louanges
380 Les nations barbares et estranges.

Trespuissant roy, doulx entre les humains,
Toutes vertus te tendoient les mains
Pour accomplir ta cronique et ta geste.
Tes nobles faiz, trop plus divins qu'humains,
385 Passoient plus en beaulté les Rommains
Que le souleil tout autre corps celeste;
Tout autre bruyt rendois sourd et terreste,

ACDHV; vieult c.o.*B;* doibt attendre *A.* 368. perserver *C;* ne *G,* et *V;* offendre *A.* 369. *Missing in A.* 370. Roy plus noble *A,* Le plus grant roy *B,* Roy le plus grant *V;* soit *A,* fut *BFG.*

No division after l.370 *in AD.* 371. Sestoit *D;* le bras fort *V;* brach *A,* roy *H;* laudatere *A.* 372. Qui *A;* rebuta *A,* osta *B.* 373. liepard *CFV;* doutable *V.* 375. glore *G.* 376. mirable *D,* muraille *H.* 377 inexpunable *CV.* 378. forche *G.* 379. flourir *G;* loenge *A,* louenges *BFGHV.*

No division after l.380 *in A.* 382. tiendrons *C;* humains *C.* 383. amplier *A,* emplir *B,* employer *corr. to* emplyer *by different hand in E,* amployer *F,* racomplir *G;* la *G;* couronne *FG;* la *G.* 384. divins]sur les *A,* divers *V.* 385. romains *BE,* humains *C,* roumans *H.* 387. *Missing in A;* rendoie *C,* rendoient

Et malgré Mort tant nous laisses de reste
De ta splendeur qu'à perpetuité
390 Resplendira en ta posterité.

Son cueur royal, de vices propugnacle,
Et de vertus le divin receptacle,
Fut consacré pour mettre ma couronne;
Le temple fut et pompeux tabernacle
395 Ouquel j'assis au plus hault du pinacle
Mon tribunal et mon glorieux trosne.
Mais la poignant et perverse matronne
Qui deul pourtrait et tristesse patronne
A desmoly l'artifice et versé
400 Dont mon estat est cheu et renversé.

Haulte maison, triumphant et royalle,
En qui le roy de l'Arche imperialle
Transmist jadis le tresprecieulx liz,
Ta grant clarté, ta main medicinalle

D, rendoist *H*, rendys *V*; son enterreste *B*; tregeste *CV*, terrestre *EG*, diestr *H*. 388. Mais *CV*; n.l.t.de r. *A*; tout *CV*; laisse *BCEFHV*. 389. resplandeur *C*. 390. Resplandiras *A*; sa *G*.

391. Ton *BCEFV*; loyal *CHV*; vice *AFHV*, biens *E*; toz *added in different hand between* de *and* biens *in E*; propugnable *AG*, propinacle *CHV*. 392. vertu *A*; receptacle *AGH*, respectacle *corr. to* receptacle *by different hand in E*. 394. fist *C*, fu *D*, fuz *EV*. 395. Lequel ·*A*, Auquel *C*, Ou *H*, Au ceruel *V*; assis *CV*; ou *FG*; pignacle *A*. 396. mon *missing in CV*. Ll.397 *and* 398 reversed in *CV*. 397. diverse *BGHV*. 398. Que *CV*; doeul *A*, dueil *BEFGV*, deueil *C*, dieu *H*; passionne *H*. 399. lediffice *B*. 400. dont je suis cheu (cheute *E*, chut *G*) et plusieurs renverse (fois verse *A*) *ABCEFGHV*.

402. l'Arche] leure *C*, bonte *V*. 403. lis *AFG*, lys *BEV*. 404. Sa *CV*; medicinable *ACGV*.

405 Dont par vertu haulte et especialle
Tous les humains et le monde embelliz,
Ton cueur, tes biens, tes sumptueux deliz
Sont rabatuz, extains et aboliz;
Car pour doulx chants et accors d'instrumens
410 Mort y a mis pleurs et gemissemens.

Traistresse Mort, en qui fureur s'atise,
Qui te maudit et anathematise
Il n'a pas tort à mon oppinion,
Quant aujourduy, par ta fiere entreprise,
415 D'un corps royal où Dieu l'ame avoit mise
Tu as rompu l'amoureuse union,
Dont en douleur et en affliction,
En cris piteulx et lamentation
Romps et despars l'amoureuse assemblée
420 Qu'espoir jamais ne sera reassemblée.

Que te grevoit sa santé desirée
En qui gisoit la vie bienheurée
Et le salut de tant de nobles hommes?
Que te nuysoit sa force incomparée

---

405. esperitable *A.* 406. Sont *CV.* 407. eur *CFV,* heur *E;* precieux *A,* soucieux *C.* 408. Sont destrins rabatuz *C,* Sont extains rabatuz *V;* et *missing in V;* amoliz *C.* 409. chantiers *C,* champs *BG.*

No division after 1.410 *in A.* 411. Traittre *A,* Tristreuse *B,* tritesse *C,* tristesse *FHV,* traistre *G.* 412. mal dist *A,* mauldit *BCFV,* maudict *E;* ou *ABEF.* 414. ta *missing in B;* folle *ABH.* 415. Du *EF;* cueur *H.* 416. Tu] En *A, missing in C.* 418. cris] cas *A;* et] en *ACEFV.* 419. Rends *G.* 420. saura *C.*

Ll. 421-430, *less* 1. 424 *which is missing, occur in the following order in A;* 429-30, 427-8, 421-3, 425-6. 421. le *V;* saincte *A,* sente *H.* 422. bien euree *BCFH,* bieneuree *V.* 423. tant de] tes *C.* 424. le *V;* craingnoit *C,* grevoit *V;* forche *G.*

425 Qui a de fait en Gaule reparée
     La liberté et la paix où nous sommes?
     Si tu pouvois porter si pesans sommes
     Que sans cesser tu ne feisses que sommes
     Tu n'auroys pas calculé le domage
430 Qu'en France as fait par ton cruel oultrage.

     C'estoit Hector, deffenseur d'Ilyon,
     L'autre Achilles, au hault cueur de lion,
     Per d'Ulyxes en douceur de faconde,
     L'autre Hercules, le trescler Scipion,
435 Portant le nom comme bon champion,
     Loué ès cieulx, doubté par tout le monde;
     C'estoit Brutus, en justice profonde,
     L'autre David, qui par ung coup de fonde
     L'orgueil anglois si durement dompta
440 Qu'onques depuis il ne ressuscita.

     Quant sans cesser Nature la descrete
     Feroit forger en sa chambre secrete,

---

425. as *CHV;* deffait *GHV,* defaict *corr. to* de faict *by scribe
B,* deffaict *corr. to* de fait *by different hand in E.* 427. pooies
A; grandes *B,* poisans *E.* 428. sans cesser] milliers *E; a different hand has added* a *between* que *and* milliers *and* tu *between*
milliers *and* ne *in E;* feisse *AE,* feisstes *BH,* feissons *CV.* 429.
ne aroies *A,* nauroies *CGV;* cartule *A,* caculle *G;* dommaige
ABCEF. 430. Qu'en] Qua; oultraige *ABCE.*

Ll. 431-440 *missing in A.* 431. dylion *BF,* dillion *C,* de lyon
G, dylyon *V.* 432. Achiles *EG,* Archile *V; a H;* grant *G;* dellion
C. 433. Par *CFHV;* Ulixes *BCEFGHV;* doulceur *BGH,* doulcur
C, douleur *FV.* 434. Herculles *B;* trescher *BC;* Cypion *BGH,*
Cipion *CDV.* 436. doubté] et craint *BCEFGV,* crains *H.* 437.
parfonde *BC.* 438. Cestoit *G;* cop *GH.* 439. englois *C;* tant
BCFGHV; durement] bien *corr. to* rudement *by different
hand in E;* bouta *CV.* 440. rescuscita *G.*

     442. Eult fait *G;* forgier *CGH.*

Où les humains organise et pourtrait,
Ou si le Dieu, qui tout juge et decrete,
445 Faisoit venir Pymalion de Crete
Pour entailler ymage de beau trait
En qui Pallas eut son tresor retrait,
Si n'en pourroit estre de mieulx pourtrait
Qui en valeur deust ce roy seignourir;
450 S'à Dieu eust pleu pas ne devoit mourir.

Les airs serains, fulcis de transparence,
Le firmament et sa noble influence
Nous ont promis tousjours de bien en mieulx,
Qu'il reviendroit en sa convalescence.
455 Comment a eu donc la Mort resistance
Aux elemens et au povoir des cieulx?
Conclurre fault qu'avons yré les dieux,
Qui l'ont ravy au trosne glorieux
Pour luy donner nom d'immortalité
460 Et nous oster nostre felicité.

---

443. Ou]Quo *C*, Qui *V;* organist *AFV*, organisses *C*. 444. si
missing in A; si le]celluy *V*. 445. Pimalion *ACG*, Pymalyon *B*,
Pigmalyon *E*, Pimalyon *F*, Pismalion *H*, Pigmalion *V*. 446.
ymaige *CV;* traict *BEV*. 447. *Missing in AB;* Palas *DEF*,
Palais *V;* en *CH*, eust *EF*, et *V;* retraict *EV*. 448. ne *AGV;*
pourtraict *ABCEV*. 449. valleur *ACE;* deubst *A*, deussent *V;*
ce]comme *A*, se *FH*, *missing in V*. 450. eult *G;* pleut *G;*
debvoit *ABE*.
No division after l.450 *in A*. 451. sereins *B;* resplendence *A*,
temperance *BCV*. 452. Le f.]Qui le servoient *G*. 453. p.t.]t.p.*B;*
bon *B*, mieulx *CV*. 454. Ou il *C*, Qui ly *H;* revenroit *A*, reven-
droit *BGH*. 455. *Missing in C;* mais puisque mort a bailli
resistence *A*, c.a donc a eu m.r. *B*, c.a donc eu la m.r. *EG*,
c.a. donc la m.eu (eust *H*) r. *FHV*. 456. aux pouvoirs *E*.
457. ire *ABCGV*, irez *EFH*. 458. trose *C*. 459. don *CHV*.

L'acteur

Icy fina ses lamentables vers
Tainctz en douleur, de tristesse couvers,
Mais son grant deul de plus en plus s'alume
Lors près du corps lequel gisoit envers,
465 De vie extainct et convertible en vers,
Prouesse vint qui tenoit une plume,
En cueur portant douloureuse amertume,
Et escripvit comme il est de coustome
Autour du roy, cui Dieu face mercy,
470 En lectres d'or cest epitaphe cy.

Premier epitaphe

Jadis fus né en maison triomphant;
Moult me greva Fortune jeusne enfant,
Mais trop plus fort pour ung temps de mon regne;
Et depuis Dieu me fist roy si puissant
475 Que je chassay le Liepart ravissant
Et si conquis Normandie et Guyenne.
Mais pour monstrer que gloire terrienne
Passe legier, la couronne ancienne
Laisse aujourduy par ung dur dessaroy

Rubric] *Missing in EH.* 461. Jai sievy *A;* ces *F,* les *H.* 462.
Tant *A,* Tains *BCFGHV;* couvert *A.* 463. grand *A;* doeul *AG,*
dueil *BEFHV,* deueil *C.* 463. se allume *E,* se alume *F.* Ll.
464 *and* 465 *reversed in B.* 465. *Missing in ACV;* De dueil
pourtraict *B;* comestible *F,* converti *G;* en]de *F.* 466. Fut
proesse *A,* Prouesse vint *B,* Prouesse estoit *CV;* tendit *AB.* Ll.
467 *and* 468 *reversed in BG.* 467. cueurs *BEH,* cuer *FV.* 469.
cui]que *ACV.*

Rubric] Proesse *AE,* Epitaphe premier de la prouesse *B,*
Proesse primum epitaphium *CH, missing in F;* pmier epitaphe
de proesse *G,* Proesse premier epitaphe *V.* 471. fut *AF,* fu
BD. 472. me greva]ne gre *C.* 473. fort *missing in CV.* 474.
ma *CV;* fait *CV,* feit *D,* feist *E.* 475. je chace *V.* 477. que
missing in C; glore *G,* gloier *V.* 478. anchienne *A.* 479. dur]
deur *C, missing in F;* desarray *V.*

480 Au propre lieu où je prins nom de roy.
        Second epitaphe
      Cy gist des Francs le puissant protecteur,
      Du veul de Mars le grant executeur,
      Chief de noblesse et le pareil des preux,
      De vieil meschief nouveau reparateur
485 A qui est deu, comme triumphateur,
      D'estre nommé Charles Victorieux.
      Nom si trescler, tant hault, tant glorieux,
      Que ja de Mort les dars impetueux
      N'y toucheront, mais tousjours demourra
490 Nom immortel, qui jamais ne mourra.
        Tiers epitaphe
      Cy gist l'amour des fins orientalles,
      L'espoir des Grecz ès cités capitalles,
      La seure paix des haulx mons Pirenées,
      La paour des Turcs, la craintes des Ytalles,
495 Dont le suppost par l'une des fatalles

Rubric] *Missing in* AEF; La ii epitaphe B, Sedm̄ epitaphiū
CH, troisieme *G* (this epitaph occurs after ll.481-490 in *G*).
481. Francs]bons *G*. 482. voeul *A*, vueil *BEFGV*, viel *C*,
vuel *H*; grand *A*. 483. Chef *AE*; des]de *V*. 484. *Missing in* A;
Des *H*; viel *BC*; vielz *H*; nouvel *CHV*, nouviau *G*. 485. deub
A. 487. O nom tant cler t.h.t.g.*A*, non (nom *EFV*) si treshault
t.c.t.g. *CEFV*, non si treshault et si tresglorieux *G*. 488. ars
CV; sumptueux *CV*. 489. mais *missing in* CV; t.d.t. lui d. *C*,
jamais d. *F*. 490. Non *BCEGH*; morra *G*.
    Rubric]*Missing in* AEF; Le iij epitaphe B, Tertiū epitaphiū,
deuzieme *G* (this epitaph occurs before ll.481-90 in *G*) 491.
Lonneur *CV*, lespoir *EF*. 492. gens *A*, gretz *C*; et *ABCEV*, en
G. 493. tresseure *A*; motz *corr. to* mons *in margin by different
hand in* A, noms *C*, nons *G*; prevees *A*, pirentables *C*. 494. de
sturcs *V*, des leurs *C*; Ytalies *A*. 495. *Missing in* A; dont] com
C, *missing in* V; par]et *F*, de *V*; liure *F*, une *G*, liures *V*.

A aujourduy ses joyes terminées,
Quant par rigueurs dures et obstinées
Celle qui mect la fin aux destinées
Fait son povoir rabaisser et descendre
500　Et convertir soubz ung petit de cendre.
　　　L'acteur
Quant en ce point, comme je vous descripz,
Furent ces trois epitaphes escripz,
Le corps porté fut par piteux mistere
Hors du chasteau. Là furent nouveaux cris,
505　Nouveaux souspirs de cueurs en deul contriz
Pour l'issue douloureuse et amere.
Querir le vint Sainte Esglise sa mere
Qui le receut en ung saint monastere;
Mais tant ploura quant vint au recevoir
510　Qu'il n'est engin qui le sceust concevoir.
　　　Le proesme sur la complainte de l'Esglise et dit
　　　　　L'acteur
De cueur rassiz et assez moderé
J'ay longuement en moy consideré

---

496. A *Missing in* CV; loix B. 497. Dont G; rigoeurs A,
rigueur C; dures *twice in* B. 498. Elle BE; mist A, met CG; la
missing in B; main CV. 499. faict AE; relaxer A. 500. sur
ACEV.

501. ce *missing in* F. 502. ses EF. 503. fut porte CV, pose fut
B; là *missing in* B; piteux A. 505. de *missing in* CV. cueur
BCHV; en]et B, et de H; courtoys C; n.s. doeul et piteux
escris A. 506. liesse G. 507. Q. le v.]Quant q.v. A; venit D. 508.
la BDFG; rechupt A, receu BDF; saint]grant C, *missing in* V.
509. *Missing in* C. 510. peust BEV, peult C.

Rubric]Missing *in* AB, Cy commence la complainte de
leglise (noblesse V) et dit lacteur CHV, lacteur D, la complainte de leglise et dit lacteur F, senssieult le proesme sur
la complainte de leglise et de rechief lacteur G. 511. et
missing in C. 512. Ay B; longuement]ja (*added in different*

Le desconfort et dure doleance
Et la pitié de l'Esglise de France:
515　Mais qui vouldroit tout dire et exprimer
Entreprendroit à espuiser la mer
Ou à nombrer les estoilles des cieulx,
Ou fol cuyder luy banderoit les yeulx
Et luy feroit soubz une obscure tente
520　De son engin descongnoistre l'estente,
Car ses regrez, piteux et desplaisans,
Noyez en pleurs, de tristesse pesans,
Ne furent pas de huyt ne de dix vers
Mais infiniz, voire trestous divers,
525　Enceins de deul et de corroux tant plains
Que s'en nos cueurs estoient bien emprains
Trop durement seroient hors des termes
Se par pitié ne fondoient en lermes;
Et qui plus est, ses tresdoloreux ditz
530　Ne furent onc qu'une seule foiz diz.
Le reciter passe donc le dommaine
Et la vertu de la memoire humaine,
Mais seroit mieulx pour nature angelique;
Nous qui usons de puissance organique
535　Enferme avons la memoire et debile

---

hand) long temps *E.* 514. De *G.* 515. tout *missing in F.* 516. espussier *G.* 517. les estoilles *twice in B.* 518. foul *BCF.* 519. Qui *B*; seroit *CV*; obscurte *V.* 520. la sente *ABDG. Division after* l.520 *in BE; B has rubric* Regrectz. 521. regards *A*, subgets *B.* 522. paissans *C*, poisans *E*, pensans *V.* 523. pas *missing in B.* 524. v. t.] et furent tous *B*, et tousiours *CV.* Ll.525-528 *missing in G.* 525. Et tant *A*, Estans *B*, En tams *CF*, Noiez *H*, En tēps *V*; tous *A*; prains *AEF*, pris *H.* 526. *Missing in B;* meurs *V.* 527. de *FHV.* 528. larmes *AEV.* 529. pis *G;* est *missing in V;* ces *V.* 530. oncq *AE*, oncques *BCGV*, pas *H.* 531. pas *H;* tout *A.* 532. vertus *V;* nature *C.* 533. par *A*, a *G.* 535. enfermez *V;* amour *A;* le *BV;* est *A;* labille *G.*

Par trait de temps oblieuse et labile.
Si ne veulx pas affermer par exprès
De dire tout ne ensuyvre de près
La gravité de sa doulce sentence,
540   Son beau parler ne sa haulte eloquence;
Mais contraint suis de dire aucune chose
De ce qui gist en mon cueur et repose,
Sellon mon sens rude, indigeste et creu,
Car ung homme est argué pour recreu
545   Qui fait ung grant ediffice lever
S'il a de quoy et ne fait achever.
Affin donques d'eviter tel reprouche
Craintivement veul entr'ouvrir ma bouche
Pour dire en gros de la tresbonne mere
550   La complainte doloreuse et amere.

      L'Esglise

Si vraye amour et pitié vous remort,
Peuple françoys, devez plourer la mort
De mon chier filz, le roy trescrestien,
Et de la Mort, qui tant durement mort

---

536. *Missing in* G; traict *BH*, traitz V; oublieuse A, oublieux
V; est H. 537. Et V; voeul A, vieulx B, vuoil C, vueil *EFHV*;
pour D. 538. *Missing in* A; touz H; ensuivir *BCF*, ensievir G,
ensiure H, ensuyvir V. 539. crainte BFV, cravite C, grevite *GH*;
doulx H; stille A. 540. *Missing in* A; ne *missing in* H. 541. Et
CV; contrains H; den *CGV*, en E; une F. 542. reppouse C.
543. *Missing in* A; rude *missing in* CV; recreu V. 544. pour]et
CV; recrez A. 545. hault *EFG*; eslever V. 546. de *missing in*
F; et *missing in* C; ne]ne la C, ne le V. 547. A.d.]Or a.d. A;
ce *CHV*; reproeuche A, reproche E. 548. Craintement *AEG*,
certainement B. 549. voeil A, vueil *BCFHV*, veulx E, voeul
G; la *EFV*. 549. tresdoulce H.

    Rubric La complainte de leglise B. 551. vray CH. 552.
P.f.plourez tous pour la m. A; venez *CHV*. 554. tres A.

555 Que mon plaisir en est extainct et mort,
     Cryez vengence au Dieu celestien;
     Vostre clameur et deul cotidien,
     Vos plains, vos pleurs me sembleront ung bien
     Consolatif, de tout autre l'eslite,
560 Car dolent cueur en lermes se delite.

     Pour mieulx plourer, complaindre et lamenter,
     Mes chiers enfans, ne laissez plus chanter
     Dedans vos cueurs Musique la joyeuse;
     S'en aille aux champs ou ès bois habiter
565 Affin qu'on puisse sa douceur eviter,
     Ou change en cris sa noyse armonieuse.
     N'escoutez plux sa voix melodieuse,
     Mais arrousez ma face doloreuse
     Incessamment de lermes infinies
570 Puis que la Mort a nos joyes ternies.

     Qui souffira à plourer ma fortune,
     Aigre à gouster, dolente et importune?
     Qui me pourra temps assez assigner?
     Je ne congnois peuple, gens ne commune

---

555. *Missing in* B; Dont V. 556. Cries V; roy ACE. 557. doeul
A. 559. Contemplatif A, consolatifs F; tous AEF; autres EF.
560. cueur (cueurs F) dolent EF; larmes ABEFGHV; de litte
AGH, delicte CEV.
    No division after l.560 *in* AV. 562. laissiez AG, laisser C.
563. En vostre coeur A; meurs V. 564. S'en voist A, S'en voise
E; ou]et CGV; au ABG, aux CHV, ung F; champs V; ou ès
b.]ouailles E. 565. *Missing in* V; puist AG, puise F; douleur
ABCDEGH. 566. changier C; voix ABCHV; amoureuse CV;
Ou c.soi en cris a.G.567. Nescoutons A. 568. arouses A, ar-
rouses G, arouser BH. 569. larmes ABEFGHV. 570. finies B;
p.q. nous a nos joyes terminees A.
    No division after l.570 *in* A. 572. au V. dolent B, dolant V.
573. assez temps ABCEFGV. 574. gens peuple BEF.

575 Qui bien peussent en tristesse commune
     Pour mon grant deul lermes assez finer;
     Car quant pitié en nos cueurs sans finer
     Ne cesseroit de lermes affiner
     Forger regrez, souspirs en pleurs confire
580 Trestous nos yeulx n'y sçauroient souffire.

     Puis que nos yeulx n'y souffiroient mye,
     Plourez o nous, saint homme Jheremye,
     Et obliez vostre captivité!
     Laissez Tarquin, Lucrece chiere amye,
585 Plourez mon filz, sans plus estre endormie,
     Et vous ferez oeuvre de charité!
     Thamar, laissez vostre virginité!
     L'oppression a chierement cousté,
     Faictes vos pleurs prendre tous nouveaux cours
590 Et nous donnez de vos lermes secours!

     Ne plourez plus pour l'exil des Troyens,
     Pour la cité ne pour les citoyens!
     Laissons Priam et le deul d'Hecuba!

---

575. *Missing in* A; puisse C, puissent H. 576. assez larmes
AFV; plourer A, finez B. 577. vos A. 578. larmes AEFGV,
plaintes B. 579. s.et p. ABC, p. en deuil E, en p.s. G. 580. vos
A; ne A; seroient G, sauroit H.
  No division after 1.580 *in* A. 581. vos A. 582. plourons A,
ploure G, pleures V; vous AEH, avons G; et hermite A. 583.
noubliez A, oubliez BCEF, oublies V. 584. Laissiez AG, laisses
V; Lucresse ABCEGHV; mie C. 585. pleures V; endormis AE.
586. feres V; leuvre B; carite AG, cherite D. 587. laissiez AG,
laisses V. 588, a c.]achienne A. 589. tous *missing in* BCV;
prenez tous nouveaux tours A. 590. donnes G; larmes ABEFV.
  No division after 1.590 *in* A. 591. plorons BEF, ploures G,
pleures V. 593. hector B, priant F, prian V; mort A, dueil
BCEFHV, doeul G.

Passons Hester et les Assiriens,
595 Laissons en paix les Macedoniens
Et leur bon roy que venin succumba;
Escripz piteulx assez sur sa tumbe a!
Mais sur tous ceulx qu'onques la Mort tumba
Pour nobles faiz de longues estendues
600 Sont à ce roy lermes grandement deues.

Conservateur de la foy catholique,
Vraye union du siege apostolique
Le puis nommer par grant preeminence.
Tousjours soustint l'election mistique
605 Et approuva la voye canonique
En reprouvant armes et violence,
Par quoy le nom de grant magnificence,
Trescrestien, en plus grant excellence
A eslevé en ses jours tresplaisans
610 Que ne feit roy depuis quatre cens ans.

Sur tous piliers de vraye foy massiz,
Il fut le chief sur lequel je m'assis

---

594. hector *ACV*. 595. Laissiez *G*. 596. qui *EV;* daire *V*, venin *changed to* daire *by different hand in E;* subcomba *BCV*. 597. Escus *V;* dessus *G;* sur *missing in G;* le *A*, la *H*. 598. iceux *A*. 599. longue *A*, lances *CV;* estendue *A*, attendues *G*. 600. larmes *ABEFGV;* longuement *G*.

Ll. 601-10 *missing in G*. 601. loy *V*. 602. *Missing in A*. 603. nomme *V*. 605. a promis *AE*, esprouva *CV;* vraye *CV*, vraye *corr. to* voye *by different hand in E;* baronicque *A*, cronicque *corr. to* canonique *by different hand in E*. 607. grand *A*. Ll. 608-10 *missing in G*. 608. grand *A*, grande *E*. 610. ny *C;* fist *CFV*, feist *E*, fust *H;* que ne fust passe a q.c.a. *A*, que roy ne fist *B*.

No division after l.610 *in AF*. 611. pilliers *ACEFGH*, pillers *B;* massifz *C*. 612. clef *A*.

En gloire, en paix et en beatitude,
Le largiteur de graces et merciz;
615 En ses grans jours d'onneur circumfulciz
Faisoit flourir toute divine estude
Dont tant s'acreut des clercs la certitude
Que nulle erreur en turbe ou multitude
N'osa penser d'entrer en quelque lieu
620 Dedans les murs de la Cité de Dieu.

Sa main tenoit l'espée flamboyant
Du Seraphin comme bon guerroyant
Sur le portail de ma maison sacrée,
Voire tant clere et tant irradiant
625 Qu'il n'y avoit riche ne mandiant
Qui eust osé approucher de l'entrée
S'il n'eust ou front l'enseigne consacrée;
Mais or la Mort, dont tout deul se concrée,
Luy est venue hors des poings arracher
630 Où roy mortel n'eust osé atoucher.

---

613. glore *G.* 614. Elargiteur *A,* illargiteur *BEFGHV,* illarg-
geur *C;* des *B;* grace *C;* merites *corr. to* merciz *by later hand
in E.* 615. circunfulsis *AB,* circonfleuriz *C,* circonfulsis *EF.*
616. la bonne *A,* dame *CV.* 617. De tant a de tous clercs *A;*
lexercitude *AG,* celsitude *BEFHV,* selsitude *D.* 618. nulle
terre *A,* heresie *B;* erreur *G.* 619. Nose *H;* passer *G;* nentrer
G; par *BCEH;* aucun lieu *ABG.* 620. Dedens *AGH.*

No division after l.620 *in A.* 621. flamboient *C,* fambloyant
F. 622. guerroyent *C.* 623. la *A,* me *G,* ma *missing in F,* sa
corr. to ma *by different hand in E;* sacre *V.* 624. trestout *A;*
cler *E.* 625 mendiant *ABEFGH.* 626. approchier *AGH,* ap-
procher *E.* 627. au *AEFV.* 628. or la] ores *B,* crulat *C;* tel *CV.*
629. a *AF,* est *missing in C;* esrachier *AG,* arrachier *CH.* 630.
attouchier *AC,* aproucher *B,* aprochier *GH,* approucher *V,*
attoucher *corr. to* aprocher *by different hand in E.*

O noble front de la pierre angulaire
Qui soubstenois en forme orbiculaire
Les plaisans fes de ma prosperité,
Ruby rayant par divin luminaire,
635   Chier ornement qui plus me povoit plaire
Pour les grans jours de ma sollenité,
Ta grant vertu, ta preciosité,
Ton cler regart plain de jocundité
Sont aujourduy comme par desconfort
640   Couchés en deul dessoubz l'ombre de mort!

Contre la Mort et ses faiz despiteux
Pourroye assez faire regretz piteux,
Mais en pitié ja pourtant ne m'orra.
Faisons nos cris monter jusques ès cieulx,
645   Cryons sans fin vengence au Dieu des Dieux;
Sa cruaulté ja pourtant ne mourra.
Pour tout confort le corps me demourra
Jusques à tant que l'ame y revenra.

No division after l.630 *in* A. 631. nobles V. 632. soustins A,
soustenois BFGH, soustenez CV; ambigulaire A, arbiculaire
CGV, obiculaire F, arbitulaire H. 633. faictz A, faiz BCH,
fais EG, faitz V. 634. Rubis ACH; variant A, rains H, rayent
V; luminere C. 635. ne p.p.p. B; me]ne BCV; pooit A, peut
C, poroit H, pourroit V. 636. biens A. 637. precieusite CV.
638. cher B, plain CV. 639. Est B; c.p.] par tres grand A.
640. Couche B, Couchiez GV; doeul A, dueil BCEFHV, doeul
G; umbre G.
   No division after l.640 *in* A. 641. faictz A, fais GH. 642.
Pourroit B. 643. pour moy ren ne dira H; ne me orra AEF,
ne mourra CV. 644. cueurs trestous H; montans C, montant
V; aux BCV. 645. *Missing in* V; crians G. 646. creante A;
pourtant ja B; morra AG, moura B, mourra *corr. to* morra
(by different hand?) *in* E. 647. la mort A. 648. reviendra CV,
revienra F, revendra G, rendra H, retournera *corr. to* retourna

Dieu doint qu'alors puisse monter ou royaume,
650 Glorifié tout en corps et en ame.
      L'acteur
      A tant se teut ceste dame excellente
      Qui bien sembloit angoisseuse et dolente
      Pour ceste mort piteuse et lamentable.
      Lors vis yssir Justice de sa tente,
655 Prudence après, qui mettoit son entente
      D'accompaigner Clemence piteable.
      Ces trois dames d'un vouloir amyable
      Vindrent asseoir comme il fut raisonnable
      En tables d'or fichées contre un mur
660 Ces vers piteux en grans lettres d'azur.
      Epitaphe de la Justice
      Soubz ce dolent et piteux edifice
      L'aigle formé par divin artifice
      Gist oppressé d'un repos trespesant,
      Qui par le vol de vertueux police
665 Tant s'approucha du soleil de justice
      Que tout son corps en fut resplendissant;
      Et chacun ray de son regart yssant
      Fut si tresdroit, si fort et si puissant
      Qu'onques fraude ne sceut par faulse estude

---

by different hand in E. 649. doint] tout *C;* qu'alors] alors quil
C; puist *AFV;* ou] en *AD,* au *CV.* 650. tout *missing in C,* cf.
1.649; et *deleted in E.*

651. adonc *CV;* taist *AB,* teust *CE,* teult *G;* celle *B.* 653. De
EF; et *missing in HV.* 654. veit *A,* vy *BF,* vey *H,* veyz *E,* vis
missing in C. 656. pitoyable *AEG.* 657. amiables *G.* 658.
comme *missing in CHV;* est *B.* 659. table *A;* fichee *A.*

Rubric]Missing in A; epitaphe de justice *EG,* Justice *F,*
epitaphe de sa justice *V.* 661. artifice *B.* 662. ediffice *B.*
663. d'un]en *E;* repoux *CF;* trop pesant *C,* si pesant *H.* 664.
voeul *A,* vueil *CV;* vertueil *C,* vertueuse *V;* prolixe *A.* 666.
plendissant *C,* replendissant *E.* 669. faulse]son *A.*

670 Faire obliquer sa vraye rectitude.
Epitaphe de la Prudence
Cy gist enclos le tresor de prudence,
L'arche d'honneur, la clef de sapience
Qui ne fut onques de vertu desnuée,
Le cler soleil, duquel la refulgence
675 Par tous les lieux de sa circumference
De bien en mieulx estoit continuée
Et ne povoit estre diminuée
Si n'eust esté la mortelle nuée
Qui est venue, comme elle est coustumiere,
680 Obtenebrer les rays de sa lumiere
Epitaphe de la Clemence
Cy gist le roy piteux et debonnaire,
De clemence le parfait exemplaire,
Tardif à nuyre et prompt à secourir,
Qui ne vouloit homme par mort deffaire;
685 Ains reduisoit son mortel adversaire
Sans faire sang sur terre decourir.
Le jour dolent que juillet feit courir
Pour vingt et deux la Mort le vint querir,

---

670. oublier *G*.

Rubric] Prudence *ADEF*, epitaphe de prudence *G*, epitaphe de sa prudence *V*. 672. le clef *AG*, le chief *B*. 673. Que ja ne fust la vertu definie *A;* vertuz *B*. 674. le cler] lesquelx *C;* sa *C*. 675. circunsistance *A*. cironfluence *BCV*. 677. Fors que par mort qui la examinee *G;* le *AE*. 679. Qui est v.] Tost venue *A;* venu *D;* est *missing in C;* acoustumiere *V*. 680. Obtenebrant *A*, obtenebrez *FH;* le *BH;* raiz *BFH*, rayes *CV*.

Rubric] Clemence *ADEF*, Epitaphe de clemence *G*, epitaphe de sa clemence *V*. 683. prospere *A*, pront *B*, prost *C*. 684. voulut *CV*. pour *A*. 686. sanc *A;* descouvrir *C*, descourir *H*. 687. *Missing in H;* jullet *A;* fist *ABCFGV*, feist *E;* couvrir *C*. 688. Par *A*, Jours *G;* et *added by different hand in E;*

Et trespassa au chasteau de Mehun
690   L'an mil quatre cens et soixante et un.

     L'acteur et le nom de celuy
   Sitost que fut ceste escripture emprainte
   Incontinent pars de l'esglise sainte,
   Moult agravé et quis lieu solitaire
   Où j'escripvy ceste dure complainte,
695   Non pas pour gaing, mais affin que fust plainte
   Grant temps la mort du roy tant salutaire.
   Requerons donc le Dieu tresdebonnaire
   Ensemble tous qu'il luy veulle au parfaire
   Bailler ès cieux, où est nostre recours,
700   Tiltre de roy pour regner à tousjours.

     Amen

---

deux]sept *A;* le *missing in C.* 689. Or *C;* au c.] au beau c. *E;*
meun *AEFV,* meung *B.* 690. Lan q.c.mil *A,* La mil iiij^e *B,* lan
iiij^e mil (milz *G*) *FG;* et]*missing in ACGV,* quon dit *B.*

Rubric] Lacteur *AEF, missing in B.* 691. fust *A.* 692. partz
E. 693. agrevee *A;* et quis]quist *A,* et queys *E,* et le *V.* 694.
je escrips *A,* jescripviz *E.* 695. pas *missing in V;* soit *AEF.*
696. de *EF;* solitaire *C.* 697. doncques *A;* roy *CEFHV;* tant
debonnaire *ACV.* 698. qui *H;* le *G;* voeille *A,* vueille *BCEV,*
veille *F,* voelle *G.* 699. ès]ou *G;* chiel *G;* en *A;* aultres *A.*
700. Cicle *A;* p.r.]araisner *C. Amen*]*Missing in ABEFGH.*

Explicit]Explicit *AH,* explicit lepytaphe du roy Charles
viime de ce nom *B,* explicit epitedium sive lamentacio Caroli
septimi regis victorissimj *C,* explicit les epitaphes du roy
Charles viime de ce nom *G, missing in EV. Text in D is
followed by a quatrain* (see p. 304). *Text in A is followed by
a ballade also ascribed to Simon Greban.*

STANLEY C. ASTON,
St. Catharine's College,
Cambridge

Notes

[1] G. de Fresne de Beaucourt, *Chronique de Mathieu d'Escouchy*, Paris, Renouard, 1863-4, 3 v. (Soc. d'Hist. de France series); see Vol. I, xliii-xlix.

[2] The MS. was given to me in 1948 by the late Rev. Dr. H. J. Chaytor, sometime Master of St. Catharine's College, Cambridge, who told me that he had bought it about 1928. Apart from the bookplate mentioned above there is no further evidence in the volume of its provenance.

[3] Listed in 1953 in Catalogue No. 722 of Messrs. B. Quaritch of London, where it is described as a sixteenth-century MS. on paper, ff. 177, with modern binding. At the end of the text of the Chronicle are seven leaves of epitaphs on Charles VII, a fact which suggests a connection with the MS. discussed here. Messrs. Quaritch have kindly informed me that the MS. was bought in 1956 by a New Haven bookseller, Mr. Laurence Witten.

[4] A member of the Belgian Legation at London from 1821 to 1867. See J. Pope-Hennessy, *Monckton Milnes: The Flight of Youth 1851-85* (London, 1951), p. 43 ff.

[5] It is tempting to link these entries with the Le Picart family of lawyers (see P. Anselme, *Généalogie des maisons de France*, 1733, especially Vol. VIII, and elsewhere *passim*) but I have not yet been able to identify the individuals mentioned. Two of them, however (Jacques and André Le Picart), are shown as holding legal appointments.

[6] See C. M. Briquet, *Les Filigranes*, Paris etc., 1907, II:304, entry 5097.

[7] This text of the Chronicle is being edited by Mr. Graham Halligan, of King's College, Cambridge, for the M.Litt. degree of the University of Cambridge. Mr. Halligan proposes to publish an article dealing with the text and its relationship with the other MSS. of the Chronicle and printed edition.

[8] See R. Lebègue, *Le Mystère des Actes des Apôtres* (Paris: Champion, 1929), p. 3 ff.

[9] In *La Plainte du Desiré* (ed. J. Stecher, *Oeuvres*, Louvain, 1882-91, III:172):

> Mais je n'ay plus un Virgile, qui plaigne
> Son Mecenas, ne Catulle, qui daigne
> Gemir la mort des petis passerons.
> Maistre Alain dort, dont de dueil mon coeur saigne,
> Qui pour Millet sa plume en tristesse baigne,
> Greban, qui pleure d'un bon Roy la compaigne,
> Si ne sçay plus desormais que ferons.

The epitaph for Milet is by Simon Greban, not by Alain Chartier; see n. 14 below. Steche's identification of Greban with Arnoul is erroneous and should read Simon.

[10] *Bibliothèque*, ed. Rigoley de Juvigny, 1772, II:408. ". . . Il a écrit plusieurs élégies, complaintes et deplorations sur la mort d'une Roine de

France, desquelles fait mention Jean le Maire en ses poésies. . . . Epitaphes sur la mort du Roi de France Charles VII, écrits en forme d'Eglogue ou pastoralle, imprimés à Paris. . . ."

[11] *Grundriss,* II:1230.

[12] P. Champion, *Hist. poét. du XVe siècle* (Paris: Champion, 1923), II:140, n. 4.

[13] *op. cit.*

[14] A Piaget, "Simon Greban et Jacques Milet," *Romania,* XXII (1892): 230 ff.

[15] A. Vérard, *Le romant de la Rose. Codicille et testament de maistre Jean de Meung ou Clopinel* (Paris, 1500). Vérard's attribution to Jean de Meung is probably due to the fact that Charles VII died at Meung and to the reputation of Jean de Meung in the early sixteenth century.

[16] In addition to the MSS. listed above, I have come across three other MSS. which, at the time of writing, I have not been able to consult. They are:

B. N. nouv. acq. fr. 4511 (formerly in the library at Ashburnham Place, Barrois Collection No. 402). Paper, end fifteen century. The text, headed *Epitedium sive lamentacio Karoli septimi victoriossimi regis Francorum,* begins on f.1. and ends on f.6v with *Explicit epitedium sive lamentacio Karoli septimi,* at 1.316 (*Qui est bien haulte a entreprendre*).

B. N. nouv. acq. fr. 4518 (formerly in library at Ashburnham Place, Barrois Collection, no. 564. Paper, fifteenth century. The text, headed *Fin d'une complainte sur la mort du roy Charles VII,* begins on f. lv with 1.317 (*Ou je suis trop de feu damour epris*) after a rubric *Sensuit le proheme de noblesse et dit de rechief lacteur,* and ends on f. 8v. with the last line of the poem (1.700).

Rennes, MS. 594 (cf. Catal. gen. XXIV, 249). Item no. 5. The text, headed *Epitaphe ou lamentation du roy Charles septieme, roy des Françoys, qui trespassa de ce siecle en l'an mil iiiicccc LX,* begins on f. 121 v. and ends on f. 132 v. The last stanza is headed *Lacteur et le nom diceley.*

[17] My thanks are due to Mr. J. C. Laidlaw, of Trinity Hall, Cambridge, who drew my attention to this fragment and kindly sent me a transcript of the MS.

[18] See *supra,* note 14.

[19] See *supra,* note 10.